Group
Communication
Pitfalls

Group Communication Pitfalls

Overcoming Barriers to an Effective Group Experience

John O. Burtis
University of Northern Iowa

Paul D. Turman
University of Northern Iowa

SAGE Publications
Thousand Oaks ▪ London ▪ New Delhi

For information:

Sage Publications, Inc.
2455 Teller Road
Thousand Oaks, California 91320
E-mail: order@sagepub.com

Sage Publications Ltd.
1 Oliver's Yard
55 City Road
London EC1Y 1SP
United Kingdom

Sage Publications India Pvt. Ltd.
B-42, Panchsheel Enclave
Post Box 4109
New Delhi 110 017 India

Printed in the United States of America.

Library of Congress Cataloging-in-Publication Data

Burtis, John Orville.
Group communication pitfalls : overcoming barriers to an effective group experience / John O. Burtis, Paul D. Turman.
    p. cm.
Includes bibliographical references and index.
ISBN 1-4129-1534-1 (cloth)—ISBN 1-4129-1535-X (pbk.)
    1. Communication in small groups. I. Turman, Paul D. II. Title.
HM736.B87 2006
302.3'4—dc22

                                2005008159

This book is printed on acid-free paper.

05 06 07 08 09 10 9 8 7 6 5 4 3 2 1

Acquiring Editor:	Todd R. Armstrong
Editorial Assistant:	Deya Saoud
Project Editor:	Claudia A. Hoffman
Typesetter:	C&M Digitals (P) Ltd.
Indexer:	Kathy Paparchontis
Cover Designer:	Glenn Vogel

Contents

Tables and Figures

Preface

R esearch demonstrates that every aspect of group activity has the potential to manifest in pitfalls that can lower the quality of group outcomes. Yet, despite the significant body of group research that identifies existing group pitfalls, few texts, if any, have focused on pitfalls to provide a useful orienting framework. The primary focus for this text is to organize potential group pitfalls into a framework that provides students an orientation for *expecting*, *detecting* and *correcting* group pitfalls as they arise during grouping.

A group pitfall is anything that can detract from or lessen the successful completion of the task, relational, or individual functions a group should serve. A group suffers some breakdown when an aspect of its desired functional outcomes suffers as the result of its experience dealing with one or more pitfalls. Group breakdowns range from minor reductions in one or more aspects of the group's functional outcomes, to substantial failure on one or more of its functional outcomes, to some catastrophic outcome. Because every group faces potential pitfalls, all groups are breakdown-conducive until they successfully navigate the pitfalls. Indeed, some groups experience improved task, relational, or individual outcomes as a result of their efforts to successfully deal with the obstacles they faced.

This text treats groups and the work involved in grouping as useful tools humans have developed for responding to the exigencies they perceive as requiring group action in response. The potential pitfalls faced by group members as they attempt to group and the exigencies for and against effective grouping need to be understood in order to overcome barriers to effective group experiences. This book is comprised of three basic units. First, chapters 1 and 2 provide you with a rationale and framework for studying group pitfalls including explanations and explorations of how communication is fundamental to any grouping breakdown and effectiveness. Second, chapters 3–7 extend the Framework for Grouping and Group Direction by providing a map of the group pitfall terrain. Specifically, chapter 3 introduces you to task and supragroup pitfalls and chapter 4 examines problems manifesting as a result of group personnel. Chapters 5 and 6 describe the pitfalls associated with group attempts to structure their behavior (techniques, tendencies, and concomitants) as they attempt to attain process prizes from grouping. Chapter 7 examines pitfalls associated with a group's attempt to establish its vision, outcomes, and attempts to provide direction to the group. The third unit includes a set of potential group outcomes and the importance of potential pitfalls to those outcomes in chapter 8, the exigencies against grouping in chapter 9, and methods for observing groups well in chapter 10.

This book helps you to (a) understand that pitfalls should be expected, (b) orient you toward *detecting* pitfalls to minimize their damage, and (c) develop your own skills for responding to or *correcting* pitfalls within the broader context of what is best for your grouping activity. When potential employers say that they want to hire someone who has good group skills, we want you to be able to say, "I know how to do that; I know how to be an effective member of a group; I know how to help the groups I am in do better work than if I am not in the group."

We gratefully acknowledge these reviewers: Phillip G. Clampitt of the University of Wisconsin at Green Bay; Kelby K. Halone of the University of Tennessee, Knoxville; M. Chad McBride of Creighton University; and Kathleen M. Propp of Western Michigan University.

1

Why Study Group
Communication Pitfalls?

❖   ❖   ❖

Some basketball teams play confused. Inefficient on defense and inept on offense, players get in each others' way, even give the ball up to the other team. There is no conformity to a unified game plan. Any tactics they try to use result in fruitless arguments about what is going wrong and who is to blame. Team members become frustrated and disillusioned. Attitude affects performance and play goes from bad to worse. Team members worry about their own playing time and about who is taking the most shots. Some shouting may occur, but mostly players are quiet and tense around each other, eager to get out of the locker room and away from basketball after a game. After several weeks, if they cannot find a way to make their play together improve, players will learn that "this team is going nowhere" and begin to believe that "this is just a bad team!" The team fails worse than anyone thought possible given the individual talents of its members.

Some basketball teams play with an excellence that defies description. Players know their roles, playing them well and creatively. Everyone sticks to the game plan except when they seamlessly work together to improvise an improvement in the plan. They take the initiative to help out if teammates struggle. They find opportunities to succeed as a group. Their play looks more like that of one entity than five individuals. Mistakes are made but quickly, even sharply, corrected, and nobody pouts because his or her feelings are hurt. Arguments about tactics result in improvements and even greater success. Players are at ease, even boisterous, in communicating with each other. They are proud of their team and they work harder than they expected when they started with the team because they do not want to let their teammates down. The team succeeds beyond what could be expected given the talent of its members.

We can learn a lesson from these basketball teams. Most day-to-day groups have a combination of effective and ineffective practices. Many achieve some modicum of success, though most group work involves some degree of struggle. Typical group experiences fit somewhere between the extremes described for the two basketball teams. Without the light that the competition with another team shines on the problems a group is having, the pitfalls faced by a group can be hard to see, even by group members. Indeed, it may be difficult to determine whether things are actually going well or poorly in some groups. Most of us have had a range of experiences with groups, from the effective to the not so effective; some are actually even awful. The differences between effective and ineffective groups may be small as they begin to manifest, but they can become very large when measured by final group outcomes. It is important to be aware of the signs that a group is not doing well and to know how to help a group begin to do better. Why? Because it enhances the likelihood that you will help create desirable group outcomes and reduces the chances that you will be involved in unpleasant groups with poor group outcomes.

Effective group communication, coupled with an orientation that *expects* and *detects* group pitfalls as they arise, gives you the foundation for overcoming barriers to effective group experiences. This book provides you with a map of the group pitfall terrain. People working well together can use the struggle against such pitfalls to improve their groups. We make use of your personal experiences in groups as well as published research findings to help you understand groups and to improve your group communication skills.

❖ OVERVIEW OF THE BOOK

Group experiences are co-constructed by group members as they talk and work together on their task. Groups can be intentionally co-constructed in ways that increase the likelihood that they will be effective and that decrease the chances of poor group experiences. The first unit in this book (chapters 1 and 2) introduces terms for understanding how we co-construct our groups by communicating with each other. The second unit identifies common and recurring pitfalls we face in our groups. The third unit describes potential group outcomes and how to make choices about your own group work. Throughout the book, but primarily in the second and third units, we provide advice (using italics) on how you can avoid group pitfalls and how to work your way through the pitfalls you do encounter.

We address three questions in this first chapter: What is group communication? Why does it matter? and Why focus on group communication pitfalls in order to study groups? The first and third questions are irrelevant if the answer to the second question is not satisfactory, so we start with that question:

❖ WHY DO GROUPS MATTER ENOUGH TO MAKE A STUDY OF THEM?

Like it or not, groups are involved in most facets of your life, and every one of these groups has to struggle to overcome common pitfalls, or you may personally bear some of the brunt of the consequences. Let's begin by looking at your life in particular. There is a plethora of groups, many in number as well as in type, with both direct and indirect connections to your daily life. Let's be explicit about how many groups there are that are important to you.

Groups Are Important to Happiness and Success

Start by thinking about your family and your work. Some families are healthy groups; others are not. Can you help your family become a healthier group? What are your goals for the future of your family? Can you help them work together to achieve those goals? Remember the childhood groups you got involved in like Girl Scouts or 4-H, youth sports teams, or study groups. Will you be able to help improve the groups that affect your own children? Think of your family and friends and their religious, professional, and social groups. Your access to your family and friends is affected by their obligations to their groups. If someone you are close to is worried because one of their groups is

Table 1.1   Reasons to Study and Understand Groups

Purpose	Individual Rationale
Happiness and Success	Personal and economic: Individual success is tied to groups.
Groups Are Ubiquitous	Inevitability: Individuals can't escape groups.
Groups Are Formative	Socialization: Individuals are inevitably shaped by groups.
Dynamics Change Communication	Competence: Individuals have to adapt to groups.
Groups Co-construct Our World	Political life: Community values are established by groups.
Better Work	Utility: Effective groups can do more or superior work.

struggling, you will feel the effects of that struggle. Can you help counsel them through difficult group experiences? The desire to answer "yes" to any of these questions provides you with a personal reason for learning how to work well in groups.

Does your job require you to work as part of a team? Are there any groups of people at work that you sometimes have to deal with? Are you a victim of whatever dynamics prevail in such work groups or can you play a productive role in helping to improve them? If you can help improve the dynamics at work, chances are that you will be rewarded for your skills. Employers regularly list "people with effective group skills" as an important consideration when they make hiring choices because of the central role effective group work plays in every strong organization. This book can help you be able to say: "I know how to be an effective member of a team. That means I personally can work well when I am part of a team. It also means that I know how to help others on the team in their attempts to do their work well." The desire to be able to make those claims provides an economic reason for learning how to work well in groups.

Groups Are Ubiquitous

Groups are ubiquitous, which means that you will find them everywhere humans are at work or play, and your life will be affected by them in a never-ending variety of ways. Groups are involved in every organization in which you are a member. All kinds of businesses and complex organizations use groups to sort through difficult tasks. Managers typically spend more than half of each day in group meetings, and the majority of work groups meet at least once a week with others meeting at least once a month (Mitzberg, 1973; Volkema & Niederman, 1995). As you attain more and more success in life, the chances are that groups of other people and meetings with teams of people will become more and more important to that success.

Once you start thinking about groups that affect you even though you are not a member, the list becomes almost endless. Think about groups beyond family and work. The curriculum you had to complete to get your education was developed by a group of individuals. The menu in public restaurants is sorted out and prepared by a group. Any time you ask someone in a bureaucracy to do something for you and are told in response, "that is against policy" or "I'm sorry, but that's not my job," you are probably dealing with a person representing the will of a group. A cockpit crew in the jet that flies you across the country is a group. How important is it to you that they work well together? The doctors, anesthesiologist, and nurses who operate on you need effective group communication. Do you know how to protect yourself against the possibility that they do not work well together? For example, when you are in the hospital, do you talk to medical professionals as though they are just one part of a team that is caring for you? You should. Groups are everywhere, helping to make organizations either stronger or weaker.

Groups Are Formative

Our experiences in groups help to shape who we are and what we believe. Some group experiences last longer than the groups themselves. Bad experiences in a group can make us not want to trust a group with any work that is important to us. Good experiences can make us feel as though our best work is done in groups. Symbolic interaction theory explains part of this formative process (Mead, 1964). It argues that we learn about ourselves, about who we are and what we are able to do well, by experiencing how others treat us as they interact with us. The self-concept that results, coupled with our implicit theories about how people in groups ought to behave, combine to form a forceful orientation for our future activities in groups. So, being in groups helps to shape who we are as individuals and it also helps to shape who we are as potential group members.

We are also affected by the value-expressive attitudes we have about the groups to which we belong. Why do you join one group and not another? Such choices are made in part based on ideas about what being a member of a particular group "says" about one as a person. Indeed, sometimes we think of ourselves in terms of the groups we belong to. "I'm a union member." "I'm a Republican." "I'm on a bowling team." "I work at Z-bar." If you make reference to a group you belong to when introducing yourself to someone, it is because you think that helps them to understand something important about you. Membership in some groups suggests how I ought to think and how I ought to behave: in a manner consistent with the values of that group. This creates a sort of mental shorthand through which we can refer to ourselves and to what we believe. The company and associations we keep help define and shape us. The groups we identify ourselves with help to tell us and others who we are and what we value.

Group Dynamics Change Communication

The communication dynamics involved in a group context are different than those that are important in other contexts. Just because you are an effective communicator in one context does not mean that you will be in another. If you are good at selling shoes, does that mean you are a good public speaker? The type of communication that is appropriate changes as the context changes in which the communication is attempted. People who write well are not necessarily good at polite chitchat during a party. People who are effective radio broadcasters might be challenged by a group context in which they must pay attention to feedback from each of the other group members. For centuries in Western culture, group communication was not treated as a particularly special and important type of communicating. During the twentieth century, that changed as research started to document the important role that informal work groups play in complex organizations and the role that effective group interaction plays in human development. Now, management theory fully integrates team-building skills with broader organizational concerns, and psychotherapists concern themselves with the nature of the groups to which their clients belong in addition to the mental health of their patients. To learn to adapt your communication to be effective in groups, you must learn how the dynamics of human interaction are affected by the group context.

We Use Group Communication to Co-construct Our World

Are there any groups where you live that make decisions affecting your home, your transportation, or your access to food, water, or energy? City commissions or county councils regulate many aspects of your life after discussing the issues in open or closed group meetings. There are political groups and all sorts of advocacy and service groups. Is there a community church or temple or mosque? Is there a local school? Do any of these community groups need your help in order to better serve your community? If so, you have a political reason for understanding groups.

To get a sense of the skills involved in shaping corporate or community values (political activity), look at the problems faced in societies with no history of democratic participation. Effective group work can be hard where people have long been punished for expressing their opinions. Krips (1992) found that people in Russia experienced difficulty working together after the dissolution of the former Soviet Union because of a history in which they were discouraged from the free exchange of ideas. The assumption was missing that group members ought to have equal opportunities to participate, and misconceptions were frequent about whether input was to be valued by group members. These are substantial pitfalls to effective group communication.

Demos, the root for the word *democracy*, means a self-governing group. We cannot self-govern; we cannot have effective democracy or effective groups if people do not learn how to work well in groups. Groups are more likely to serve useful purposes when everyone in them takes responsibility for what the group decides. There is nothing more fundamental to citizenship than learning how to work well with others. Having a political reason for learning how to work well in groups does not mean that everyone needs to be a politician, but everyone does need to be able to understand and engage in the processes that shape how values will be represented in the policies and the laws that govern the places where we live and work.

Effective Groups Do More or Better Work

The final reasons for making a study of groups are found in the various utilities to be served by working in groups. Groups can help us to do stuff. Groups can be powerful, because they are the way that we harness the efforts, energies, and intelligence of several people in service of a common task. In simplest form, some groups have tasks to do that are enhanced by having more people doing the work. Pulling a heavy load is made easier the more people you have pulling it. Picking dandelions is done faster the more people you have picking them. "The more the merrier" represents such additive tasks. The kind of group work we focus on in this book is different. It does not involve additive tasks; it involves conjunctive tasks that require coordinated interaction. Some groups have tasks where a greater and greater number of members is not better and better. Conjunctive tasks require integration of thought and action and become more difficult as the group gets larger. "Too many cooks spoil the stew" represents such tasks. Even with conjunctive tasks, though, there should be a utility served by having a group do the work.

Throughout this book, we refer to such utilities as the process prizes a group might attain if its members work well together. When a group of people is effective, it is more powerful than individuals working alone, and its effectiveness means that better work gets done. The better work is "value added" to the task by having it done in a group rather than by individuals working alone. We call these prizes because they are especially desirable outcomes and we call them process prizes because the desirable nature of the outcome results from the interaction of the individuals working together, not from the individuals themselves. Process prizes from effective group interactions are (a) the group does better creative thinking or work than the individuals alone would do, (b) the group does better critical thinking or work than the individuals alone would do, or (c) group members accept group outcomes more because they played a part in the group. The first two process prizes are measured in enhanced quality outcomes. The third is measured by how well those outcomes are treated by group members when their work is done. The three process prizes manifest as the value added to the work because it was done in a group.

Can you get a group to help you? Groups can help you to do more work than you could ever do on your own. Can you turn group utility into personal utility? Some entrepreneurs find the transition to be difficult from their single-proprietor new business to one that employs several people because they do not know how to work well with others. Successful professionals often find that their success increases the number of times that they have to work in groups of people (e.g., a successful accountant becomes a partner in the firm and then has to start helping manage the other accountants in the firm, which requires being able to work well in a group). Groups can help you become more creative in developing options or to better test ideas critically before you adopt them. Groups can create acceptance of and support for a plan of action by employing the efforts of others in the process of developing the plan. Knowing about these important process prizes can help you to get more done in groups, because you understand the purposes that are supposed to be served by groups.

In sum, for all the above reasons, it is wise to make a study of groups. In your daily life, you can practice the study of groups by observing the groups you are in at work and play, by observing the groups that are depicted in the movies you watch and the books you read, and by trying to determine why people behave as they do. Whenever the action involves a group, try to determine how that fact might be affecting what you observe. Becoming a student of how groups work can actually be fun. It is exciting to begin to have insight into why people behave as they do and also to learn ways to help increase your own effectiveness.

Every business, organization, and community enterprise depends on groups. When you were very young, others had already set up the groups that nurtured you and that provided you with protection. Groups make possible all sorts of wonderful things. For instance, you do not have to organize the food production process that allows you to do your job instead of spending your own time every day hunting for or gathering the food you need to survive. The ability of any society to perpetuate itself comes down to the health of its groups. As people mature, they need to help shoulder their share of that work. Every worthwhile group needs people to do its work in order for it to stay healthy. As human beings, we each either help or hurt (even if only through benign neglect) the groups that are necessary for the survival of us all. Groups live, grow, and evolve either into stronger or into weaker entities over time as a direct consequence of how we choose to involve ourselves in them. If too many people choose not to be active, society and cultural advances stop. Over time, any organization or culture can fade away.

❖ DEFINITIONS OF *GROUP* AND *COMMUNICATION* AND *PITFALLS*

This book is focused on group communication pitfalls. Defining the three components of this subject matter, *group* and *communication* and *pitfalls,* provides the organization for the remainder of this chapter. Because it takes communication to cocreate a group as well as to co-create and/or to address group pitfalls, we start with this question:

What Constitutes Communication?

We use a combination of two quite different and yet basic definitions of communication (Burtis, 1989). The combination of the two covers the realm of what is important for defining communication in a group. First, communication is the *transfer of information from one source to another.* The quality of this aspect of communication is judged by a fidelity criterion: effective messages are clear in that the receiver of the message learns exactly what the source intends. The necessity in any effective group for members to share information accurately is represented by this definition. Second, communication is *making and sharing meanings.* This implies an ambiguous process affected by the personal perceptual filters and frames the people involved bring to each communicative episode. Communication in this sense is not outcome (accurate or otherwise) but process. Effective communication evolves only as sources and receivers work together to co-construct an understanding of what matters with regard to the issue at hand.

Group communication involves the transfer of information among members and also the co-construction of meanings that will enhance or bedevil the group. In a very real sense, a group is a co-construction of the communication among its members: the attempts people make to form and to maintain an effective group through their talk. Both the information transferred and the meanings that are co-constructed during any attempt to communicate are affected by a group's communication network: who speaks to whom. Lines of communication must be open to all group members in order to increase the chances that the people involved will be able to serve the purpose for doing their work in a group: attaining a process prize from their work together. Open and active talk among all of the group members co-creates an all-channel network, which is characteristic of effective group communication. In the ideal, everyone must be able to talk with, listen to, and give feedback to everyone else in the group in order for the communication to be "group communication." Our definition of a group gives a primary role to communication; group communication is the co-construction of the group.

What Constitutes a Group?

A group is people who co-construct both a common purpose (task or goal) and shared perceptual membership boundaries through regular communicative interaction that allows them to work interdependently to serve desired task, relational, and individual functions.[1]

Purpose. A common purpose is a shared desire to achieve an agreed-on goal. If group members are working toward different ends, they will only appear to be a group until their desire for different things results in efforts by them to separate their activities. Group members can have many different purposes, but there must be at least one common goal (e.g., accomplishing a particular job, keeping each other company) from being together in order for there to be a group. The group's task is usually where we find a sense of joint purpose, so it is appropriate to say that groups share a common task, though sometimes there are different exigencies that motivate group members to the same task.

Interdependence. Interdependence is when the actions of each individual member affect and are affected by the others in the group. Although people may be working on a common task, they may or may not be influencing each other as they do so. Influencing each other requires a common process; group members must be involved in a manner that affects each other. One cannot succeed or fail without the other succeeding or failing, too. In the ideal form, a group's interdependence means that the success of the group depends on the contributions of each member and that the members rely on each other to reach their shared goals. For example, three strangers riding an elevator at the same time are not a group. They are just an aggregate of individuals because they lack a shared goal and an interdependent process. Three people working together to fix a broken elevator are a group. Consider a more complicated example. Three telemarketers sit next to each other at a table with a bank of phones. Each tries to make sales. This is a *nominal group*, or group in name only, because it lacks the interdependent process though they all share a common task—talking on the phone trying to make sales. They can fail or succeed alone. The distinctions among aggregates of people, nominal groups, and groups turn out to be quite important when we get to a discussion of how interaction can help and also hurt group performance. Groups with members who fail to realize and to capitalize on their interdependence are more likely to underperform or to fail as a group. Reliance on one another is a part of interdependence as is the need for each member to contribute to the group, and both are directly related to the ability of a group effort to attain the process prizes intended from doing work as a group.

Perceived Boundaries. Perceived boundaries are perceptions of who is and who is not a member of the group. *Boundary* is a metaphor representing the need for members to identify themselves as part of the group. The ability to do this depends on the presence of shared characteristics that help participants identify themselves as members of the group. Shared characteristics allow members to differentiate themselves from those outside the group. That means that members know who is *not* a member. A perceived boundary works like a virtual fence you have between your property and your neighbor's. You use a fence to make clear what is on your side and to separate that from what is on the other side, the side that is not yours. You can describe your property according to its characteristics, and you can describe your group according to its characteristics. Often, that means describing the signs of group membership—the signs there are that someone is a member of the group. These characteristics of your group help you understand and enforce the group's perceptual boundary. Does your favorite team have a mascot, special colors, inside jokes, or stories about their history? A dress code in a private school or a uniform in the military provide common examples. Fraternities and sororities use Greek letters to designate themselves and conduct rituals of membership that may even involve hazing to let new members know how special they are. "The curse of the Bambino" was part of the folklore for fans of the Boston Red Sox who once blamed their failure to win a world series on having been the team that traded a youthful Babe Ruth to the New York Yankees long ago. The point is to find ways to distinguish between those who are in and outside the group, clarifying perceptual boundaries.

Interaction. Interaction involves communication and is required to co-construct each of the first three elements of a group. We have already described how communication involves the co-construction of meaning. Communication is used to co-construct groups and what is meaningful to a group. Members of a group need to talk and to share their ideas with each other. They must work together, coordinating their efforts in order to do the work of the group. Have you ever started to work in a group only to find that the rest of the potential members of the group want immediately to divide up the work and then to proceed to work on it alone? Perhaps that is a good idea. Perhaps it is not. It depends on whether there is a process prize to be desired from interacting as a group on the particular task at hand. When people divide up a project so that they no longer have to work together in any way to accomplish an assignment, they are not working as a group on the project. When they cut off interaction, it means that they will not be able to attain the process prizes that can only be achieved from the process of working as a group.

Our description of these four elements, which are necessary to comprise a group, begins our description of what a group must be and do in order to accomplish the purposes people have for groups. Working alone is one alternative to working in a group. There are also other ways for people to accomplish tasks without interaction or interdependence or shared boundaries or shared goals. Alternative entities to groups may share one or more but not all of the above elements (e.g., a nominal group that lacks shared process and interaction but uses several people to work on the same job). In some cases, those entities are preferable to groups. In other cases, they are not. A goal you should set for yourself is to learn when it is appropriate to employ a group to accomplish a task and when it would be better to use an alternative entity. A decision about what entity to employ for a given project should be informed by the nature of the task as well as by the relationships among those involved and their individual needs.

All groups serve task, relational, and individual functions (Benne & Sheats, 1948; Mudrack & Farrell, 1995). Every group must serve these three functions in order to be judged an effective group. Task functions are the reason a group is called together or put to work on a subject in the first place. A task involves the group's mission, goals, and outcomes. When a group does its work, it does so in ways that manifest in task outcomes. The work gets done as the group structures its experiences together. Even recreational or social groups have a task. People in a bowling league have bowling as their task. People in self-help groups have sharing their experiences and making therapeutic gains as their task. People in a family have the work of feeding, clothing, sheltering, and nurturing each other as a task. People in a business group have the jobs assigned them by the organization as their task. Every group should be assessed in part by how well it has served its task function.

The relational function is served by the ability of group members to work well together as they approach their task. If group members do not get along, if they do not learn to relate well with each other, they will struggle. Consider three synonyms for *relational:* maintenance, socioemotional, and people-orientation. Maintenance means the group's ability to keep the necessary processes in place (to maintain them) as it works on group tasks. Effective relationships among group members help maintain the group's ability to do its work. The maintenance staff that care for a building are not doing the task the building was designed to do. Instead, they maintain lighting and equipment and an environment that is clean and free of hazards so that the task that the space is designed for can be done. The socioemotional metaphor describes the fact that people feel good or bad about the social aspects of their relationships as they work with others. The emotional aspects of life in a group can enhance or diminish your desire to get to meetings and to do well when you are there. A group that is people oriented is one that cares about the relationships among its members and also about how each individual member is doing. How well a group serves its relational and individual functions are parts of an assessment of the group's effectiveness.

A group serves its individual function well when group members grow and benefit as individuals from the process of being involved in the group. We are concerned with the individual function because group membership comes at a cost to the individual. Consequently, members should anticipate some individual satisfaction or positive outcome from their work in addition to strong task and maintenance outcomes. Bormann (1996) claims that "each individual ought to have the opportunity to grow and develop his or her potential within the group. . . . The praiseworthy group . . . is one in which the member's potential for achievement and self-transcendence is realized" (p. 280). That individual functions ought to be served by a group seems to be self-evident to us.

Contrary to our orientation, some group scholars argue that when individual functions are served by a group, they distract or detract from the group's task and maintenance functions. Yes, some selfish acts are quite clearly pitfalls to effective group communication, such as the withdrawing, blocking, and status- and recognition-seeking activities that Brilhart, Galanes, and Adams (2001) identify as well as the aggressor, blocker, and dominator roles Mudrack and Farrell (1995) identify. Poor personal behavior certainly has pitfall potential when individual purposes are served at the expense of the group. But the obverse may be true as well. Sometimes individual group members are hurt by their

Table 1.2   Summary of Group Functions

Type	Outcome Type	Examples of desirable outcomes
Task	Work outcomes	Complete a report; finish a job; develop a solution; win a game.
Relational	Maintenance, social-emotional, or climate building	Ability to work or play together well; group solidarity; cohesion.
Individual	Person-oriented or self-serving outcomes	Sense of accomplishment; increased group skills; friendship.

service to a group; sometimes individuals are even sacrificed for the good of the group. We believe that a healthy, sustainable balance is attainable only when a group serves all three functions well: its individual function as well as its task and social functions. The disagreement about the role individual functions should play in groups provides a transition to the final question addressed in this chapter:

What Constitutes Group Communication Pitfalls?

Group Pitfall. A *group pitfall* is defined as anything that might reduce the effectiveness of a group; anything that might diminish its desired outcomes. Whether a pitfall is anticipated or unforeseen, whether it is a problem created by the group or a problem that the group is just unfortunate enough to have to face, a group pitfall must be addressed during the group process in order for the group, in the end, to improve its performance. Common group pitfalls tend to recur. Every group must face at least some of them. If, by the end of a project, your group has failed to address the common group pitfalls it has faced, the effectiveness of your group will have been diminished. That is when group breakdown has occurred.

Group Breakdown. A *group breakdown* is defined as a diminished group outcome. A breakdown occurred if, by the end of its work on a project, a group failed to accomplish its ideal potential performance given the resources that were available to it. Breakdown is indicated by the group's failure to attain a process prize while serving all three functions a group is intended to serve. In practice, this means that group breakdown has occurred when a group produced less than it should have in terms of the group's task (task function), in terms of the ability of the group's members to maintain their capacity to get along well while working with one another (relational function), or in terms of the group's service to its membership (individual function).

Pitfalls and breakdown are closely related but different. We mentioned at the start of this chapter that it is sometimes very difficult to tell how well a group is doing while they are still in the process of working together. Group members may not even be fully aware of how well their group is doing, regardless of their optimism or pessimism. The difficulty can be explained as part of the nature of a dynamic and unfolding process. For example, individual group activities may not appear to be much of a problem, but small pitfalls can sometimes lead to quite negative outcomes. Further, an activity that helped create a pitfall for the group at one meeting can end up getting corrected by group members at a later meeting, turning out not to be a problem after all. And it is possible that the members co-construct a stronger group when they have to work together as a team to address a pitfall. In that case, what appears at one point to be a problem for the group actually leads to improved outcomes for the group over time. These are reasons to separate the conception of potential pitfalls to group communication (from the actuality of group breakdown). Every group has a variety of possible ways to achieve a potential outcome. Every group faces pitfalls in group processes that have the potential for diminishing group outcomes. How the group responds to these pitfalls shapes whether there is actual diminution or reduction in final group outcomes: breakdown.

Both pitfalls and breakdown manifest in a variety of shapes, colors, and sizes. Pitfalls range in intensity and importance from the slightly inconvenient, to the addlepating, to the completely discombobulating (sounds pretty bad, doesn't it?). Group breakdowns also range from a minor reduction in how well a group function was served, to a failure on one or more of a group's functions, to a catastrophic outcome of some sort. Gouran and Hirokawa (2003) indicate that "the reasons for faulty performance in decision-making and problem-solving groups are many and varied, and not fully identified or completely understood" (p. 27). Our approach to these pitfalls and the uncertainty surrounding them is to cast the widest possible net with our definitions of what constitute group pitfalls and group breakdown so that we can be certain to have oriented you to the potential problems you may face when working in a group.

❖ CASTING A WIDE NET TO INCLUDE
   ALL PITFALLS AND BREAKDOWN

Casting as wide a net as possible means we need to consider two forms of group breakdown. First, when a group fails, it has broken down. That form is easy to understand and to accept as breakdown. Second, when a group succeeds to some extent but underperforms given the resources it had available to it, that, too, is a group breakdown. This second form of breakdown requires some justification. Why should underperformance be called breakdown? The reason is that the underperforming group wasted available resources, especially the time and talent of its membership, on a mediocre outcome. In addition, if a smaller number of people could accomplish the same outcome as an underperforming group has, a smaller number of people should have done the work. That is because less energy would then have been used, lowering the costs of the group to match the outcome attained. (The exception to this rule is when the need to attain the process prize of group member acceptance justifies tying up additional member resources in the group's work.) Finally, underperforming groups risk setting individual or group norms for performance at substandard levels for future work by that individual or group: they learn to expect to underperform. These reasons justify setting the standard for effective group performance at optimum levels and also for including underperforming groups among the ranks of groups that have broken down.

The potential for group productivity should be assessed by whether an optimum or ideal standard has been met. Our definition of group breakdown is based on the premise that potential productivity in a group equals actual productivity plus whatever losses there were due to faulty group processes (Steiner, 1972). *Potential productivity* is defined as the most a group could be expected to accomplish under good circumstances, given the resources available. That implies the use of an ideal as the criterion to measure how well a group actually does. Using the ideal to measure functional outcomes (task, relational, or individual) suggests the possibility of finding a number of ways for a group to improve its performance. Put another way, it suggests that there are all sorts of group pitfalls that could result in diminution of group outcomes. Potential productivity is a useful ideal for a group to seek as part of their goals and also a useful criterion for assessing group outcomes.

❖ GROUP COMMUNICATION PITFALLS
   BY COMMISSION OR BY OMISSION

Potential communication is a second aspect of group work where some assessment can be made regarding optimum quality. Gouran and Hirokawa (2003) argue, in their functional theory, that the "performance level of decision-making and problem-solving groups can be traced to the extent to which communication among group members contributes to the fulfillment of particular requirements of their task" (p. 27). In this sense, communication pitfalls can manifest in two ways: by commission and by omission. First, if the communicative interaction among group members actually diminishes their capacity to serve the group's functional outcomes, they have used their communication to co-construct a barrier to an effective group experience. Consequently, their communication has not contributed as it should to their attempts to serve their group's functional needs. This is a pitfall by communication commission. Second, if problems that are not created by the group must, nonetheless, be faced by the group in order for them to succeed, and if those problems are not identified and talked through by group members in a manner that enhances their ability to get past the problems, then the absence of such necessary communication has become a pitfall to the group's work. Again, the consequence is that the group's communication has not helped them to serve their group functions. This is a pitfall by communication omission. Again, an ideal, in the form of optimum group communication, becomes the standard for assessing how well a group addresses the pitfalls it faces.

Our position is that all groups are ripe with possibilities: for effective group actions and for potential group pitfalls. In fact, group work is conducive to pitfalls. *Conducive* means "contributing to the possibility of" or "providing the circumstances necessary for" something to occur: in this case, group pitfalls and breakdown. That means that group work involves circumstances that can naturally lead to some problems for the people in the group as they attempt to work together. Their actions can co-create both effective group work and group pitfalls. Communication is the only process for avoiding or for working through group pitfalls. But communication can also be involved in the co-construction of group pitfalls (pitfall by communication commission), or groups can fail to communicate about important problems facing them (pitfall by communication omission). In addition, the three functions groups are intended to serve make groups conducive to pitfalls because it is difficult to achieve each of the three functions and because it is difficult to balance all of the three functions. These observations form the basis for what we call the Breakdown-Conducive Group Framework.

❖ THE BREAKDOWN-CONDUCIVE GROUP FRAMEWORK

The Breakdown-Conducive Group Framework justifies treating group pitfalls and group breakdown as normal, recurring, to-be-expected-and-dealt-with phenomena. In part, the Breakdown-Conducive Group Framework argues: (a) every group is subject to recurring types of pitfalls that can lead to the diminished success (breakdown) of the group, and (b) a focus on recurring forms of potential group pitfalls can help a group member *expect, detect,* and *correct* the pitfalls. The Breakdown-Conducive Group Framework is the basis for this book; it justifies the heavy focus we place on group pitfalls. Because all groups face potential pitfalls, all groups are breakdown-conducive, even ones that manage, eventually, to successfully navigate the pitfalls and do not, in the end, suffer any diminution of performance (group breakdown).

Some groups co-construct improved outcomes on their task, relational, or individual functions as a consequence of their efforts to deal successfully with the obstacles they faced. That they were breakdown-conducive, in effect, helped them become a stronger group because they had to work together as a group to avoid or to overcome the pitfalls they faced. Salazar (1995) postulates that the number of obstacles encountered by a group is positively related to the number of attempts made by group members to facilitate effective group work (in addition to the increase in potential for those pitfalls to be disruptive). So, the more pitfalls faced by a group, the greater the possibility that overcoming those pitfalls can lead to a stronger group (though the possibility also exists that the pitfalls may overcome the group). Having to work through pitfalls can help strengthen your group, and understanding pitfalls can help you in your efforts to work through them. This provides the beginning of the answer to one final question:

❖ WHY SHOULD WE FOCUS OUR STUDY OF
GROUPS ON GROUP COMMUNICATION PITFALLS?

Focusing your study of groups on group pitfalls and breakdown can help you overcome barriers to effective group experiences. For example, a focus on aspects of diminished group performance helps encourage setting higher standards for effective group action: a standard, which suggests that a group should raise its performance goals to achieve an optimum outcome unless they have a good reason not to. In addition, the focus on pitfalls in the Breakdown-Conducive Group Framework makes it very evident, from the onset of group work, how common it is to experience group pitfalls; they should certainly be expected whenever one works in a group. Understanding the breakdown-conducive nature of groups helps create realistic expectations regarding work in a group. Properly framed, group pitfalls and breakdowns are viewed as natural phenomena whenever people work together.

If pitfalls are natural in any group, we should learn to expect them. That expectation encourages us to develop both a prepared stance and a humble approach to recurring group pitfalls. Preparation allows us to hone the skills necessary to avoid some pitfalls and to work through other pitfalls. Most of us develop our own personal strategies for avoiding group pitfalls and tactics for working through the problems that our groups do end up having to face. But, to do those important things well, we need to understand the nature of and potential for common group pitfalls. Humility allows us to keep our own potential culpability for the co-construction of the group's pitfalls in mind when dealing with a group problem. Humility gives us perspective when struggling with a group. It allows a more levelheaded approach to the group's problems. Greater effort can be directed toward avoiding or working through pitfalls than toward becoming defensive and attacking other group members because of the role they played in helping to co-construct the problem. You can teach yourself to shift your focus away from just your own experiences in a group. Try to include also a consideration of the difficulties that the group is facing and the experiences other group members are having. Then, your knowledge of the nature of pitfalls can improve the quality of the strategies you develop to help you avoid pitfalls. This knowledge also helps you to develop reasonably intelligent tactics for correcting pitfalls that are encountered: in short, to overcome barriers to effective group experiences.

Figuring out how to overcome a problem is made easier by understanding the problem. Your group communication skills can be enhanced once you decide to (a) accept that pitfalls and breakdown in your group efforts are inevitable; (b) expect pitfalls and be prepared to detect and to understand them as they unfold; (c) be humble in such circumstances, anticipating and accepting your own possible complicity in co-constructing the pitfall and the group's ensuing response; (d) when you must, work your way through pitfalls trying to minimize the natural human tendencies to be ego-defensive and to scapegoat someone else for the problem; and (e) try to anticipate how you might better deal with such problems the next time you face them. Learning to expect and detect common group communication pitfalls during any group project begins the process of getting you ready to be a more effective group member.

❖ CHAPTER SUMMARY AND CONCLUSION

In this book, we provide you with a map of the group communication pitfall terrain. We also describe how groups of people working well together can use the struggle against such pitfalls to improve their groups. Effective groups are very important to us all. Knowing how communication is supposed to work, what a group is supposed to be and to do, and the intended functions for a group can all help you to figure out where pitfalls may manifest. Unfortunately, there are many aspects of group communication that diminish the group's capacity for serving its three intended functions and attaining a process prize.

We use an orientating framework that includes the idea that you ought to *expect* group pitfalls in order to develop an enhanced ability to *detect* such pitfalls in order to discover or create ways to *correct* such pitfalls. Our emphasis is on the first two parts, expect and detect, because those are the primary ingredients for overcoming barriers to effective group experiences. Any group will suffer if its members do not know to expect and to detect the problems that reduce group effectiveness. Learning ways to correct these problems is important too, but the details of an individual group situation can vary so much that a technique, which may work in one group to correct a problem, may fail to work at all in a second group and may work to create new problems in a third. Consequently, our advice in this book is oriented toward helping you co-construct effective group practices through your communication with other group members rather than toward providing specific answers for fixing each new problem you encounter. Effective group communication processes, coupled with an orientation that expects and detects pitfalls as they arise, gives you the foundation for overcoming barriers to effective group experiences.

2

How Grouping and Group Direction Help Create Effective Group Experiences

❖　❖　❖

Imagine that you are at a party. What would you do if your host at the party got the room quiet and then told everyone to "get into groups"? What actions would you need to take in order to get into a group? What kind of activity would be involved as you begin to group together?

Probably you would establish eye contact with other people around you and say something creative like, "hi there" or "what's up?" or "do you want to group with me?" You might keep an eye on your host even as you started to move into physical proximity with a few other people to start to group together. Someone you don't know says, "Hi, I'm John. What's your name?" Your friend Shanlyn responds with, "Do you know what they are going to make us do?" Someone else you don't know says, "I'm April; pleased to meet you, John." Some guy you think is named Marcus, ignoring the others gathering around him, whispers to another friend of yours named Shauna, "Do you want to get out of here and go someplace quiet for awhile?" Shauna, looking at John, says, "No, this party is too much fun; let's play the game." Shanlyn asks Shauna, "Are we going to play a game; do you know how to play?" April says to John, "Do you want to play?" John says, "I am great at games." Marcus says, "I wonder where I can get a drink." You see that he is still eyeing Shauna, who is standing by John, trying to get his attention.

All sorts of confusion and possibilities, including conflicting desires to leave and to play (or to leave and play), are evident in this example. Someone (the host) from outside the future group is influencing the behavior of people who may become a group. People begin to respond to the host's charge by introducing each other, speculating on what their group might do and whether it will be fun, and by describing their own interest in and capacities for doing what the group task might be. Probably every one of them is trying to figure out who the others are and what they will be like. Probably every one of them wonders, "what should I do?" and "how do I fit in?" What do you think—is this party bunch a group?

A *group* is people who co-construct both a common purpose (task or goal) and shared perceptual membership boundaries through regular communicative interaction that allows them to work interdependently to serve desired task, relational, and individual functions. The party bunch does not meet those standards yet, but groups are co-constructed through talk. People can only become a group through the interactions they share as they co-construct meanings, for example, about what to do and how to do it. In a very real sense, a group is its communication: the attempts of its members to work together and to maintain their ability to do so by interacting with each other. So a group is not just an entity or thing, it is the ongoing efforts by people to use communication to allow themselves to successfully coordinate and complete their activities. In that sense, it appears that the people at the party may be trying to form a group. Their efforts to group together constitute grouping activities (except Marcus, who tries to separate himself and Shauna from the others).

People with a specific idea about what a group should do will try to get others to move with them in the same "direction." If they are successful, they will have gotten the others to work together to help co-construct a common purpose and shared perceptual boundaries.

Grouping activities are what people have to do if they are going to start a group going in one direction or another. Grouping activities and working to influence group direction are necessities for overcoming barriers to effective group experiences.

Humans have developed the skills for working in groups because of our need to address certain recurring types of problems that we are not best-suited to dealing with alone (e.g., protecting ourselves, finding and processing food, building shelter, learning about our world). Some problems (e.g., I feel too tired to work) may require only one individual to solve (I go to sleep). Other problems require an expert to solve (e.g., my new business is producing an unmanageable blizzard of bills and invoices, so I consult an accountant and hire a bookkeeper). And, some problems are best addressed by a group of people working together (e.g., I am lonely and bored, so I call up three friends to come play poker with me). The problems that a group of people are needed to address create their own specific kinds of issues: potential group pitfalls and breakdown. We have to work at grouping together effectively or we will fail to be of much use to each other and may even do some damage. Any attempt to group is conducive to pitfalls, so we have to refine our skills for working effectively with the tool that a group provides us.

This chapter is about how grouping and group direction are employed as tools by people who seek to have effective group experiences. We introduce you to a framework of key terms that are useful in our study of groups. We discuss how people attempt to group— specifically, how they get a group going and how they develop a direction for their group. These are basic requirements for co-constructing an effective group experience. The Framework for Grouping and Group Direction we describe in this chapter provides the nomenclature (the vocabulary of terms used in the framework) and grammar (the interrelationships among those terms necessary for you to employ your new vocabulary) for the rest of the book. We introduce you to this framework to help you orient to common aspects of every group experience.

❖ THE UNIVERSALS OF GROUPING ACTIVITY

Grouping activity may come from a desire to start a new system or to change the direction of a current system. There are two universal truths about groups. First, every group must form. Second, every group must change and, in particular, end (the most dramatic change). Groups form and change. Some groups finish their work and stop grouping. Some groups just come apart, whether their work is finished or not. And some groups evolve into a new group.

Over time, changes in a group's direction can signal fundamental alteration in what the group is and what it is intended to do—perhaps even its mission and members. Sykes (1990) argues that to understand groups, we must figure out "When does an aggregate become a group?" and "When does one group change and become another group?" The first question frames the first universal of grouping: groups form. Sykes's second question orients us to the second universal: that groups change, at some point either ending their activity or becoming a different group entirely. These two universals of grouping can be used to develop a basic framework for understanding groups.

Grouping is at the center of human activity. Johnson (2001) explains the tendencies for complexity to emerge from apparently independent, even chaotic, activities. His study finds emergent complexity across such diverse cases as the creation of computer software design, in ant colonies, and even in seemingly random phenomena such as the development of sprawl in cities over decades and centuries of time. In each case, Johnson's work demonstrates that small groups of activity are at the center of, and provide the impetus for, much larger organizational systems and designs. This understanding of the central role played by grouping activity in human affairs is reflected in an article by Poole (1998) that says, "The small group should be the fundamental unit of communication research" (p. 94). Small groups and the grouping activity they involve are keys to understanding the human experience.

Grouping is the centerpiece of human action and is at the heart of our framework for understanding group pitfalls and the co-construction of effective group experiences. *Grouping* and *group direction* are metaphors we use to represent ongoing and active processes that are dynamic in the moment and that change over time. Grouping and helping determine group direction represent recurring, universal types of activities people tend to engage in when they perceive an exigency for working in a group. Consequently, grouping and group direction are representative metaphors: representing the ongoing and dynamic changes co-constructed in recurring forms of activities that are basic to the human experience.

We need to take a moment here to describe how representative metaphors, such as grouping and group direction, are used in this book. What is a representative metaphor and what purpose is to be served by the use of a representative metaphor? First, let's understand metaphor. A metaphor names something in one domain as something from another domain (e.g., time is money, group work is a struggle for survival). Because metaphors are, by definition, cultural phenomena (Lakoff & Johnson, 1980), they represent "a culturally informed way of communicating" (Gershenson, 2003, p. 315). By drawing together two domains within the metaphor, a mental shorthand is created, allowing one to communicate much about the new concept or domain (group work) by making quick reference, through the metaphor, to aspects of the familiar domain (the struggle for survival). The mental shorthand helps evoke a sense of understanding about what is involved in the subject at hand.

A representative metaphor provides an evocative focus on a particularly important and recurring aspect of the human experience. A representative metaphor "turns up" and makes lucid (clear and vivid) the dramatic action that is being co-constructed in a situation (Burke, 1945; Madsen, 1993). Dramatic action indicates the human engagement in any setting. For example, when a person in a group interprets what is going on in his or her group, that individual then responds to the group rhetorically in a manner that is consistent with his or her interpretation of that situation. The individual's interpretation and his or her rhetorical responses to it constitute his or her engagement or dramatic action in the group. An individual's response to a group situation creates dramatic action, which helps others in the group co-construct their own interpretations of the group and their own rhetorical responses to the grouping experience. All grouping action is dramatic action and an indication of human engagement. The recurring nature of the basic aspects of such dramatic action requires representation in order to be noted and understood.

When we select metaphors to represent recurring, universal aspects of dramatic action in groups, we employ the basic shorthand of metaphor to draw the sort of comparison that helps create a cogent or powerful understanding of what is always involved in a group situation. This is consistent with Poole's (1990) claim that good theory requires compelling metaphors. So, for example, when we use *direction* as a representative metaphor in this book, it is our intention to take the familiar concept, direction, with its connotations of location in space, movement, and intended destination. We use it to represent the struggles all people have when they attempt to make sense of their situation as members of a group; theirs is a struggle to co-create group direction. As a device, a representative metaphor articulates a central idea that helps hold dramatic action together while providing a dynamic focal point around which diverse ideas and actions can cluster and connect.[2] A representative metaphor is a starting point for discovering the rhetorical elements in a situation and how they interact (Madsen, 1993).

The Framework for Grouping and Group Direction includes a set of representative metaphors used to evoke recurring aspects of the human engagement in groups (see Table 2.1). The framework is based on an understanding that each group is unique and yet shares with all other groups a certain few characteristics. For example, Burtis (1995) argues that a relatively small set of different types of direction givers (e.g., guides, managers, and leaders) are needed to address a wide range of grouping exigencies in order to help groups form, maintain themselves, or change their direction. The Framework for Grouping and Group Direction provides a set of metaphors that represent the recurring aspects of human experience in groups.

❖ THE FRAMEWORK FOR GROUPING AND GROUP DIRECTION

The Framework for Grouping and Group Direction describes how grouping activity helps co-construct group direction. It helps us understand group beginnings, changes, and endings as well as the potential benefits from grouping and the recurring pitfalls that challenge grouping efforts. It includes three propositions: (a) All groups form and all groups change, (b) forming and maintaining groups involve grouping activity and group direction, and (c) perception of an exigency for grouping (which serves as the impetus for grouping activity and group direction) creates a base for the rhetorical resources available to those who want to group or to affect group direction and a base for potential group pitfalls. To understand these propositions requires the use of several terms. The terms are the nomenclature and grammar for understanding the processes of grouping and of group direction (see Table 2.1).

Table 2.1   Framework for Grouping and Group Direction: Nomenclature and Grammar

Representative Metaphor	Definition
Aggregate	People who are unrelated by a common task or process or history.
Aggregate Puddle	The state of individuals who are neither grouping, nor experiencing an exigency to group, together. A relatable bunch of people who may be brought together by a grouping effort if a Purgatory Puddle begins.
Direction-Conducive Group	People who perceive an exigency to consider or to accept direction, or to try to provide direction to others. Indicates a Purgatory Puddle and rhetorical resources.
Direction Givers	Provide grouping direction by doing a task alone (doer); provide support or momentum for direction provided by another grouping member (follower); answer the question, "What do we do next?" (guide); serve formal authority functions (manager); or personify vision made salient by crisis (leader).
Direction Giving	Helping to move a group along or helping to change or stop a group's direction.
Entropy	Randomness. Prior to any exigency for grouping, it is the altogether absence of any order or grouping effort or group direction. After grouping ends, time passes, and the effects of grouping wane, randomness results.
Exigency	Anything perceived to provide an impetus for action; grouping-conducive exigency is perceived to invite grouping action; e.g., a problem or task that needs doing, an imperfection that needs correcting, an obstacle to overcome, an improvement to be attained, or the desire of an individual that requires grouping to satisfy. An exigency for grouping perceived is a Purgatory Puddle created.
Group Direction	Co-constructed sense of where the group is going and how. Indicates the momentum and effectiveness of grouping activities compared to eventual or desired grouping outcomes. Moving the group along.
Grouping	Activities and efforts of people responding to an exigency they perceive invites group action. Any attempts to create or to change group direction.
Inertia	The tendency for people and groups to continue what they are doing and how they are doing it until an exigency is perceived for making a change. Grouping requires effort to overcome inertia. Changing the direction or processes of a group also requires effort to overcome the inertia of normative group practices.
Purgatory Puddle	A rhetorical situation where people perceive an exigency for grouping to change or escape the status quo: purgatory impels escape. Comprised of a *supragroup*, a group-conducive *task*, and *personnel* available for grouping. (Scene exigency.)

Representative Metaphor	Definition
Rhetorical Situation	An exigency is perceived that invites a rhetorical act (e.g., a Purgatory Puddle is a rhetorical situation that invites grouping activity as a rhetorical response).
Savior Complex	Any attempt to get the group to follow a particular individual as direction giver. The negotiation of who will give and who will receive direction. Co-constructed relational dance among personnel in a Purgatory Puddle. (Agent exigency.)
The Quadrad	The four bases of exigencies, rhetorical resources, and pitfalls for grouping: Purgatory Puddle, The Way/Process, Vision/Outcome, Savior Complex.
The Way/ Process	The means for grouping. Any coordinating of activity to address grouping exigencies: the *techniques* (communicate, meet, and use a procedure); *tendencies* (norms, roles, and communication network); *process prizes* (creation, critical work, or member acceptance); and *concomitants* of grouping (confusion, conformity, conflict, and consciousness—climate, cohesion, culture). (Agency exigency.)
Vision/ Outcome	The ends desired from, or products of, grouping. Represented by the Promised Land. Final manifestation of the task in a Purgatory Puddle. (Purpose exigency.)

Grouping and Group Direction

The first terms, grouping and group direction, represent the sense of action and purpose in interdependent human interactions. People must blend their efforts in order to become and to operate as an effective group. Grouping is the activity of people attempting to address exigencies, which, they perceive, suggest interdependent human interaction in response. Grouping includes any attempts to create or to change group direction. Group direction involves a co-constructed sense of where the group is or should be going. An assessment of group direction can indicate a sense of the momentum and effectiveness of grouping activities as compared to eventual or desired grouping outcomes: an assessment of the progress and health of grouping activity and of the group enterprise. Sometimes a group will seem to lose its way or to stagnate. Even then, the representative metaphor (direction) helps us to describe such groups (as lacking direction, as having lost their way, as going nowhere, as wandering aimlessly, or as getting off track and not making any progress). Grouping members attempt to provide direction in order to help move the group along or to change where the group is going.

Burtis (1995) argues that all systems, from the small group to the complex organization, require basic grouping activities. At the start of this chapter, we describe a party scene in which people are asked by the host to get into a group. The response of individuals receiving the instruction to "get into a group" is to physically start to move together, to look at one another, to strike up conversations, to listen together for further instruction, to talk about the nature of the potential task and their interest in it, to describe their personal skills for doing the task, to make suggestions regarding how to proceed, and so forth. These efforts are grouping attempts. Such efforts start to affect the individuals involved and may begin to affect a group if the efforts to group are successful and continue over sufficient time.

To group is to gather together, and such gathering or grouping can be hard work because it requires care and attention. People are apart, they are moving alone (or in other groups), and they must now start to move together to co-construct a new group: a sense of shared purpose and shared perceptual boundaries. They must begin a symbolic convergence (Bormann, 1996), a sense of shared meaning about what is important to them and who they are as a group, in order to start moving in the same direction. Grouping messages are created and exchanged in attempts to co-construct some shared sense of meaning. Grouping processes can involve many tens, hundreds, or even thousands of communicative interactions over time in these efforts to co-construct a shared sense of meaning.

Fuhriman and Burlingame (1994) understand groups through the lens provided by chaos theory in order to explain that grouping involves apparently small or unimportant aspects of activity that can become big or vital aspects of a system later in its life. Structuration theory (Giddens, 1979; Poole, Seibold, & McPhee, 1985, 1986) says that any system is the "observable pattern of relationships among members" and the various "rules and resources used by members to construct the system." The structuration process is the continued "production and reproduction of . . . social systems" (Poole, 2003, p. 50). Grouping is dynamic, dramatic action in which interaction between group members is used to form and maintain their system.

Direction Giving and Direction Givers

Direction giving is the metaphor representing what happens when a group member helps to move a group along: helps to effect, affect, or stop a group's direction. Typically, grouping involves members taking turns suggesting or providing direction to their group. It also involves receiving direction from others in the group. For people to group effectively, they must begin to converge symbolically in order to start moving in the same direction. Direction giving is accomplished in a group any time one of its members commits an act or makes a statement that commands the attention and/or resources of others in the group.

There are five basic types of direction givers: doer, follower, guide, manager, and leader. Each direction-giving type is represented by a metaphor that evokes its key aspects as a recurring type of attempt to provide direction to groups. Doers and followers might seem unlikely names for direction-giving activity, but they turn out to be essential in almost every effective group. Guides, managers, and leaders are types of direction givers that are traditionally lumped together under the umbrella of leadership, but they are actually responses to different kinds of grouping exigencies (Burtis, 1995). The five types of direction giving and direction givers are metaphors that represent the potential for any grouping member to provide direction to a group.

Doers provide direction by working alone from start to finish on something necessary for the group. If a group needs to have baked items to sell, a doer bakes cakes. A doer's work encourages the group to make use of the completed effort (changing or perpetuating group direction) and frees group resources for other action. If the group does not make use of the doer's work, it takes a position in opposition to that work by attempting to move in a different direction.

Followers provide support or momentum for group direction by receiving and making effective use of the direction provided by another grouping member. Unlike the solitary action involving a doer, action that requires a follower will fail when proposed if no follower emerges in support. For example, if a group member has an idea for the group but nobody acknowledges the merits of the idea or supports it, the idea will likely not provide direction to the group. If a follower throws her or his support behind the direction suggested by a group member (e.g., by "seconding" or speaking on behalf of a motion in parliamentary procedure), she or he helps provide momentum for getting the group to move in the proposed direction. Some members become what Bormann (1996) calls a *lieutenant* when they actively support and help to articulate the position taken by another group member. Their efforts help to recruit additional support for the cause. Doers and followers play key roles in direction giving and are always necessary for effective group experiences.

Guides provide an answer to the question, "What do we do next?" For example, a guide can provide direction by giving a reason to try to change some aspect of the status quo or by showing a way for the group to proceed or by suggesting a destination or outcome for the group to consider. Guides help orient the group to the moment at hand. All grouping members can move in and out of the guide role, each providing direction to the group when they have some expertise or opinion that can help orient the group. Guideship approximates the activity of responsible group members in a participatory democracy: each contributes his or her expertise as needed when the group lacks direction. Guides are essential to every effective group experience.

A *manager* has formal authority over other grouping members. In some groups, managers have a job description that gives legitimate, formal authority to whomever holds that position to hire, assign tasks to, reallocate, and fire other personnel. Even when there is no such formal authority, there may be some issues sufficiently thorny or problematic that a group will vest a semblance of formal authority in one of its members, cocreating their manager. Leadership is vision made salient by crisis (Burtis, 1995). A *leader* personifies the vision co-constructed by the group and, consequently, is a type of direction giver needed only when grouping members perceive crisis exigencies. Managers and leaders may not be essential in every group experience; they are important, however, whenever grouping members perceive an exigency for them.

The direction-giving metaphor, though inclusive of what are traditionally considered leadership phenomena, is intended to signify no particular value or quality regarding the direction offered to a system. If your manager or leader tells you to do something, there is an assumption that doing that act is appropriate. If a direction giver tells you to do something, there is no such assumption. Offering to give direction to a group can include opposition to the group's current direction. Even the sense of need for direction can be in dispute, with some individuals in an aggregate arguing for grouping and others against.

The Direction-Conducive Group

Direction-conducive group is a metaphor representing people who perceive an exigency for interdependent human interaction. People in a direction-conducive group will tend to give serious consideration to the direction others attempt to provide to their group. They may also attempt to provide some direction to the group themselves. These people are open to the consideration of issues relating to their group's direction. When group direction is a salient issue, perceived by grouping members to be important, it increases the possibility that a direction-giving attempt will succeed. Consequently, a direction-conducive group has potential tactical or strategic rhetorical resources for any grouping member who wants to try to provide direction to the group.

Groups tend to maintain their direction (because of inertia) until group members get a sense of, and appreciation for, a new direction. Complaining about some aspect of their grouping may start a change and so might the suggestion of an alternative direction that people perceive sufficient exigency for taking. When a person acts to provide direction to a group, the rest of the group members can support that attempt or they can ignore or oppose the action. Support means expending energy to help continue the direction the grouping action provides. Ignoring or opposing a grouping attempt means expending energy against it or in favor of some other action.

Inertia

Inertia is a metaphor representing the tendency for people and groups to continue what they are doing until exigencies are perceived for making a change. To begin a new group requires effort to overcome inertia. To change the direction or processes of a group also requires effort to overcome the inertia of normative group practices. In physics, inertia means that bodies at rest stay at rest and bodies in motion stay in motion unless acted on by another force (i.e., something like how friction helps bring a rolling ball to rest). As a metaphor, inertia represents the tendencies toward continuation of current human activities that have a sense of direction to them. Consequently, new grouping activities require overcoming inertia to get started both because it takes new efforts to get started with a new grouping attempt and because the people who might group together are already engaged in doing other things.

Inertia is especially pronounced among people who have been grouping for some time as members of a successful group. Their strong sense of group direction leads to efforts to try to continue to group in ways that are familiar or similar (bodies in motion stay in motion) until and unless they get a reason for change (unless acted upon by another force). Their experience with successful grouping teaches them to presume that appropriate actions in the past indicate appropriate actions for the future. Consequently, co-constructing a new direction for a group requires both working toward the new direction and working at over-coming inertia against change within the established group or order. Extant or ongoing grouping activities may be harder to change than new activities are to start because the former get support for perpetuation from the inertia that "favors" continuing to do what is already being done. Patterns of human activity become normative, or like a habit, once we become used to doing certain things in certain ways.

To get a sense of how groups and patterns of grouping activity are co-constructed and then become normative, it is helpful to start by conceiving of an absence of any such dramatic action: the complete absence of grouping, group direction, or engagement in a setting. That involves a state of entropy. Conceiving of entropy allows us to appreciate the actions that help us move from a state of entropy into increasingly complex human interactions.

Entropy

Entropy is a metaphor representing randomness. Prior to grouping, prior to overcoming inertia and getting group direction, there is entropy or randomness: there is not even a sense of a potentially desirable new group. Entropy is important to groups only as a description of the obverse of grouping (e.g., when no exigency for grouping is perceived and no history of grouping is in place). Entropy is the absence altogether of any order or grouping effort or group direction. And, after any group ends, time passes, and the effects of grouping wane, randomness and entropy return. Because all groups end, there is a tendency toward entropy, which in human terms is the randomness from a complete absence of dramatic action or engagement in a setting. The metaphor has its limits. People who have not yet become interested in grouping together are at least already in existence as individuals (an individual, certainly, is not entropic) and are probably already engaged in other forms of grouping activity (also not entropic). But entropy can give us a sense of what precedes a particular grouping enterprise.

Common misinterpretations to avoid are to treat entropy as though it is the confusion or the uncertainty about how to proceed that commonly accompanies any grouping attempt or to confuse entropy with the times in the life of a group when its members are not making the effort necessary to group well together. Entropy is neither confusion nor the lack of sufficient effort to group well. Where entropy indicates a total lack of grouping impulse, history, or mechanism, these other conditions are mere pitfalls to effective grouping. Indeed, confusion and uncertainty are essential parts of the impetus for trying to make grouping more effective. The concept of entropy allows us to conceive of an aggregate of individuals, unrelated in any way, and also of what is required for them to try to change into a group. This allows us to consider several more terms in the Framework for Grouping and Group Direction.

Aggregate and Aggregate Puddle

Before any group can form, there must be an aggregate of potential people to consider doing the group work. *Aggregate* represents people who are unrelated by a common task, process, or history: without a shared sense of perceptual boundaries. In construction work, aggregate is the material to be formed together in concrete or building blocks; aggregate is not the stuff that binds the block together nor is it the block. For geologists, aggregate is the sum mass of material in a rock; it is not the rock. An example of an aggregate in a human context is five strangers who are walking in different directions down different streets in a city. They are an aggregate because they are unrelated in any way. They share no common task, no perceptual boundaries of membership, and no communicative interaction or interdependence.

Aggregate Puddle is a metaphor representing the state people are in before they begin to consider becoming part of a group. Because they are an aggregate, people in an aggregate puddle are neither grouping together nor experiencing an exigency to group together: they are independent of each other in terms of the future group effort. But, an aggregate puddle is comprised of people who are "relate-able" in some way other than grouping. They might be relate-able by their proximity (e.g., strangers riding the same elevator together but going to different floors, folks interviewed when a police officer looks for potential eyewitnesses who live near the scene of a crime). They might be relate-able by the need some unknown person has for grouping them (e.g., a CEO who sees "potential employees" among an "educated population" near where her company is thinking about locating a new plant). They might be relate-able by similar activity (e.g., strangers riding an elevator together) or by an impending external event (e.g., strangers working for different companies in a World Trade Center tower just as crashing planes send them streaming together down the stairway into a joint act of heroism on September 11, 2001). Aggregate Puddle represents a conceptual "place" where someone who wants to begin to group can find others who might be stimulated to group.

Recall Sykes's (1990) question: "When does an aggregate become a group?" Perception of an exigency can become the impulse for such a change. Bormann (1996) suggests that individuals do not actually stop being an aggregation until "members go to work and get to know one another [as] they divide up, coordinate, and structure their working procedures" (p. 2). In our terms, they stop being an aggregate when they can somehow be related to each other. They stop being an Aggregate Puddle when they begin to perceive an exigency for grouping together. The practical difference between an Aggregate Puddle and the beginning of a group is that grouping requires members to first perceive, and then to respond rhetorically to, an exigency for interdependent human interaction.

Exigency

Exigency is anything perceived to provide an impetus for action. Bitzer's (1968) conception of an exigence (hereafter exigency) is as "an imperfection marked by urgency; it is a defect, an obstacle, something waiting to be done, a thing which is other than it should be" (p. 6). A grouping-conducive exigency is anything perceived to invite grouping action: anything that helps create a desire to group or for group direction. Exigency as a metaphor represents the needs, desires, motives, and attitudes evident in the dramatic action of people engaged in a situation: in how grouping members frame and respond to their situation. Once grouping is attempted in response to a perceived exigency, that grouping attempt becomes a potential exigency for the actions of other group members.

When people perceive exigencies for grouping or for changing group direction, their actions in response are rhetorical. They try to bring a new group or group direction to life. Though not all exigencies invite rhetorical response (e.g., being hungry is an exigency for eating and no rhetorical action is involved), some exigencies do. An exigency perceived to require rhetorical action stimulates an act of discourse in response. Any attempt to group or to provide direction to a group is a rhetorical act.

Understanding the nature of rhetoric and rhetorical action is necessary in order to describe how grouping activities co-construct effective group experiences. Do not be confused by negative connotations for the word *rhetoric*. Rhetorical action is communication created to modify a situation. Brock and Scott (1972) explain that rhetoric is a "human effort to induce cooperation through the use of symbols" (p. 16). Symbolic action includes any use of language or of nonverbal behavior to help create or modify meaning. Rhetorical action in groups includes tactical or strategic attempts to provide a grouping impulse or direction. Grouping skills are rhetorical. Rhetorical competence includes the capacity to note what symbolic resources are available and then employ those resources well in the cause of effective grouping: to frame, articulate, and support good ideas, and to help others understand and respond effectively with their own actions.

An Aggregate Puddle may begin to consider grouping when they perceive an exigency—for example, if the elevator that several strangers are riding in got stuck between the second and third floors. Once stuck, the potential for grouping activity manifests in whatever exigencies are perceived from being stuck. Each person frames the situation (e.g., as a claustrophobic event worsened by the need to go to the toilet, as an opportunity to get acquainted and to share some tasty chips and salsa, as the sign of a terrorist attack). Each framing of exigencies has rhetorical resources that may be used to suggest a response to the situation. Some framings may oppose grouping (e.g., a desire to wait for an authority figure to get the elevator moving, the idea that it is unsafe to violate cultural norms by talking to strangers on an elevator, a negative reaction to others on the elevator). It is an open question whether grouping will be attempted and, if it is, whether it will succeed. An exigency that is perceived provides potential germination for grouping activity and direction.

❖ RHETORICAL SITUATION AND A PURGATORY PUDDLE

Any perceived sense of common purpose begins to change the nature of the situation and of how people might respond. Individuals who begin to share a sense of exigency for action are no longer only an Aggregate Puddle and yet neither are they a group. We again borrow one of Bitzer's (1968) terms to represent this circumstance: rhetorical situation. A rhetorical situation exists when someone perceives an exigency that invites rhetorical action in response. Rhetorical situations are not limited to settings that invite grouping in response. Groups are just one tool humans have at their disposal; grouping is just one kind of rhetorical action. However, if the exigency is perceived to require grouping in response, a special type of rhetorical situation is in play. Consequently, we use a more specific metaphor to describe a scene that involves a grouping-conducive rhetorical situation. When a rhetorical situation is grouping conducive, or a group is direction conducive, it is what we call a Purgatory Puddle.

Purgatory Puddle is a metaphor that represents a rhetorical situation where people perceive an exigency for grouping in order to change their status quo. They may seek to use a group (or a change in group direction) to modify or to escape their current state of affairs. The purgatory metaphor has connotations of a temporary and unpleasant setting. A Purgatory Puddle is a setting that people perceive will require them to work as a group in order to escape, purge, or expiate their problem. The perception of grouping exigencies within a Purgatory Puddle impels grouping members to try to change the status quo because it has become flawed or otherwise uncomfortable. A Purgatory Puddle involves people in transition.

A Purgatory Puddle is a conceptual place; it represents the recurring human experience of need for group action to seek desired change. As such, the Purgatory Puddle represents the bias toward action that manifests as the perception of exigencies for grouping and the readiness to respond to those exigencies by employing rhetorical resources available in a group's setting: the scene for their dramatic action (Burke, 1945). Every Purgatory Puddle is a setting consisting of three components: (a) a group-conducive task someone believes that grouping members should address, (b) the personnel available for grouping, and (c) supragroup issues, which are external-to-group contingencies that may motivate or affect grouping action. Consequently, supragroup issues are important to, but sometimes are also beyond the direct control of, grouping members. All of these are unpacked for their pitfall potential in chapters 3 and 4. In addition, these three components of a Purgatory Puddle are potential bases for grouping exigencies and for rhetorical resources to respond to those exigencies.

Every Purgatory Puddle is a potential or existing group setting. Every group begins as a Purgatory Puddle. As the group evolves, so, too, does its Purgatory Puddle. A Purgatory Puddle indicates that the scene is conducive to an attempt to create change through grouping. However, the presence of a Purgatory Puddle does not guarantee that there will be a group. If the exigency perceived for grouping is not sufficiently strong and salient, then other activities may be more engaging.

Consequently, they might not attempt to group or to change group direction in spite of perceived exigencies to do so.

If, and only if, a Purgatory Puddle is acted on, grouping activity begins. At that time, three additional representative metaphors come into play: The Way/Process, Vision/Outcome, and Savior Complex. These three, and Purgatory Puddle, comprise the Quadrad: four recurring types of dramatic action in grouping (Burtis, 1996, 1997, 2004a, 2004b). We use the Quadrad to extend the Framework for Grouping and Group Direction in three ways: first, to organize the recurring types of exigencies for grouping and group direction; second, to organize the recurring types of rhetorical resources available for co-constructing grouping and group direction; and third, to organize the recurring types of potential pitfalls that face people during any attempt to group. In short, the Quadrad metaphors represent the recurring forms of human engagement in attempts to co-construct effective group experiences.

The Quadrad metaphors apply as soon as any exigency perceived for grouping is responded to with a grouping attempt. The Quadrad terms help tell the story of grouping by representing the experience of a grouping member and of the group. The metaphors represent the dramatic, recurring forms of human action in systems whose members are oriented toward grouping: who think that working in a group is the right tool to use given the issues they face. Grouping members orient to their system with a bias toward action that the perception of grouping exigencies creates, and they show this orientation in their readiness to respond with rhetorical attempts to group or to affect group direction. The Quadrad metaphors represent that bias for action and readiness to respond.

There is the potential for varying intensities of perceived exigencies for grouping, of rhetorical strategies in response, and of system member engagement in grouping processes and purposes. Low intensity dramatic action involves the weakest exigencies for grouping, the weakest rhetorical response, and, consequently, the least engagement of grouping members in their group project. High-intensity dramatic action involves the strongest possible exigencies for grouping, the strongest possible rhetorical calls to action in response, and the strongest possible levels of engagement for members in their system. The metaphors in the Quadrad are intended to represent all these various intensities, by naming the strongest forms.

To put it succinctly, every aspect of grouping activity is accompanied by potential rhetorical resources for grouping members, in particular for those who attempt to give direction to the group. "Every aspect" means that rhetorical resources can be found (a) in the germinal conception of any need for starting a new system or for changing the direction of an existing system (Purgatory Puddle); (b) in the ongoing processes necessary to start a system, to continue to maintain the direction of a system, or to change its direction (The Way/Process); (c) in the ends desired by, and the purposes for, the system (Vision/ Outcome); and (d) in the various struggles involved in trying to act successfully as a direction giver in the system (Savior Complex). The possible exigencies perceived for grouping activity recur as one or more of these four types. The resources for grouping rhetoric, for the strategic and tactical communication of grouping, similarly recur as one or more of these four types.

The four terms in the Quadrad are not discrete. They represent symbiotic (interdependent) and synergistic (generative) aspects of any dramatic action involved in grouping: each affects and helps effect the other (see the integrated model in Figure 2.1). Each is also affected by the suprasystem and the historical, social, and cultural context in which the group works. The combination of these four terms, the Quadrad, represents the recurring aspects of dramatic action or of human engagement in grouping action.

The Way/Process metaphor represents any means employed for putting order to grouping activity. This includes any attempt to coordinate the interactions of grouping members so they can address grouping exigencies and attempt to achieve a process prize. The recurring aspect of human experience is the need for, and attempt to provide, order in group processes. Although almost every group has several possible ways to co-construct desirable outcomes, there is a need, stronger in some people than in others, to do things "the right way." Others are happy if there is any small semblance of order. The Way metaphor has connotations of a correct path or procedure. Any thought about what is an appropriate way to group results in the perception of exigencies for encouraging appropriate processes. Such conceptions also affect whether grouping is perceived to be done well or poorly. The Way/Process includes any grouping effort that responds to Purgatory Puddle exigencies by trying to develop a means for escaping the Purgatory Puddle.

The Way/Process represents the bias toward action that manifests as exigencies for organizing grouping attempts. The Way/Process also represents the readiness to respond by employing rhetorical resources available in a group's means or processes: the agencies of their dramatic

Figure 2.1   The Quadrad: Bases of Grouping Exigencies, Rhetorical
Resources, and Group Pitfalls

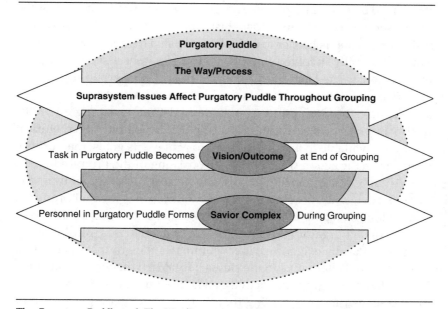

The *Purgatory Puddle* and *The Way/Process* each affects and helps effect the other. The *Vision/Outcome* and the *Savior Complex* in turn affect and effect ongoing changes in the Purgatory Puddle and The Way/Process as well as in each other. "Spilling over" the boundaries in the model indicates the symbiotic (interdependent) and synergistic (generative) relationships each base has with the cultural, social, and historical context in which the grouping takes place, and with all and each of the other bases. Outside the Purgatory Puddle, other groups involve or affect grouping members in the Purgatory Puddle.

action (Burke, 1945). The Way/Process agencies of action are comprised of the techniques (communicate, meet, use a procedure), tendencies (norms, roles, communication network), process prizes (creation, critical work, or member acceptance), and concomitants of grouping (confusion, conformity, conflict, consciousness—climate, cohesion, culture). All of these are unpacked for their pitfall potential in chapters 5 and 6. Throughout the life of the system, The Way/Process will be co-constructed synergistically and symbiotically with the evolving Purgatory Puddle, Vision/Outcome, and Savior Complex.

Vision/Outcome is a metaphor that represents the final products of, and purposes for, grouping. Vision/Outcome exigencies and rhetoric are based in trying to articulate where the group should go and what should comprise the completion of its task or project. *Vision* has a connotation of foresight or special insight into where a group ought to be headed or of what the group should attempt to accomplish. It also connotes a special sense of purpose: the importance of the group and its work. The outcomes of any group can be assessed by how well the group served its three functions: task, relational, and individual. The vision of a group is harder to articulate and also harder to assess, but it can be integrally involved in how grouping members see themselves, their co-constructed activities, and their purpose for grouping.

Vision/Outcome represents the bias toward action that manifests as exigencies for attaining the ends desired from grouping attempts. It also represents the readiness to respond by employing rhetorical resources available in a group's desire to achieve its goals: the purpose for its dramatic action (Burke, 1945). Consisting of the Promised Land, the Vision/Outcome includes both the *promise,* or desirability of the group's goal, and the actual substance of its *land,* or its final products. The Vision/Outcome is the evolved co-construction of the task component of a Purgatory Puddle. Vision/Outcome is a resolution of Purgatory Puddle exigencies; it consummates the grouping act with a co-constructed alternative to the status quo. When the Vision/Outcome is completed and grouping activity ends, the Purgatory Puddle ceases to be co-constructed, assuming that there is no longer a perception of an exigency for grouping.

The Savior Complex metaphor represents the co-constructed dance in which grouping members learn how to give and to receive direction in their group. The easiest glimpse of some aspect of the Savior Complex is found in any attempt to get the group to follow a particular individual as a direction giver, but the dance involves all grouping members. *Savior* has connotations of hope for being saved, rescued from the Purgatory Puddle. Some people put their hope on having someone else provide direction for their group. For others, *savior* connotes the idea that there might be one best or right person to provide that direction or that there might be one best or right way to give direction to a group. Complex has connotations of pathological behavior and also of complexity. Both meanings are intended and are helpful in representing the complex, and sometimes unhealthy, amalgam of dynamics and relationships involved as group members interact and attempt to co-construct common purpose, process, and direction. All of the attempts to provide direction to a group affect Savior Complex, even those focused on describing problems in the Purgatory Puddle, providing The Way/Process, or the suggesting Vision/Outcome.

Savior Complex represents the bias toward action that manifests as exigencies for receiving direction from another group member or for attempting to provide direction to others. Savior Complex also represents the readiness to respond by employing rhetorical resources available in the personal credentials of grouping members: the nature of the agents involved in the group's dramatic action (Burke, 1945). Savior complex has its origins in the personnel component of a group's Purgatory Puddle. As grouping activity unfolds, grouping members develop a patterned sense of each other as grouping members and of the relationships among grouping members. All of these are integrally involved in the Savior Complex dance.

❖ CHAPTER SUMMARY AND CONCLUSION

In this chapter, we introduce you to a Framework for Grouping and Group Direction, which includes metaphors that represent recurring forms of the dramatic action typical of human engagement in grouping activities. In the following chapters, we use the nomenclature and grammar introduced in this chapter to talk about successful groups, failed groups, and about how communication increases the likelihood that a group of people will be able to avoid or to work through potential group pitfalls (see Table 2.2 for an overview of pitfalls addressed in Unit II). The representative metaphors in this chapter help "tell the story" of grouping and direction-giving action as people make rhetorical attempts to overcome the barriers to effective group experiences.

Table 2.2   Partial Summary of Grouping Pitfalls by Quadrad Base

Metaphor	Pitfall Type	Definition	Pitfall Examples
Purgatory Puddle	Task Issues	Wrong task for a group	Task never understood by group. Task does not command interest. Task is too simple. Task with means-independent process.
	Personnel Issues	Wrong group of members for task	Group with too few/many members. Members lack necessary personal resources. Negative assembly effect (e.g., dogmatic, hidden agenda).
	Supragroup Issues	Factors beyond group's control	Competition with other groups. Resource obligation to other groups. Poor boundary spanning. Poor consciousness raising.
The Way/ Process	Technique Pitfalls	Inappropriate procedures	Inadequate communication. Problems with meetings. Lack appropriate procedure or use of faulty or hurtful procedure.

(Continued)

Table 2.2 (Continued)

Metaphor	Pitfall Type	Definition	Pitfall Examples
	Tendency Pitfalls	Development of norms and roles	Lack constructive norms. Inadequate enforcement of norms. Lack of constructive roles. Problems with communication network.
	Process Prize Pitfalls	Inappropriate critical or creative thinking	Too much or too little critical or creative thinking. Inadequate or flawed deliberation process. Use of fallacious reasoning.
	Concomitant Pitfalls	Confusion, conformity, conflict, and consciousness	Inadequate framing. Too little or too much conformity or conflict. Lack of cohesion or productive climate or culture.
Vision/ Outcome	Promise Pitfalls	Group member perceptions	Inadequate sense of grouping salience to justify continued effort. Inadequate attraction to goals or outcome group is working toward.
	Land Pitfalls	Aspects of accepted inferior outcome	Opportunity costs. (Un)anticipated bad consequences of change. Failure to attain goals or solve problem.
	Finishing Pitfalls	Inappropriate grouping completion	Poor implementation. Poor group acceptance or commitment. Poor follow-up and follow-through.
Savior Complex	Conception Pitfalls	Over-/ underreliance on direction giver	Failure to want direction giver. Overreliance on direction giver. Overattribution of credit or blame to direction giver.
	Ascension Pitfalls	Inappropriate choice of direction giver	Appointment versus emergence. Inadequate follower or lieutenant recruitment and support. Inadequate or flawed credentialling.
	Poor Choices Pitfalls	Inappropriate choices by direction giver	Poor direction-giving choices (e.g., wrong direction-giving type, style, base of power, or balance of group functions).
	Transition Pitfalls	Inappropriate cultivation of direction givers	Failure to cultivate new direction givers. Failure to pass baton. Failure to acculturate new direction giver or group to new direction giver.

3

Pitfalls in Task and Supragroup Exigencies

❖ ❖ ❖

H ave you ever been in a group where you got frustrated because you could have done the group's work better or faster if you had just worked alone? Ever cheered for a team that was hampered because the organization that managed it was lousy? Ever had someone you were working with not pull his or her own weight because of trouble with his or her home life? Ever been asked by someone to speak on behalf of a group you belong to in a way that was uncomfortable because you had no authority to do so? Ever been part of a group that struggled to find new members? Ever had a turf battle against another group? Such experiences are common. They all involve pitfalls that arise because of the nature of the job a group is working on or because of the circumstances in which the group must work. We begin our specific discussion of potential group pitfalls with some that may even be evident before group interaction begins. Purgatory Puddle pitfalls manifest from the *supragroup* in which the group will work, from the nature of the *task* on which a group will work, and from the *personnel* available for the work.

❖ GROUPS AS SYSTEMS

Every human group is an open system. Everything that goes on in a system has the potential to affect every other thing in the system (interdependence). Although there may be many component parts and processes in a system, if you change any one of those, the system itself is changed (wholeness), so we cannot reduce a system to its parts, study just one of those parts, and still succeed in understanding the nature of the whole system (irreducibility). Even if a system is focused on one task, there may be several ways to do the job well (equifinality—many ways to equivalent outcomes: i.e., "there is more than one way to skin a cat"). Every human system is comprised of subsystems and is also enmeshed in suprasystems (hierarchical embeddedness), which provide a context (environment) for the system and a source of necessary resources (inputs). These features of systems help us understand some of the dynamics of the dramatic action in groups.

The dynamics of a system make linear predictions of cause and effect almost useless. Consequently, our attributions of who or what causes problems in our groups tend to be simplistic. Henman (2003) explains:

> [A] "domino effect" is apparent whenever group members interact because the effects of any action will cause consequences to ripple through the system. Explaining how or why an outcome occurred is very complex because all the reasons for a result are not obvious. Often group members never find the answers to their questions because they try to look at just one aspect of the group's system, which is frequently the most recent action of an individual in the group. No one answer is likely to provide the complete story. (p. 6)

Grouping members are interdependent by definition, and a change in one member or in how one member behaves can affect the relative effectiveness of each of the others in a group and of the very nature of the group they co-construct. The ongoing structuration of processes and meanings as people co-construct their groups makes it important to avoid simplistic conclusions regarding the potency and effects of a particular pitfall or person. Unfortunately, the efficient way to transfer to you the information regarding potential pitfalls is in the form of seemingly static lists of phenomena. Beware: though we define and describe pitfalls for you one at a time, none of the issues we are about to discuss is discrete or fully independent from other grouping activity.

❖ PURGATORY PUDDLE PITFALLS

The *Oxford Essential Dictionary* (1998) defines purgatory as a "state of temporary suffering or expiation" (p. 486), which makes *purgatory* an effective representative term for the transitory nature of exigencies that are perceived by people for trying to change their status quo. The Purgatory Puddle is not an actual place; it is the group members' conception or understanding of the circumstances that give birth to a group. A Purgatory Puddle exigency is some sort of charge or complaint against the status quo, against the current way or state of things. A charge is a task given to a group to complete. A complaint is an expression of desire for change. After a salient charge or complaint is stated, members feel obligated to make some sort of response.

Any rhetorical situation is impermanent because perceived exigencies change with dramatic action. A Purgatory Puddle is similarly dynamic because perceptions of exigencies for grouping are temporary and evolving. Once grouping has begun, for example, shortage of time or inadequate effort by group members can become salient exigencies in the evolving Purgatory Puddle. The evolving Purgatory Puddle endures as a dynamic grouping-conducive circumstance of expiation, transition, and change.

Groups, as co-constructions, are only as strong as their interactions to overcome the challenges they face. Our description of Purgatory Puddle pitfalls is organized as supragroup, task, or personnel issues (the latter are dealt with in chapter 4). As you read these pitfalls, remember that the challenge from a pitfall can help a group grow stronger as they work together to avoid or to overcome the pitfall.

❖ SUPRAGROUP PITFALLS

Supragroup issues are external-to-group contingencies that may motivate or affect grouping action. *Supra* means above, beyond, or transcending. Supragroup pitfalls manifest as environmental constraints, which may diminish or overpower grouping exigencies or grouping efforts. There are some dynamics that are beyond the control of a group, at least in terms of the fact that they predate grouping, but none of them are beyond the capacity of a group to talk about. Failure to expect, detect, and attempt to avoid or to work through such problems constitutes a group communication pitfall by omission.

Table 3.1   Summary of Purgatory Puddle: Supragroup Pitfalls

Supragroup Pitfall	Examples
Inappropriate Resources	Insufficient time or usable space or materials.
Crisis in Supraenvironment	Community crisis becomes an excuse for failure.
Competition With Other Groups	When competition is used as an excuse for distorted behaviors. When group member attentions turn to joining a better group.
Obligations to Other Groups	Time or energy needed for one group are obligated to another.
Norm Competition	Preference for "the way we did things in my old group."
Values Mismatch With Supragroup	The organization wants a lot done fast, whereas the group wants to put out the best product possible, which takes more time.
Poor Boundary Spanning	Poor coordination of activity and jurisdiction with other groups.
Poor Recruiting and Consciousness Raising	New members are not recruited or socialized well. Needed support from outside agents is not cultivated.
History Between Members	Past relationships affect or interfere with future grouping options.

Inappropriate or Inadequate Resources

An environment that includes insufficient or inappropriate resources for grouping can become a potential pitfall to group efforts. Potential for success is diminished when environmental contingencies allow too little time or in some other way retard the resources necessary for effective grouping. Being forced by a plane crash to share a small lifeboat as the group's only potential workplace and a shortage of food or water necessary to allow members the sustenance needed while paddling themselves to safety are two examples. Physical resources can be conducive to grouping or they can hinder, even hurt, the attempt. Effects of a resource shortage may manifest throughout the life of grouping activities. Faced with inadequate or inappropriate resources, grouping members change what they would otherwise do in order to orient to their struggle against environmental constraints. When poverty or being reared in an abusive family is used to explain aberrant behavior, it is recognition of the effects that environmental variables can have on individuals and on their actions. The group co-constructed under such circumstances may become jaded by its ongoing responses to the circumstances, just as it might also find ways to become strengthened by how it overcomes its challenges.

Crisis in the Supraenvironment

Crisis in the group's supraenvironment also diverts energy away from grouping. Examples include a building that is on fire while a group is trying to meet or when group members try to work though their company is facing bankruptcy and may lay off some of the group's members. Although a supragroup crisis may sometimes be turned into a point of opportunity, it also always competes for the attentions of group members. A group's response either helps strengthen or diminish the group. Temporary delays in grouping can be appropriate, but not when a group uses them to construct an excuse for failure. Environmental issues that command the attention of group members threaten to divert energies from grouping and to provide an excuse to fail.

Competition With Other Groups

Competition between groups manifests two ways. Either can be responded to in beneficial ways or in harmful ways. First, competition occurs in disputes regarding allocation of resources or outcomes (who gets the resources; who gets to win). Second, competition occurs in disputes regarding how to frame the Purgatory Puddle, which can influence the loyalties of individuals engaged in task issues involved in that Purgatory Puddle. Sometimes competition with other groups helps a group to accomplish more than if they were working without such an external basis for comparison. Some co-constructions of competition may, however, divert grouping energies toward destructive aspects of the competition at the expense of more important grouping activities. How grouping people frame and co-construct competition with other groups is the key to whether they create more or less energy for their grouping.

When two or more groups require the same resource, and only one of them can actually have the resource, they co-construct a *zero-sum game* (e.g., only one team can win a game: the other team loses). Sometimes intergroup competitions involve a zero-sum game. Sometimes grouping members just co-construct the perception of a zero-sum game out of their preference for the energies such competition provides them. Sometimes grouping members are just too limited in their vision to conceive of other possibilities such as co-constructing a *win-win* situation in which energy and value are added to both competing or cooperating groups. The real question is whether beneficial or harmful effects result from their framing and co-construction of their Purgatory Puddle. Competition helps if it enhances the ability of the groups involved to serve their three functions (task, relational, individual).

When competition is harmful, however, its negative effects may go beyond the loss of the energy required for grouping. Bormann (1996) elaborates on the possible negatives of competition. A modified version of his list of ills includes (a) when one group belittles members in another group, (b) when nonmembers are treated unethically or when the ethical code of group members is violated, (c) when group members are encouraged to behave badly to demonstrate their loyalty, (d) when turf wars focus energy on getting resources rather than on using them wisely, (e) when the group protects or advances itself at the expense of the suprasystem, and (f) when group members try to elevate their status to gain exemption from the laws or norms that govern other members in society. When such harmful effects become evident as a result of competition, a pitfall is in play and should be responded to with a change in grouping practice.

The second manifestation of competition involves alternate framings of a Purgatory Puddle. Multiple groups sometimes form from the same Purgatory Puddle if the task or issue involved is sufficiently salient in the perceptions and rhetoric of grouping members to become constitutive of a number of different kinds of grouping responses. Each different response is probably based in a different framing of the Purgatory Puddle. Such alternate framings may stir an interest among grouping members in alternatives to their own current grouping attempts. For example, civil rights issues in the mid-twentieth century spawned many grouping activities in response. Some were attracted to the framing of the Purgatory Puddle advocated by the Reverend Dr. Martin Luther King, Jr., and others were attracted to the framing articulated by Malcolm X. All ongoing groups need to recruit new members. Members of one group may use their framing of the Purgatory Puddle to compete for the attention or loyalties of people who are already involved in another group. Members may start to rethink their loyalties as they see how their group behaves versus how an alternate group behaves. Different exigencies may become salient as experience

with the topic broadens. Again, the co-construction of the framing for such competition determines whether it helps or hurts the involved groups.

Members' Obligations to Other Groups

Grouping members' obligations to other groups can diminish the personal resources still available for them to bring to the new grouping effort. If you were kept late at work and that keeps you from attending to the obligations you have for a family or community group, you experience this tension. We discuss this same issue from an individual's perspective in later chapters. Right now, we focus on the issue from the perspective of the resources available to a group. Limits created by obligations to other groups in the suprasystem are always a potential issue. Those demands vary according to the changing dynamics and circumstances of the other group. It makes sense to recognize from the beginning of any attempt to group that grouping is limited by member obligations to other groups.

Norm Competition

Norm competition may result when a group member belongs to two different groups where the behavioral norms are at odds. Poole (2003) describes the tendency for group members to try to re-create conventions from one group to the next. Bormann (1996) explains that "when people are members of several groups and discover contradictory norms, they . . . often try to resolve the conflict by adopting one norm consistently. When this happens, they will adopt the norms of the more attractive of the two groups" (p. 188). The pitfall can also manifest with norms set during an earlier grouping experience, as in, "We didn't do it this way where I come from." When a new player on a college or pro team chafes at the new team's conventions, the issue is probably her or his preference for the more familiar norms of the old team. Experiencing a significant change to one of your basic conventions for how grouping should be done can make the transition to any new group difficult.

Kelman (1961) describes compliance with group norms as proceeding from *conformity* (doing what the group expects because the group expects it), to *identification* (doing what the group expects because one likes doing it), to *internalization* (turning a group norm into one's own value; trying to employ that value in one's other groups). Cross-fertilization of experiences across groups is a healthy form of diversity. If a member's identification with or internalization of a norm from one group creates problems in another group, however, it becomes a pitfall that must be addressed before a benefit from the diversity of experiences and outlooks can be attained.

Values or Goals Mismatch Between Group and Suprasystem

A poor match between the values and goals embraced by a group and the values and goals embraced by supraorganizational entities upon which the group depends can prove to be a pitfall to both. Supra-organizational values should manifest in the support they provide for some grouping activities and the neglect or damage they inflict on other grouping activities. Otherwise, that is a pitfall in and of itself. When organizational rewards are in line with organizational values, then grouping will be enhanced when grouping members' values and practices line up with the supragroup's. When they do not line up, there is a poor match between what the group does and values and what the supragroup wants done and valued.

Differences in values are common and the effects can be damaging. Broome and Fulbright (1995) identify a typical issue when cultural forces operating within organizations value quantity over quality and result in group members being pressed for immediate results, when they would prefer spending more time to develop better results. Another issue concerns long- and short-term goals. When team management is trying to implement a "youth movement" to build for success in future years and the team is trying to win the pennant this year, the two entities are at odds. In any such cases, supragroup actions will tend to confound the group, and supragroup values will tend to reward alternatives to what the group attempts. The mismatches can become deterrents to grouping activities, creating tensions in the group as it struggles to preserve its own integrity. Even when the group complies with supragroup values (as opposed to identifying with or internalizing the values), the quality of their work is no doubt affected.

When members of several different groups within an organization have to group together, similar tensions can be involved. Putnam (2003) says such problems are to be expected in any *bona fide group* (groups that have to negotiate their boundaries with other groups in an organization or community).

Members bring to the group setting divergent interests, disparate values, and specialized jargon that reflect occupational and departmental differences. Through making sense of their organizational roles, groups form stereotypes of other departments. . . . Moreover, members of "warring factions" may take their intergroup perceptions into their team meetings in ways that construct internal dynamics. (p. 13)

These are common concerns in bona fide groups because they are accountable both to their supraorganizational group and community as well as to their own group. Effective group work can enhance both the group and the supragroup. Sometimes, however, otherwise excellent people and processes can be laid low by such tensions. Such mismatches in values or goals can lead to reductions in ability to serve all three grouping functions.

Poor Boundary Spanning

A key to addressing some supragroup pitfalls is found in how group members interface or communicate with the supragroup. When group members talk to members of other grouping entities, they are *boundary spanning* and, as with any grouping activity, boundary spanning provides the potential for pitfalls. Poor boundary-spanning processes with supragroup entities can limit group or individual member effectiveness. If groups do not succeed at negotiating their boundaries with the other groups their members belong to (whether or not they are part of the same organizational entity), the group's chances of success are reduced. If issues regarding how a group should try to accomplish its needs for boundary spanning are not discussed openly, pitfalls are more likely to manifest. Boundary spanning, according to Putnam, involves coordinating actions among systems. Each group must work out its desired level of isolation and of integration for its communications and activities with other groups. Groups negotiate jurisdiction and autonomy into patterns of communication, affecting their accountability and responsibility. All of this involves the need for effective boundary spanning.

Consider the role communication plays in the negotiation of group boundaries. It is through boundary negotiations that the "internal and external dynamics of a team" are realized (Putnam, 2003, p. 9). A group must have perceptual boundaries that members use to distinguish between who they are as a group and who they are not. Those boundaries, however, are co-constructed and dynamic. Putnam and Stohl's (1996) bona fide group perspective recognizes that fluid boundaries are a natural feature of groups. The growth and longevity of a group are tied to its members' success negotiating boundaries with other systems. Poor boundary-spanning processes are a fundamental source of potential pitfalls in any grouping activity.

Poor Recruiting and Consciousness-Raising Processes

Any grouping activity must begin with some concern about getting others involved. Poor recruiting and poor consciousness-raising processes both hurt effective grouping. Poor recruiting can inhibit the necessary flow of new members in general; poor consciousness raising can inhibit the translation of personnel into well-socialized group members. In addition, poor consciousness raising, which involves helping others understand the purposes and processes of the group, can limit the group's ability to generate support for grouping causes from important constituents and stakeholders who are not group members. Recruiting mines the ore (people); consciousness raising refines it into useful form (grouping members or support from key constituents). Properly socialized new recruits understand and appreciate what a group is, does, and means to its more experienced members: its co-constructed common purpose and perceptual boundaries. Putnam (2003) suggests that "new members import new ideas to the group and former members carry a residue of the past into new groups. As membership changes, boundaries change and can alter a group's identity, goals, and even its unique niche" (p. 11). At issue are the potential pitfalls facing any group as it attempts to extract from its supragroup circumstances sufficient personnel and support.

History With Group or Grouping Member(s)

You may find yourself involved in a new group with group members who are already familiar. The final supragroup pitfall may manifest anytime one begins to group with an individual or group of individuals who are already familiar, whether the shared history was good or bad. In such cases, you are likely to perceive the new group based in part on the good or bad baggage that individual helps bring to your mind. This can affect your desire to group; it can lead to your increasing, reducing, or changing the nature of your grouping efforts. It is interesting to note that the potential exists for past bad history to be overcome in a group as people find out that "old so and so" is not such a "bad so and so" after all. And, some good friends find that grouping together puts a strain on their relationships. Communication involves looking for and creating common meanings; the history you share with others can serve as a help or hindrance to that. So, the issue again boils down to how well grouping members are able to co-construct their current and future interactions. The past should be kept in perspective as just one set of information, and not be viewed as determinative of the future.

A group is only as strong as the interactions it co-constructs. Many key interactions are with its supragroup.

❖ WRONG TASK FOR A GROUP

The "wrong task for a group" is a mistaken response to a rhetorical situation. The mistake is to treat the situation as a Purgatory Puddle, which requires grouping in response, rather than as a situation conducive to the efforts of an individual, a dyad (two people), or a nominal group instead. The important decision of whether to use grouping as a tool should be an open question for any group. Some projects should not be done by a group. In addition, every project that requires the attention of a group may include some activities better done by an individual. The questions that help to determine whether to use grouping are, "What type of tasks should be done by a group?" and, if a group is the proper tool, "Which aspects of the project should be done by the group?" Part of the answers are found in three aspects of the role played by communication in completing the task and part of the answers are found in three aspects of how grouping members relate to the task. The decision of whether to group around a task involves all six issues. Judging well when not to use a group is a useful skill.

A group is not always the best tool. There is a substantial history of research comparing the relative strengths of individuals and groups on problem-solving tasks. After a review of that research, Hirokawa (1990) explains why groups are better for some tasks and individuals are better for others. First, the *task structure* influences the need for procedural order or planning. As the complexity of the task increases, so, too, does the need for a group because a group may be able to develop

Table 3.2   Summary of Purgatory Puddle: Task Pitfalls or "Wrong Task for a Group"

Issues based in the role communication plays in completing the task.	
Task is too simple	Group members already know what to do without discussion.
Task is means independent	Group members can work faster and better alone.
Task has clear solution	Group members do not need to figure out or test the answer.
Issues based in how grouping members relate to the task.	
Task is incoherent	A poorly conceived charge is not understandable even to creator.
Task is not salient	Group members do not perceive exigencies for doing the task.
Task needs no acceptance	The outcome can be successful without any group commitment to it.

a better set of procedures to address the task. Second, as the *information requirements* of the task increase, so does the need for a group in which there can be more information exchange and information-processing behaviors. Groups are better than individuals when members are "required to coordinate their efforts to collectively analyze, interpret, and apply available information to complete the task" (p. 196). Finally, *evaluation demands* can increase the need for a group. When it is unclear how to assess alternative solutions and there is a need to develop suitable evaluation criteria, a group is better suited for the task. In all three cases, the primary distinction is how inherently essential communication is to the nature of the task. Tasks that require interaction for success are better for groups, and those that do not are better for individuals or some other entity. Tasks that require the most interaction tend to be complex, have means-interdependent information requirements, and equivocal evaluation criteria. Table 3.3 provides additional details for each consideration, as does the following discussion of each type of pitfall.

Task Is Too Simple

Some tasks require discussion before one can feel competent to begin to address them. Others are simple enough to work on without discussion. If any individual, upon seeing the situation, understands

Table 3.3   Individual Vs. Group Task Components

Task Structure Requirements	*The difference between simple and complex tasks involves:*
Goal Clarity	Extent that group is conscious of final goal for task completion.
Goal-Path Clarity	Extent that group recognizes method for achieving desired goal.
Goal-Path Mechanics	Total number of steps necessary to achieve group goal.
Goal-Path Obstacles	Total number of obstacles that hinder completion of group goal.

Task-Structure Continuum

Simple Task		Complex Tasks
Better for Individual	-----------------------------------	Better for Group

Information Requirements	*Effort required to achieve group goal involves:*
Information Distribution	Do all members hold all necessary information to complete task?
Information Processing	Quantity and complexity of information needed for task.

Information Requirement Continuum

Means-Independent Task		Means-Interdependent Task
Better for Individual	-----------------------------------	Better for Group

Evaluation Demand Requirements	*Effort to determine appropriateness of choice involves:*
Solution Multiplication	Total number of choices believed to be correct or appropriate.
Criteria Clarity	Degree to which evaluation standards are offered.
Objective Verifiability	Extent that group choice is clearly correct or acceptable.

Evaluation Demand Continuum

Unequivocal Tasks		Equivocal Tasks
Better for Individual	-----------------------------------	Better for Group

the nature of the task and can go to work on it alone and in a manner seen as appropriate by concerned stakeholders, the task is too simple for a group. Task structure requirements (see Table 3.3) indicate when a task is too simple to require interaction to address. Assigning such a task to a group can create pitfalls (cf. Newell, 1980). Letting people work alone can be more efficient than if a group is convened and everyone is made to wait to proceed until they have discussed together the basic nature of a simple task. In such cases, group processes and interaction can actually create confusion or other problems. Grouping members may tune in and out of the conversation, listening to part of what is discussed and not to other parts. Further, group dynamics always involve the risk that a concomitant to grouping, such as a negative aspect of conformity or conflict, will diminish group outcomes. In the case of simple tasks, such risks are avoidable. Tasks should be scrutinized by grouping individuals before they decide that the task is sufficiently complicated to be conducive to group work.

Task Is Means Independent

Tasks with processes that can be engaged effectively alone have pitfall potential when addressed by a group. Driving a car is a *means-independent* process, better done by one person at a time. Other tasks require coordinated effort and communication to accomplish well because of the nature and dispersion of the information involved in addressing them. Playing football or a game of bridge are means-interdependent processes, better done by a group than by a dyad, individual, or nominal group. The information requirements for group interaction (Table 3.3) indicate when a task is means independent. Group tasks should have "integrative complexity" (Gruenfeld & Hollingshead, 1993). When a task requires group members to share information and to interact about complex information, they must work well together to do well. If the task does not require such interaction, the potential for pitfalling increases with the use of a group.

A warning is in order: This is not an argument against groups whenever people can find ways to work alone. People with a bias against doing work as a group often make the mistake of dividing a group task up into individual assignments so that they do not have to interact much. That is a mistake on tasks that would benefit from the process prizes available only through grouping. Just as the ability of a group to work on a task does not automatically justify using a group to work on it, the ability of individuals to do a task does not justify working alone. The issue is not ability; it is the quality of work, which is based in the part interaction plays in doing a given task. Consequently, discussion is helpful regarding when group interaction is appropriate.

Clear Solution Is Available

Groups are less necessary for tasks with clear, easily identified, and objectively confirmable evaluation requirements (see Table 3.3), which indicate when a clear solution is available. In such cases, a group is not needed to decide what constitutes success. Individual members and stakeholders each know a successful outcome when they see or do it.

Group discussion of the communication requirements given the task should occur in every group. When a task appears to be better suited for a group than for an alternate entity, on any one of these first three potential pitfall issues, people should err toward addressing the task as a group (at least the aspects of the task better served by grouping). Even when people decide not to engage a task because it is a "wrong task for a group," they should agree in advance to be willing to reconsider the decision not to group, if new exigencies for grouping become salient to them. Finally, whenever a grouping member makes a compelling case for grouping action, people should err toward grouping in response. The reason for that is related to the next three "wrong task" issues, the ones involving how people relate to their task.

Task Is Incoherent: Cannot Be Understood

Some tasks lack sufficient coherence ever to be understood by group members (Gouran & Hirokawa, 2003, p. 29). If the entity issuing a charge (giving an assignment) to the group fails to understand and articulate a reasonable task, the task may never become clear to the group either, making it more likely to struggle without the benefits that can come from such a struggle. This does not mean that tasks must be immediately clear to the group in order to be suited for group work. Indeed, tasks that are simple and clear are generally not suited to group work either. Tasks with ambiguities in them, which can be managed through grouping processes, can help strengthen a group (Salazar, 1995). Groups excel, relative to individuals working alone, when faced by difficult or equivocal material and situations. However, some tasks are so inherently unclear, perhaps even to the individual who assigns them to the group, that they become part of a recipe for failure. If a group co-constructs what they consider appropriate outcomes to such an incoherent task, there is still the possibility that the individual who gave them the charge might be dissatisfied, having expected some other kind of outcome. *Any such supragroup entity should be consulted by the group or its representative until a mutually agreed-on understanding of what the task comprises can be co-constructed and documented. The effort to co-construct and to document (in writing if necessary) a mutually agreed-on framing of the task can be an excellent use of grouping energy.*

Task Is Not Salient

A group is a tool used in response to the perception of a salient exigency for grouping. A task that is not sufficiently salient (perceived to be important) to command the interest and efforts of group members can create pitfalls. Such a task limits a potential source of energy for the system. Group members do not have to be initially excited about a task in order to take it on or have it assigned to them. As they work on the task, their interaction can help them create some of the energy needed for effective grouping. However, a task cannot be perceived as so uninteresting or tedious that it drains the energy out of the grouping effort without posing a serious potential problem.

When a group is not engaged by its task, its members can become bored and aimless when addressing the task. This response may signal that grouping is not taking place because of the task. Grouping without interest in the task may signal that the exigencies for grouping emanate from some Quadrad base other than the Purgatory Puddle. The attraction of having a process to engage in or a journey to take that helps structure one's day may involve some members in the group, though they might not be much interested in the task that spawned The Way/Process that engages them. The attraction of a Promised Land (e.g., of getting rich) may attract others to the group, though they are not very interested in the task or process needed for attaining that Vision/Outcome. Grouping may manifest from a desire to serve a relational function (wanting to share time with other people) or from an individual's personal desire to act as a direction giver of some group. In such cases, grouping might still succeed, but the members' low regard for the task aspects of their grouping provides pitfall potential from insufficient attention to the task.

Task Lacks Need for Group Acceptance

The final "wrong task for a group" pitfall is found in tasks that can be accomplished just as well by a group direction giver or by some other entity and for which no group member's acceptance will be required or is in dispute. Meier (1963) suggests group work on any tasks requiring a high level of member acceptance and use of an individual or expert for tasks that do not. The problem is in figuring out how potential grouping members perceive a task. There are some tasks that a group will want to address or to have some input into in spite of the seeming simplicity of the task. And, there are other tasks that groups hope can be taken care of on their behalf and without their effort. The more mature the group and the more experienced its direction givers and members are with each other and with the kinds of tasks they typically face, the more likely that orientation to tasks can be negotiated successfully. Vroom and Yetton (1972) provide a calculus for managers to use for deciding when to employ direction-giving styles that are participatory and when to make decisions on their own. Their decision tree is one way to address such issues. But stay alert and flexible. The key to judgment about whether a group is required rests with the group.

❖ HOW TO EXPECT, DETECT, AND CORRECT THESE PITFALLS

Our discussion of these pitfalls boils down to whether the communication involved in group interaction will serve to help the work on a task or to hinder it, and how grouping members orient to the task at hand and to their supragroup. The key role played by communication should not be surprising. Grouping is a communicative co-construction. Through their talk, group members learn how to explain themselves and to pool their resources and their efforts. Effective group members find a way to work together to formulate processes for and orientations toward doing their work. Their co-constructions include efforts to help members of the group understand their situation and task, to help group members understand a useful approach to the task, and to help group members develop alternative approaches to addressing the task. Interaction is always required for assessing the merits of task alternatives, which allows the group to assess the quality of the work they have done on a task. Active engagement in all of these activities helps group members feel that they played an important part in the development of their group's work, which helps them become more committed to their group outcomes. All such discussions can improve the group's ongoing ability to serve its functions as a group and to attain potential process prizes.

It may not always be clear to people in advance what supragroup issues they will face and which tasks will require them to work together. Groups should be willing to ask, and later in their grouping to re-ask, "Is this sort of task one we should all be working on together?" and "Are we communicating outside of our group in all the ways that we should be?" It is healthy, as an orientation, to expect a group to address the "wrong task" issue and boundary-spanning issues with some regularity. If group members orient this way, the chances may be reduced of a group co-constructing a pitfall that pertains to these issues. Whether or not a particular task or any of its subtasks are better done by a group or by some other entity should become a regular part of the considerations of an effective group. Concern with how the group is managing its boundaries should also be a regular consideration in effective groups. The more difficult it is to get a sense of task and supra-group issues, the more likely that group interaction should be used to explore them.

Once you accept the general orientation of this book, which is that you should expect, detect, and correct (avoiding, if possible) group pitfalls, you have the basic information you need when the nature of potential pitfalls has been identified, as has been our goal in this chapter. Your understanding that interaction, though it can help co-construct pitfalls, is also the only way to work through pitfalls, provides you with the best general strategy for proceeding. We want to add to that strategy the idea that *broaching the subject* of a potential pitfall can help you orient your group toward the work you know they may have to undertake when a potential pitfall begins to manifest.

Broaching the subject involves engaging group members in conversations germane to potential pitfalls before the pitfall arises in the group. For a new group, this can be done at the first meeting or first few, perhaps even at several points during those meetings. For an extant group, broaching the subject can be done at any meeting when you feel the need to begin to lay the foundation for future attempts to deal with a potential pitfall. Obviously, the discussion of a pitfall is also possible at any meeting after the group appears to be experiencing a problem, but, by then, the benefits from broaching the subject in advance are lost.

What is meant by broaching the subject of a pitfall before it manifests? In a moment, we will provide several examples of conversational prompts that can help you broach the subject by asking the group to address a topic germane to the pitfalls we discuss in this chapter (see Table 3.4). To bring up a potential problem before it manifests can be tricky; it can often result in a fairly unenthusiastic group response. Members may say something general about wanting to do a good job and to use effective group processes, but they probably will not find the subject very salient or engaging until a pitfall manifests. Regardless of any initial lack of enthusiasm, broaching the subject at an early group meeting puts the topic into the group's history of conversation. It then serves as a sort of precedent, giving group members "permission" to raise the concerns again, later in the life of the group, should they suspect a pitfall has begun to surface as they are working together. When that happens, even their earlier half-hearted conversation on the topic can become very useful in efforts to engage the pitfall.

Research demonstrates that the use of "reminders," which are either indications of generally effective group processes (Schultz, Ketrow, & Urban, 1995) or specific references to a goal the group previously agreed to try to attain, can improve group performance. A reminder can take such forms as, "Is this what we meant when we said we were going to try to . . . ?" or "Have we really done our best to . . . ?" or "Do we have enough evidence that . . . ?" or "Have we looked at enough reasonable alternatives?" According to Hirokawa (1980), the one difference that is relatively clear between effective and ineffective groups is that effective groups spend some of their communication time talking about what processes they should employ as they proceed and, as their work together unfolds, about whether their grouping processes are working well for them. When you broach the subject of potential pitfalls in advance, it gives you material to work with when it comes time to remind the group of their good intentions.

Disagreements about the nature of a task and how to negotiate group boundaries can serve the group, if they are willing to engage such discussions as potentially useful exercises. We encourage groups to discuss a number of aspects of their task and supragroup before they decide whether and how to proceed as a group. For example, we think *groups should analyze the group's purpose and the nature of the situation that resulted in someone charging the group with addressing the task. They should define key terms in their charge and in their understanding of the task and situation. They should attempt to identify key stakeholders, individuals beyond those in the group who might be affected by or interested in the issues to be addressed by the group. They should discuss their goals and any limitations they anticipate in terms of the task they face.* What follows is a set of prompts that can help you to raise these issues: to broach the subjects that can help your group co-construct its way around or through the pitfalls described in this chapter (see Table 3.4).

Table 3.4   Expecting, Detecting, and Correcting These Pitfalls

Prompts for Broaching the Subject on Purgatory Puddle Pitfalls: Task and Supragroup

Getting to work: Why are we here?
1. *Discuss the task in general.* What do we think that we are supposed to be doing?

Focus on the task.
2. *Define key terms* in the charge or task or problem. Identify the key words. Are there any we do not understand and need to look up? What do they mean to you? To me? To our supervisor? What do our various stakeholders think that they mean? What do experts on the subject think that they mean? Are there any implied terms or concepts we need to consider as well? Don't just ask if everyone understands what all the words mean (they will probably just nod); try to make the definitions explicit and to discuss them.
3. *Discuss constraints and resources.* What external issues might make our task more difficult? What might keep us from succeeding with the charge? What resources are there outside of the group that we might access to help us? Are there any personal obligations to other groups that might make it more difficult for us to work together?

Time out: We need some perspective taking.
4. *Identify possible exigencies* for the charge. Why did someone give us this assignment? What exigencies do you suppose she or he perceived that resulted in this charge? What do you suppose they think ought to be accomplished by asking us to address the charge? Should we take their exigencies into consideration when we set our group goals?
5. *Identify possible stakeholders.* Are others outside the group going to be affected by our actions? Could others in the future be affected? Could any of the people we live or work or play with outside the group be affected by how we group or by the outcomes of our grouping? How should we take these people into consideration?

Is grouping really the way to proceed?
6. *Is this the right kind of task for a group?* What role should our communication play in improving how we approach the task? Are there any aspects of this task that we should work on alone or in dyads or by consulting an expert? How do we avoid the temptation to work alone on issues the group should decide, though it might take us longer as a group to do so?

If so: How do we ensure that we do an effective job of grouping?
7. *Do we have enough time and other resources* available to us? What other resources will we need to find in order to do our work well? How should we generally approach or divide up the time we have left before this project is due? Can we develop a time line?

Be willing to be recursive, to return several times to the topics related to these prompts. These topics include issues that need to be raised again and again, sometimes to get any real traction on them, other times to make adjustments in how the group responds to them. Forcing some talk on each issue broaches the subject and invites future conversation on a topic, even if the first run at the topic is not particularly fruitful.

❖ CHAPTER SUMMARY

Any exigency for grouping poses potential pitfalls even before a group begins to form. Supragroup pitfalls may manifest in the interface between a group and its context. Mostly these involve difficulties in co-constructing appropriate and effective boundaries between the group and its suprasystem. Additional pitfalls manifest in tasks that receive inappropriate grouping responses: treating a different kind of rhetorical situation as though it were a Purgatory Puddle. There are tasks for which an individual working alone or some other human entity is a better choice, a better tool, than grouping. Pitfalls are complicating dynamics with the potential to reduce group performance or outcomes. Pitfalling can be by commission, when grouping members do something that gets them into trouble. Pitfalling can be by omission, when grouping members fail to anticipate and avoid, or to address and work through, a problem. Expecting to need to use communication as a means for anticipating potential pitfalls and for working your way through the pitfalls you cannot avoid is the best general strategy available to you as you attempt to overcome barriers to effective group experiences.

4

Personnel Pitfalls

❖ ❖ ❖

As many as 22% of the problems facing groups manifest from their personnel and other premeeting issues (DiSalvo, Nikkel, & Monroe, 1989). In chapter 3, we covered two of the three major categories of potential Purgatory Puddle problems (task and supragroup pitfalls). Now we complete the Purgatory Puddle pitfalls as we focus on those evident in the *personnel* available to group.

❖ "WRONG GROUP FOR THE TASK" PITFALLS

Personnel pitfalls, when the wrong number or combination of individuals are available for work on a grouping task, manifest in unfortunate ways as the group attempts to do its work: demonstrating that the individuals involved are the "wrong group for the task."

Inappropriate Group Size

A key variable in group interaction is the number of people involved. When you are alone, thinking requires one set of skills; when with another person, someone whom you wish to impress, thinking is complicated by the need to communicate with that person. Add a third

Table 4.1   Summary of Purgatory Puddle: Personnel Pitfalls or "Wrong Group"

Personnel Pitfall	Examples
Inappropriate Group Size	Too many members.
	Too few members.
Members Lack Personal Resources	Lack subject matter expertise.
	Lack group communication skills.
	Lack authority or credibility.
	Lack personal capacity.
Negative Assembly Effect	Trait, orientation, style, and circumstance-based issues

person to the mix and the complications continue to multiply: you now must attend to each person, to their relationship with each other, and to how they orient to you (individually and together).

Consider the potential interaction time available to each member. A meeting with three members gives each the opportunity to contribute 33% of the talk. Six members reduces talk time to 17%, 12 members to 8%. Each interaction also requires attention from other members, whose work gets more difficult with each additional member. In short, communication dynamics change once the context becomes a group; they then become more difficult with each additional member. Such dynamics can serve the group when grouping is done well. However, they can also be a problem, so as a general rule, *a group should not be larger than necessary.*

The first "wrong group" pitfall is when a group has too many or few members. Too many group members may get in each other's way and will be a waste of resources, reducing member productivity. Too few members may render the group unable to complete its task (i.e., because of limited resources or viewpoints). When an organization downsizes or experiences budget cuts, groups attempt to accomplish old outcome levels with fewer members. Increased productivity results when a group learns to need fewer people to do its work, but harm to individual members may also be a consequence. Even if they succeed on task, too few members taxes each for his or her participation, resulting in diminished health or quality of life.

What is the right size for a group? The answer will vary depending on what you want a group to be able to do and on the personal resources of its members (see below). *Three to seven members are typically ideal* for serving the three group functions. Some skilled group practitioners might be able to sustain small group dynamics (the kind needed to attain process prizes) among 8 to 15 or so members, but that is hard work to accomplish.

A number of dynamics are of concern, even within a small range of group size. Carron and Spink (1995), who summarize the research on the subject, say that direction giving tends to be more shared, less difficult, and more informed by interaction among individual members when there are fewer members in the group. Direction giving is more likely to be autocratic when there are more members. Members tend to feel less satisfaction, less personal involvement, and more anxiety as the size of a group grows. Larger groups tend to be better at additive tasks but less effective at conjunctive tasks, and there appears to be a curvilinear relationship between group size and cohesiveness.

A final issue is that small *groups can benefit if there is an odd number of members* so that role and direction-giving emergence issues are easier to sort out when, for instance, a majority of members prefer a particular role assignment (Bormann & Bormann, 1996). The concern is not with tie votes (voting should be discouraged in groups anyway, as it stops efforts to achieve consensus) but with the process through which direction givers emerge. In such role competitions, having a group size that allows one person to be a favorite among group members for a particular role function is helpful to the healthy evolution of group processes. In sum, too many or too few members is a potential problem.

Members Lack Personal Resources

Member resources and orientation are integral to effective groups and are synergistically related in ways that are difficult to assess in advance of a grouping effort.

Lack of Expertise. Individuals available for grouping may lack expertise on the task facing the group. This may be because nobody in the world has sufficient knowledge regarding some new problem (such as was the case when people first started to die from AIDS but nobody knew its cause or how to treat it). It may be because nobody available for grouping has the necessary expertise. The question of expertise is difficult to sort out because some may use it as an excuse not to try. People can learn some of what they need to know about a task by working on it, but there are some tasks that require subject matter expertise. *If you are required to work on a topic about which you know little, keep in mind that value can be added to a group by an individual who knows little about the subject but is an effective group member; he or she can help even the experts.*

Lack of Group Communication Skills. Even experts in a subject may lack grouping skills and consequently fail in their efforts regardless of their expertise in the subject matter. For example, the people involved in the Challenger and Columbia shuttle disasters were experts in engineering and/or in aspects of public policy. Two important group skills deserve special attention. First, individuals who work well in groups have probably developed the ability to *accomplish a discussional attitude* toward working in groups. Among other things, this involves *keeping an open mind, working hard to articulate one's own ideas, and trying to get contributions from all other grouping members*. Second, effective group members have probably *developed deliberation skills*. These are the analytical skills necessary to be able to *generate and test ideas* and evidence rather than letting the dynamics of grouping determine which ideas become group outcomes. Such skills are why employers are so interested in hiring people with group communication skills.

Lack of Authority or Credibility. A group of individuals may lack the authority necessary to do or to implement the work assigned them, or they may lack credibility because key stakeholders are not represented among those doing the work of the group. The shortage of authority or credibility can render meaningless an otherwise potent group process and outcome. A lack of authority can only be fixed if an entity with authority over the task assigns authority to the group (a supragroup issue) or if a member who has the necessary authority is added or recruited to the group. If the group fails to represent key stakeholders, group processes and outcomes may lack credibility or legitimacy. Some form of representation either in the group or through the group composition process is the solution. *An inclusive and effective process of group construction* does not put everyone interested in the group, but it *ensures adequate authority and it includes opportunities for representation of, or other form of input from,* stakeholders.

Lack of Personal Capacity. Group members may lack other personal resources needed to accomplish their work. The best examples of this are individuals who do not have sufficient time or cognitive complexity to do the work. Does the individual member have the capacity to do the work required? Time is often a determining variable in how individual capacities play out. Cognitive capacity may work to exacerbate or ameliorate the effects of time constraints. For example, one's cognitive complexity (not intelligence), the ability to conceive of and to work with multiple meanings attached to particular ideas, may be involved in one's ability to address complex problems or to multitask. *Change in group composition is the only remedy to this pitfall. More or fewer members may be needed, contingent on the capacities of those involved.*

Personal capacity provides a transition to the largest set of potential personnel pitfalls: individual characteristics. These characteristics may combine in problematic ways during attempts to group, which produce the potential pitfalls we call a *negative assembly effect.*

A Negative Assembly Effect

Each individual is an individual because of his or her characteristics and because of how he or she behaves. Some characteristics and behaviors tend to enhance an individual's performance in a group and others tend to diminish performance; many of these effects are heightened when individuals are mixed together in a group. The concept of an *assembly effect* means different things to different scholars: trying to build a cohesive group prior to the first meeting by who is put into a group (Bormann & Bormann, 1996); or the effects in group behavior from combinations of people, though not because of their characteristics (Shaw, 1981). We find the obverse of these concepts to be useful as well. A negative assembly effect could result from problems because of the nature of the people put into the group or because of how combining them together affects group behavior and outcomes. We define a negative assembly effect as putting individuals together in a group who may tend to co-construct grouping activity that accomplishes less than expected given the resources they have. Obviously, contradicting Shaw, we include effects that result from their individual characteristics in our conception. Negative assembly effect represents how individual characteristics or combinations thereof might tend to increase the propensity for a group to struggle.

As you work your way through this material, be careful how you respond to it and try to keep in mind how you can make use of it. As you read these sections, ask yourself, "Is this true of me?" and "How frequently is it true of me?" and "Is it descriptive of others with whom I group?" You should recognize that how people respond to these characteristics and behaviors is more vital to grouping success than is the actual characteristic or behavior. In fact, understanding and adjusting to these characteristics and behaviors as they manifest in a group may actually enhance your group's ability to do its work. There is no personal characteristic or behavior in the following synthesis that is always useful or always hurtful.

Figure 4.1   Individual Characteristics and Behaviors From Traits to
Circumstance-Based Tendencies

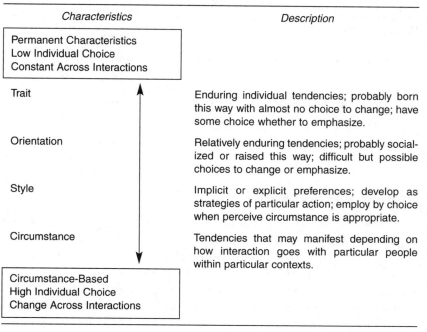

Characteristics	*Description*
Permanent Characteristics **Low Individual Choice** **Constant Across Interactions**	
Trait	Enduring individual tendencies; probably born this way with almost no choice to change; have some choice whether to emphasize.
Orientation	Relatively enduring tendencies; probably socialized or raised this way; difficult but possible choices to change or emphasize.
Style	Implicit or explicit preferences; develop as strategies of particular action; employ by choice when perceive circumstance is appropriate.
Circumstance	Tendencies that may manifest depending on how interaction goes with particular people within particular contexts.
Circumstance-Based **High Individual Choice** **Change Across Interactions**	

The remainder of this chapter provides an extensive set of personal characteristics and behaviors that may play out in groups in unfortunate ways. Our organizational matrix (see Figure 4.1) employs four metaphors (trait, orientation, style, circumstance), which represent the origin, duration, and choice involved in the characteristic.

❖ TRAITS

Traits are enduring individual characteristics that change little if at all from your birth through your lifetime (see Table 4.2). One would expect you to exhibit these characteristics in any context that provides opportunities for the trait to manifest. Impossible or very difficult to change, some traits may help you in grouping attempts and others may complicate successful grouping. Each is important only to the extent that it affects grouping, but each has been identified as a phenomenon of importance that recurs across a variety of groups.

Table 4.2   Summary of Trait-Based Pitfalls for Groups

Trait Pitfall	Examples
Demographics and Personality	Age; sex; intelligence; self-esteem; physical attractiveness.
Communication Tendencies	Extroversion, introversion, and communication apprehension; self-monitoring.
Ascendancy Tendencies	Aggressiveness, assertiveness, and argumentativeness; Machiavellian; dogmatism and perfectionism.

Demographics and Personality

These characteristics are born with the individual or determined in large part very early in life. Biological sex of the individual, age, intelligence, height, body type, physical appearance (which becomes a cultural marker of physical attractiveness), and self-concept are examples. Research in the middle third of the twentieth century tried to determine if there are ideal combinations of traits for effective direction giving or group membership. Much of that research suffered from problems with *test tube groups,* which are carefully controlled, one-shot experiments in which group dynamics differ from those in bona fide groups and longer-term group experiences in natural settings. However, the fact that scholars asked such questions in the first place is a sign that they thought the nature of an individual might affect her or his performance.

Grouping members can tend to believe the same thing. For example, numerous scholars have found evidence that member perceptions about sex and gender roles can be influential in determining who eventually emerges to lead a group (Bormann, Pratt, & Putnam, 1978; Gemmill & Schaible, 1991; Rosenfeld & Fowler, 1976; Yerby, 1975). Even though the sex of a group member does not predict his or her potential grouping capacities, combinations of that trait in the group can be expected to have effects because of the responses of grouping members. Would it matter if you were the only woman or man in a group? Would it matter if everyone else in your group were 30 years older than you? Would that affect your grouping or theirs? Imagine that Indira is obviously the smartest person in your group; how might that matter? We base our expectation that traits may affect grouping in the perceptions group members have regarding the traits of their compadres. A trait has pitfall potential if grouping members let it constrain grouping effectiveness: *avoid that tendency when you detect it.*

Communication Tendencies

Because grouping requires communication, one's orientation toward talk and other aspects of communication is fundamental. Because *extroverted* individuals are outgoing and interested in interacting with others more than are introverted individuals, we might expect them to have fewer problems grouping. That is not necessarily the case. *Introverted* individuals may start interacting more slowly and may never interact as much as the extrovert, but their performance can enhance grouping just as the extrovert's can become a problem. Making negative causal attributions about individuals because they tend more toward extroversion or introversion is the most predictably problematic behavior; *avoid doing so.* These individual characteristics need to be worked around; *avoid the impulse to try to make somebody change.* A version of this pitfall is communication apprehension, which manifests differently for different people but may involve a general sense of unease whenever one is required to interact with others in a group. This goes beyond shyness so that the apprehensive person has to wage a battle with herself or himself in order to be a group member. It serves no purpose to add negative attributions from other group members in response.

Self-monitoring (Snyder, 1974) is looking to external cues to determine which emotional cues are appropriate to present within the context. If everyone is sad and mournful, telling jokes and being lighthearted would not appear to the high self-monitor to be appropriate; the low self-monitor would tell a joke if she or he thought it was funny, regardless of the emotional tone of the context. Each of us falls on a continuum between being a high or a low self-monitor. High self-monitors will tend to adapt to show appropriate emotional cues and probably are adept at doing so. Low self-monitors will not base the emotions they show to others on external cues but rather on how they feel in the moment. This distinction can actually have quite an effect on a group. Some research indicates that individuals who are high self-monitors may be more in tune with the emotional state of other grouping members and may, consequently, be more likely to emerge as direction givers. If a member appears emotionally out of sync, it can be off-putting to other group members. When someone attempts to adapt to group emotions, other problems can result. *No general advice is in order, beyond understanding the phenomenon when it manifests, because either tendency might help groups in some cases and be a problem in others.*

Ascendancy Tendencies

To ascend is to move to the top. Ascendancy tendencies are manifestations of the needs some people have to come out on top. An example might be a tendency toward being *aggressive*. Grouping may be enhanced by cooperative or by competitive activities, but aggression is almost always a sign of trouble. Aggression is activity undertaken to hurt others. It comes at the expense of others. When aggressive behavior is used during grouping, it is almost always a pitfall, though it can be part of a response to other aggression. Regardless, aggressiveness may feel normal to some people. Research indicates that some bullies are less aware of how their behavior "feels" to their victims than we might expect. The use of aggression in response to provocation is one form of assertive behavior, designed to protect self-interests. *Assertive* behavior is also appropriate and necessary if one is to contribute to the flow of active grouping behavior: the ready exchange of information, ideas, and opinions involved in effective grouping. However, assertive behavior may "feel" aggressive to some members, regardless of whether or not it is done appropriately and with good intentions. *These difficult dynamics need to be talked about openly if you perceive that they are manifesting in your group.*

There is a time and place for well-constructed and supported arguments, which are carefully articulated claims with clearly expressed reasons to accept or to support them. Consequently, groups require some argumentation to improve the quality of their work. Some people, however, do not seem to know when to tone down their argumentative nature and others shrink from any communicative exchange involving competing ideas. Scholars say *argumentativeness* is the variable involved. Some people love to argue. Others are put off by that tendency. As long as there is sufficient argumentative capacity in the group to carefully test ideas, the potential for pitfalling locates in any combination of individuals that places one or more members at a disadvantage. If you know that you like to argue, you probably know that others are sometimes turned off by your skills and you need to *find ways to check your tendencies without losing their benefits; do not assume that others agree with you just because they cannot answer your arguments* anymore than a victim who succumbs to physical aggression agrees with the aggressor. If you tend toward the other extreme, *try to recognize the benefits your group can attain through careful testing of ideas and evidence, adapt to allow such exchanges with minimized irritation (breathe deeply), and make your unease known to the group so they can adapt to your needs as well.*

The *Machiavellian* (Mach) does whatever is necessary to achieve what he or she wants in a group. If you know someone who always finds a way to come out on top, even if that means having to take advantage of friends or colleagues, then you may know a high Mach. High-Mach behavior can be helpful or not for a group, depending on if it happens to also serve the group's goal. Those who played against Michael Jordan (in basketball) describe his work ethic and court demeanor in manners that suggest to us he may be a high Mach and, arguably, as a consequence, the best basketball player ever. *Accepting such an individual for what he or she is, and protecting your backside by keeping careful records of key interactions, are reasonable tactics. If you are a high Mach, you ought only consider involvement in grouping activities that match your interests well and you need to consider the effects your behavior may have on your own future success after you construct a reputation for mistreating your compadres.*

The *dogmatic* member is inflexible, insensitive to cues from others, emotionally committed to her or his own idea or process, and may be a perfectionist. He or she takes unequivocal stands on issues and may be seen as domineering, bossy, or pigheaded ("my way or the highway"). Such behavior is a pitfall to any co-construction and can only serve a group in times of crisis or flagging energy (assuming the dogmatic did not cause the crisis or energy drain). Unlike the high Mach, the dogmatic may not be adept at getting what she or he wants except by digging in his or her heels and refusing to budge. *Dogma* suggests there is a "truth" that must be obeyed. Dogmatics may believe they are serving a high purpose, they may choose the comforts of certainty over the unpredictability of grouping outcomes, or they may just not understand how systems work: that equifinality means there is more than one way to attain excellent outcomes. Dogmatism is antithetical to a discussional attitude and to deliberative skills.

Groups should attempt to achieve consensus. The dogmatic group member can stymie consensus or cause the group to redirect efforts or outcomes in problematic ways. Neither can be allowed to stand. *After careful consideration of a dogmatic's ideas and controlling against the complete rejection of the ideas because their advocate is so off-putting (remember that his or her motives may be good), grouping members must combine forces to overrule the dogmatic person. A dogmatic member must (be made to) allow the will of the group to manifest, once they have been given their say (or expect expulsion or a future of being shunned, ignored, or ostracized).*

❖ ORIENTATION

An *orientation* may be nurtured into the person and becomes a fundamental characteristic of who she or he is as she or he interacts. Bormann and Bormann (1996) say that trait-based explanations of grouping behavior have mostly given way to interest in relatively enduring, difficult-to-change personal *orientations* (see Table 4.3). They give two examples, group members' orientations toward achievement and toward preference for procedural order. We add several more.

Orientation Toward Achievement

Orientation toward achievement manifests as a pitfall when disparate approaches to grouping result from a significant mismatch between the members of a group in their desire and work toward excellent outcomes. The member or members with a very high orientation toward achievement may spend time and energy between meetings working on the group project only to find that others in the group are not thankful for their hard work. Individuals lower in orientation toward achievement may feel threatened and also shut out of important

Table 4.3   Summary of Orientation-Based Pitfalls for Groups

Orientation Pitfall	Examples
Achievement	High versus low focus and effort toward group success.
Procedural Order and Time	Desire for agenda and group structure; felt time versus clock time.
Information Processing	Critical and creative process preference; needs for cognition and closure.
Interaction	Orientation toward authority.

decision-making or role-determining processes because they have not "paid the same price" the high achievers have paid. Note that the pitfall is not from the mismatch itself (though that can be problematic) but from how the mismatch is co-constructed into group life. *Knowing that differences in orientation toward achievement can become a pitfall should be used by all members as the impetus for early and explicit discussion of goals, perception of grouping exigencies, and the processes that should be co-constructed given any disparate orientation toward achievement. If the group cannot agree, once their cards are on the table, they should not be a group. They do not share the joint purpose, process, and sense of perceptual boundaries (what it means to be an effective member in this group) necessary to succeed and should adjust membership accordingly.*

Orientation Toward Procedural Order and Time

Putnam (1979) identifies *preference for procedural order* (PPO) as a basic orientation toward how grouping should unfold, and she documents how mixing individuals with different PPOs can result in pitfalls for a group. Each of us has a greater or lesser PPO (Hirokawa, Ice, & Cook, 1988; Putnam, 1979, 1982) and neither tendency is necessarily indicative of effective grouping. High PPOs want the group to have and stick to an agenda and time line, stay on task, and complete its obligations. Low PPOs want to work more organically, focusing on tasks and ideas as they come up, and not relying so much on structure or process but rather on a general feeling of progress. These individuals are more likely to work well with ambiguity, yet low PPOs may be called "lazy," "disorganized," or "addlepated" by colleagues with a high PPO (who are called "fascists," "anal," or "control freaks" by their low-PPO compadres). In addition to pitfalls from mixing high- and low-PPO members, there can be problems if a group only has members with too much or too little PPO, or if a grouping context conducive to high or low PPOs is dominated by members with the other orientation. *Where possible, group composition should involve individuals with context-conducive PPO levels. Regardless, the competing benefits of structured and of more organic processes need to be appreciated, accepted (perhaps explained to the unknowing), and put to work through role constructions that use members' strengths.*

Orientation toward time involves whether one considers time a resource to be used or an organic part of one's experience (Hall, 1959, 1983). The former stance is "clock time," or regimented time, and the latter is "felt time." In a macro sense, if one's cultural upbringing tends more toward the ongoing flow of human experience and "issues of the clock" are not particularly important, one is used to operating on felt time. If you are raised that way, it feels uncomfortable and unnatural to regiment your life according to some arbitrary and external thing like what the mechanism of a clock says is an appropriate time for action. There are seasons, there are days that come and go, and those are the rhythms of life, not a clock. If you were raised "on the clock," people who operate using felt time can be infuriating. You can get a sense of your orientation to time by thinking about how much it bothers you to be late: to a meeting, to a party, to work. Are you always the first or the last to arrive? Do you still attend if you are 5 minutes late, 20, an hour? If all but one group member arrives on time and the final member comes an hour late, does that bother you? Do you want him or her to give a reason and apology?

Orientations to time and order can affect individual and grouping behavior in helpful or negative ways, whether the orientations are mixed or all tend toward one extreme. The vigilant group member asks, *"Are our orientations getting us into trouble?"* Do not just ignore aberrant behavior (defined as different than whatever group norms seem to be). If you don't ask, the chances of experiencing a pitfall increase, as do chances of misdiagnosing behavior that could also indicate a more serious problem. *Understanding and discussing any competing orientations can almost always result in the co-construction of a mutually acceptable process for proceeding.* Ignoring the discussion inevitably manifests in irritated feelings and negative causal attributions.

Orientation Toward Information

Each of us has a preferred learning style, some preferring hands-on experience, others more theoretical or abstract explanations, and others the opportunity to watch or see a model. Each of us has different information processing preferences (e.g., reading about it, discussing it, "tossing solutions around," "sleeping on it"). When we must work with others to group, the risk is that such preferences can become pitfalls either to the individual whose preference is ignored by the group or to the group, which is not well served by the orientations of its members given the task. Some people do their best creative work when there is a period for incubation. They get an idea, chew on it awhile, and then leave it alone, perhaps for several days. Others want to stay on task and to continue to play around with an idea in the group. Both types of members may get frustrated if their orientation to processing information is ignored. *Opportunities for both types of processing need to be co-constructed into The Way/Process techniques whenever possible.*

Two particular processing preferences have been talked about in recent research. First, the *need for cognition* (not an indicator of intelligence) varies across people according to whether they are more interested in mental relaxation or mental stimulation (Scudder, Herschel, & Crossland, 1994). The low-need-for-cognition individual might be adept at complex games or crossword puzzles (that delight high-need-for-cognition folks) but doesn't have much desire to engage in them because of the effort involved. Second, the *need for closure* (Webster & Kruglanski, 1994) varies according to how much one needs to have a definitive answer and sense of completion on the subject at hand. An individual with a high need for closure wants to see a line of thought or project through to its end or it will continue to bedevil her or him. Mix these individuals in a group and there may be different levels of enthusiasm for continuing to work through a difficult idea or for finishing one thought before moving on to the next. *Again, a co-constructed process that protects the interests and strengths of all involved individuals is made possible through conversation.*

Orientation Toward Interaction

Orientation toward interaction is a stance toward the nature of grouping and of the authority relationships that tend to evolve from any grouping. An example is the *authoritarian* group member who perceives that it is appropriate that status and power differences exist to separate group members and their roles. Such individuals "... are demanding, directive, and controlling in their relations with those less powerful than themselves. When they are in a subordinate position, they are submissive and compliant; they accept their subordinate roles as natural and appropriate" (Shaw, 1981, p. 192). On the other extreme are those who reject any authority. If they perceive that the group or one or more of its members is getting too strong, they may reject even the conformity necessary for basic group membership. *Co-construct your grouping processes to protect and to tap the benefits of each orientation to the greatest extent that you can make possible.*

❖ STYLE

The third category of personal characteristics is *style* (see Table 4.4). Your personal style involves choices you make regarding appropriate action or activity, given your perceptions of a Purgatory Puddle. Your personal style might become fairly difficult to change, and there will probably be aspects of it that are implicit, that you are not even aware of. In spite of how ingrained style choices have become for you, they are still easier to change than a trait or orientation. That is because style choices are based in utilitarian attitudes. Utilitarian attitudes are functional: they help you accomplish what you want, or you can change them. Your style choices guide your own grouping and direction-giving activities, because you think that they will work.

Style From Theories of Interaction

Grouping and group direction are fundamental activities for humans. Consequently, each of us has developed, through our lifetime of experiences, a set of expectations or prototypes about how grouping and direction giving ought to be done. Think of the best direction givers you have ever known or heard about. Now, look for common characteristics among them: the aspects that you think makes them effective direction givers. That might give you a sense of your own *"implicit theory of direction-giving"* (Keller, 1999; Lord & Maher, 1991) as well as any explicit ideas you have about how direction givers ought to behave. It could be very difficult to figure out what your *implicit theory of grouping* or of direction giving is, because it is not an explicit

Table 4.4   Summary of Style-Based Pitfalls for Groups

Pitfall	Examples
Theories of Interaction	Implicit or explicit theories of grouping or direction-giving; conceptions of appropriate action.
Personal Impression	Masking/impression management; hold back/blend in; face work.
Theories of Communication Utilities	Rhetorical sensitivity; need to facilitate discussion versus to be the center of attention.

prescription but rather a more deep-seated set of assumptions probably located in the "blind" part of your personal nature. But both implicit and explicit theories of grouping and of direction giving manifest in your behaviors. You behave differently because of what you think appropriate behavior is. You probably tend to judge others according to how well they play what you think are appropriate group member or direction-giver roles. Conceptions of appropriate action manifest in style choices.

Early research into styles of direction givers asks which style is always best: *autocratic* (the direction giver decides), *democratic* (the direction giver facilitates process so that the group can decide), or *laissez-faire* (the direction giver keeps her or his hands off the group and lets them do what they like). The answer to which style is best is: it depends. Our view is that direction-giving styles need to be selected according to the exigencies perceived within a grouping system. If one style of direction giving can work better in certain circumstances, use that style. Because style choices can help or hinder grouping and group direction, they become the source of potential pitfalls and of rhetorical resources. *An interaction style should always be employed rhetorically, with its pitfall potential in mind, which leaves open the possibility for needing to change one's grouping or direction-giving style during the course of any grouping enterprise. Willingness to talk openly about one's style decreases the pitfall potential for changing one's style to adjust to new grouping contingencies. Style is choice born of experience with effectiveness and should be talked about that way and treated that way.*

Style of Personal Impression

The style choices each of us makes regarding personal impression affect how willing we are to share ourselves with others. Dramatists say that each of us is involved in dramatic action during everyday life as we play out the roles we take on as friend, student, worker, confidant, child, parent, lover, and so forth (Burke, 1945; Goffman, 1967). For example, if you have been promoted at work and have to supervise people who are your friends, you may have to decide how and when to wear your "boss mask" or your "friend mask" as you try to play an appropriate role given the new group contingencies. This *impression management* (trying to get others to see us as we want to be seen) occurs across cultures, and is called *face work* (Ting-Toomey, 1988, 1991). It is face work to try to make the right impressions on others in your group.

For example, some feel the need to fit in so strongly that they tie their effort to group norms, lowering their performance in order to fit in.

During a first meeting of a new group, members experience what Bormann (1996) calls *primary tension,* because they do not yet know what to do or how they will be expected to behave in the new group. "People do not ask many questions in the period of searching for a role and for status, because they do not wish to appear ignorant or stupid. They may, therefore, act as though they understand much more than they do" (p. 256). *Withholding what you really think and feel, including statements of your confusion, lack of understanding, or disagreement can create problems for the group. Without becoming rude, spouting your unpleasant thoughts and feelings in the moment they occur to you, you can still find ways to encourage yourself to give important data to your group. If you are confused, say so. If you disagree, say so. Those actions help grouping quality improve. If you are overwhelmed by the desire to make a good impression, promise yourself that you will take a chance at least twice each meeting to express a concern with some aspect of process or with some idea being discussed. Do not let impression management overcome your ability to contribute. Agreeing with whatever everyone else in the group thinks is not making a contribution: it is passive behavior and works against attaining a process prize.*

Style From Theories of Communication Utilities

Hart and Burks (1984) argue that each of us tends toward being more or less *rhetorically sensitive.* At one end of the continuum are those who tend to think communication is for getting anything that you feel or that bothers you off your chest: expressiveness utility (low rhetorical sensitivity). Those who think of communication as a tool for accomplishing desirable ends (functional utility) adapt their communication to accomplish those ends (high rhetorical sensitivity). There is a parallel here to our discussion of self-monitoring in that the rhetorically sensitive individual is probably better able to be effective in most grouping activities, though he or she may also deprive the group of what might be useful information about his or her thoughts. The individuals who express themselves without regard to consequences may hinder grouping, or may help "shock" the group out of negative behavioral patterns. Individuals who become "group clowns" may do so for expressive ends (to become the center of attention) or to break tension in the group in a functional attempt to help the group get on with its work. *To the*

Exercise 4.1 Style Based on Interaction Theory: Impression or Utility?

How do you behave when you think your opinion is in the minority in your group? Think now about your answer. Decide whether you would express your dissent or just go along with what the majority clearly wants. Ask yourself if you do express your dissent, how forceful and frequent would you be. Once you decide your answers to those questions, ask yourself?

Did I answer that way because of my understanding of appropriate grouping behavior?

Did I answer that way because of how I want myself to appear to others in the group?

Did I answer that way because I think I should try to express myself or because I have some other purpose that can be served by saying what I think or by keeping quiet about my disagreement?

---

extent that individuals can appreciate how their behavior is helping or hurting grouping efforts, they can make reasoned choices for which style of communication utility best fits the context. If they judge poorly, grouping compadres should tell them so.

When you hold what you perceive to be a minority view in the group, do you keep your opinion to yourself or share it with your group (see Exercise 4.1)? If you hold back your concern or idea, you reduce the possibility of someone else learning from it or using it to develop a new idea. A minority opinion, once it is well understood by everyone in the group, may no longer be held by the previously dissenting member, or it may become the majority opinion in the group. Even if the dissenter remains alone in her or his position, expression of the minority viewpoint serves the function of helping the rest of the group understand better why their majority view is preferable, where it may be somewhat flawed, and what the alternatives are that they rejected. Consequently, even minority opinions that are wrong can be useful if shared with the group.

❖ CIRCUMSTANCES

The final category of Purgatory Puddle, personnel, personal characteristic pitfalls is circumstance (see Table 4.5). These are personal tendencies that manifest as interaction effects for particular people within a particular context.

Table 4.5   Summary of Circumstance-Based Pitfalls for Groups

Circumstance Pitfall	Examples
Interaction Sources	Experiences become the base for interaction and innovation.
Interaction Reducers	Social loafing is actual or perceived.
Interaction Changers	Hidden agenda; sexual interest; dislike another member.

Interaction Sources

Communication requires some shared base of experience. Some experiences so shape us that we are different people because of them. Does it matter if you grew up in a large city or on a farm; male or female; rich or poor; Muslim, Buddhist, Baptist, or atheist; African, Norwegian, or Taiwanese? Have you been in the military, had someone close to you die, been married, had children? We find it easier to communicate with those similar to us because common experiences are a basis for talk. But, those with different experiences bring diverse skills and backgrounds to the group's problem, which may make different exigencies salient and different tests of grouping processes and outcomes necessary. Process prizes may be attained as a result.

Interaction Reducers

Social loafers do not carry their fair share of a group's work. They are not engaged or involved in the group task. They may talk or remain silent, but any talk and activity are not well focused toward advancing the work of the group. When there are assignments, the social loafer may seek the easiest one or not complete an assignment at all. Social loafers are those doing less than they can to help the group (Lantane, Williams, & Harkins, 1979). Obviously, such activity is a pitfall to grouping. Unfortunately, so is the perception of such activity when the "loafing behavior" really signifies something else (see Table 4.6). Both actual and perceived social loafing can result in pitfalls. *Perceived loafing should be sorted out through conversation, attempting to determine motivations for behaviors that appear to be loafing and then co-constructing a way to get group benefits from the situation. Actual loafing is also sorted out through talk that changes the behavior, finds alternative useful activities that engage the loafer and enhance the group, or draws a line between the*

Table 4.6   Explanations for Social Loafing During Grouping

Actual Social Loafing	Perceived Social Loafing (member is trying to stay engaged with the group progress despite difficulty)
Member does not care.	Member believes self-censoring is appropriate given her or his personal style of interaction.
Member is lazy and wants a free ride.	Member feels too new to group or too ignorant of process or task or relationships to talk yet.
Member feels that the focus of the group at this moment is not his or her job or responsibility.	Member trusts the rest of the group and wants to do what they say/decide is best.
Member is angry or turned off by grouping choices, processes, or direction.	Member feels inadequate for the task, as in, "I'm too stupid to be of help."
	Member is introverted or suffers from communication apprehension.
	Member is intensely interested but neutral because he or she cannot decide what he or she thinks.
	Member is overwhelmed by work that feels too hard to do.

loafer and full group benefits. Treating loafing as a communication construction (Allen, Mabry, & Halone, 2004) makes rhetorical responses to it appropriate.

Interaction Changers

Have you ever known someone who joins a group because of a reason at odds with the group's goal (e.g., she or he wants to pad her or his resume; she or he wants to date a group member)? When such issues play out openly, they can cause problems but they can be addressed. If such issues are hidden from the group, they can be damaging because a *hidden agenda* can affect grouping and group direction without the group's awareness. A hidden agenda is most damaging when the member's agenda is incompatible with group goals and exerts negative influence on group processes or outcomes. Related examples are when one group member has a sexual interest in another member (Bormann, 1996) or when a group member develops a dislike for another member ("She [or he] just rubs me the wrong way!"). *Hidden agendas need to be uncovered; hidden intentionally, they are unethical actions. Openly discussed, group priorities take precedence because individual functions are to be served by effective grouping, not by under-mining it.*

❖ HOW TO EXPECT, DETECT, AND CORRECT THESE PITFALLS

This chapter provides an extensive set of personal characteristics and behaviors that may play out in groups in unfortunate ways. *Remember, there is no characteristic among those we discuss that is always helpful or always hurtful. Recognize that it is how people respond to characteristics and behaviors that is more important to grouping success than is the actual characteristic or behavior.* Understanding and adjusting to these characteristics and behaviors as they manifest in a group may actually enhance your group's ability to do its work.

How can you make use of information about such pitfalls? You can work to change a characteristic behavior or you can try to ameliorate its negative effects in a group. What about traits: they cannot be changed? True, but they can be understood well enough to be allowed to manifest rhetorically. *Ask yourself, "What can I do to make use of this trait or orientation?" and "How can I minimize the damage I might cause because of it?" and "Under what circumstances can I allow it to manifest in a way that actually helps my group?" and "How can I help co-construct ways to allow competing characteristics of my colleagues become group resources?* Such questions are a rhetorical orientation to this material.

It all boils down to how your interaction can help groups overcome whatever personnel difficulties they face by co-constructing potential limitations into group resources: at minimum, co-constructing ways to avoid or to overcome the pitfall. Effective group members work together to construct processes and orientations for doing their work, which enhance that possibility. The Breakdown-Conducive Group Framework argues that part of each group's work should be the co-construction of ways around or through the pitfalls they face. That may be more difficult when some personality types are involved, but the challenge, if effectively addressed, can ultimately strengthen the group.

Remember the idea that broaching the subject of a potential pitfall can help you orient your group toward the work you know they may have to undertake when a potential pitfall begins to manifest. Broaching the subject involves engaging group members in conversations germane to potential pitfalls before the pitfall arises in the group:

beginning to lay the foundation for future attempts to deal with a potential pitfall by co-constructing a conversational history and group norms conducive to such work. What follows is a set of conversational prompts that can help you raise these issues (see Table 4.7).

Table 4.7   Prompts for Broaching the Subject on Purgatory Puddle: Personnel Pitfalls

---

Is grouping really the way to proceed?

1. *Is this the right group for this task?* What are our strengths and weaknesses as individuals given this task? Is there anyone who should not be in this group or someone we need to add to this group? Is this the right size group for the task? Can we use extra members to benefit the group? Should we release any members?

If so: How do we ensure that we do an effective job of grouping?

2. *How do we hold each other responsible* for the work we are supposed to do? Should we discuss a process now in case someone stops attending meetings or does not seem to be meeting their obligations to the group?

How do we want to do this: What do we want to get out of this?

3. *Discuss grouping goals.* What expectations do we have for interactions as a team trying to work together? What sanctions will we use against ourselves if we fail to do so?

Humans are quite creative at adapting to difficult circumstances once we experience and understand them. Once the nature of potential pitfalls has been identified, you have the information you need to begin to expect, detect, and correct them. Keys to correcting such pitfalls include *(a) dispel the notion that a trait, orientation, or style of interaction is "good"; (b) reduce the natural tendency to cast aspersions at persons who are different; and (c) find ways to build the benefits of alternative characteristics into group process. Checks and balances* are grouping processes that allow benefits from competing processes and priorities to all serve a common purpose. Humans created the technique of checks and balances to enhance our odds for successfully co-constructing dramatic action. They are part of our wisdom. *Through your discussion of the issues raised in this chapter, you can* tap a similar wisdom among group members, in order to *co-construct your own checks and balances into grouping processes.*

Now that we have introduced you to potential Purgatory Puddle pitfalls, it is a good time to introduce a specific technique that can help you expect, detect, and correct such pitfalls. This technique, called *Orienting the Group,* is an example of putting a check on natural grouping processes and tendencies in order to encourage grouping members to be vigilant, to help them so that they do not miss something important (see Table 4.8).

The following framework for problem-solving discussions is based loosely on the work of John Dewey (1910) and that of functional theorists Gouran and Hirokawa (2003). We have assimilated some of their work with the thinking in this book. Although our general advice is to start a new group with some sort of social icebreaking activity, to address the primary tension, and then to proceed through each of the following steps, two caveats are in order. First, because human grouping is rarely a linear process and will always be responsive to perceived exigencies that change as grouping unfolds, do not expect a group to proceed in a step-by-step manner through all of these prompts, especially through all of the detailed suggestions under step number one (Analyzing the Purgatory Puddle). Rather, groups should consider each of these as a potential prompt to stimulate consideration of worthwhile aspects of their work. In short, group members should ask themselves, "Have we considered this prompt or idea?" and "If not at this meeting, then when?"

Second, the best group interaction may move back and forth between topics several times over several meetings, even reconsidering decisions and processes the group might have thought were already completed. This is called *being recursive* and, as the functional perceptive (Gouran & Hirokawa, 2003) makes clear, an effective group must be willing to reconsider its work, "even to the point of starting over" in order to improve the quality of its problem-solving and decision-making processes.

The first step in the Orienting the Group technique involves a careful analysis of the group's Purgatory Puddle, providing you with prompts to consider issues that often get ignored even by fairly successful groups. The second through fifth steps in the technique focus on Vision/Outcome processes and pitfalls. More details on how to analyze the Vision/Outcome will be added in chapter 7.

❖ CHAPTER SUMMARY

Communicative interaction is the most important dynamic affecting group effectiveness, in spite of our focus in this chapter on personnel and how personal characteristics can have a presence in the life of your

Table 4.8   Orienting the Group: A Technique for Detecting Potential
Pitfalls

1. *Analyze the Purgatory Puddle.* Discuss all aspects of the situation before
   working on (or completing work on) the Vision/Outcome.
   a. Define key terms in the group's charge or assignment. Ask each
      member to be explicit about his or her own meanings; ask, "Would
      experts or stakeholders have different meanings?"
   b. Analyze the group's charge including the problem it must solve or
      task it must do.
      i. What is the nature (qualities and quantity) of the problem?
      ii. What caused/contributed to the problem (where do we find
          evidence and facts on this)?
      iii. What is the duration of the problem—will it solve itself if left alone?
      iv. Is the problem a good task for a group to address?
   c. Identify stakeholders and the nature of their stakes in
      i. The problem.
      ii. The group's charge.
      iii. The group's The Way/Process.
      iv. The group's Vision/Outcome.
   d. Identify and discuss the exigencies
      i. That led to this charge being given to this group.
      ii. That will be important to each of the different stakeholders.
   e. Discuss limitations on the group:
      i. Resources available and problems anticipated and resources that
         are lacking.
      ii. Nonresource-based problems likely to be encountered.
   f. Discuss and set group goals. Develop criteria for testing: "How will
      we know whether we succeeded in reaching each goal?"
      i. Goals for individual contributions to the group.
      ii. Goals for the nature and quality of The Way/Process the group
          will use.
      iii. Goals for the nature and quality of the Vision/Outcome.

2. *Generate potential Vision/Outcomes.* Identify a relevant and realistic set of
   alternatives.

3. *Test Vision/Outcomes.* Carefully examine each alternative against
   previously agreed-on criteria for group goals and for an acceptable choice.

4. *Pick best Vision/Outcome.* Try for consensus for each decision the group
   makes.

Plan to implement Vision/Outcome and to gather feedback on effectiveness. Give the
group an opportunity to debrief after their work is completed and allow time
for a clear and hopefully celebratory meeting or event to signal the termination
of the group's work.

group interaction. "Wrong group for a task" pitfalls include the wrong number of members, members who lack personal resources, and any negative assembly effect. Our objective is not to provide an exhaustive list of such phenomena, nor is it to predict particular effects from any of these variables. Rather, our objective is that you understand and consider the nature of personnel constraints within a Purgatory Puddle, so that you can co-construct your responses to them: do not allow such important pitfalls to be unexpected, go undetected, and remain uncorrected.

5

Pitfalls in Grouping Techniques, Tendencies, and Process Prizes

❖   ❖   ❖

Remember the first day you went to school when you were 5 or 6 years old? Imagine if, gathered with 10 or so of your new friends, you were told, "All right, listen up. Your charge is to become educated. You will need to invent the concept of school. Decide what to do at school. Figure out what subjects need to be taught, who will teach them, and which ones everyone must take in order to be educated. You have a week to accomplish your task, after which you will be expected to go to school until you are educated." What's wrong? Oh, you think that a bunch of children are the "wrong group for the task?" Good for you. Going to school for the first time is hard enough without having to invent school. Do you remember how your first day of school actually went? Did you know where to go and what to do? Think of all that you had to learn about going to school before you could even begin to learn the alphabet or numbers. You had to "learn the ropes"—what to do; how to behave; how to orient yourself.

Now that you are older, you are more adept at organizing difficult tasks on your own. Trying to start a new group is always difficult. You may not know where to begin, but you know you have to figure that out. Joining any extant or ongoing group is a little like trying to go to school for the first time. Or, like your first day on a new job, your first day at college, or coming home with your first baby. All are situations where you have a new task, new people to get to know, and a new supragroup in which to work. Each situation involves figuring out how to proceed. The Way/Process represents the recurring aspects of human attempts to make sense of any such situations that involve grouping. The first day a new group meets, everything is uncertain, except you know you have to figure out how to proceed.

Put metaphorically, any grouping enterprise is a journey from one place to another. The origins of the journey are in Purgatory Puddle exigencies, which evolve throughout the life of the group: some task to do and some personnel or supragroup desire for action. Purgatory Puddle exigencies are experienced as something group members want to change, to escape, and to get behind them. Vision/Outcome exigencies serve as a beacon or magnet, the attraction of the desirable outcome. What is missing are the means for taking the trip. Organizing the trip, the logistics involved, and the meanings that are co-constructed while working those things out combine to form The Way/Process. All Quadrad bases of dramatic action involve "unknowns" before grouping begins. Perceived exigency for action, shrouded in uncertainty about how to proceed, results in rhetorical acts of interpretation and framing: grouping and direction-creating attempts.

The Way metaphor in the Quadrad represents the desire people can have for stability, organization, and some sense of orientation within a system. Such connotations are especially evident in a new group, which can feel like the first day of a new job or of school. The metaphor The Way represents the bias toward action perceived in exigencies to get organized and the readiness to respond rhetorically by creating order in grouping situations: either to learn the way things work here or to create ways for things to work here. The Way represents connotations of the comfort in having (following or creating) a path for the journey. To have a process and appropriate orientation to it is perceived as desirable, even when one does not fully understand how or why the process is supposed to work.

Groups begin to structure themselves in two ways as grouping begins: establishing a pattern of work and creating a social system of relationships (Bormann, 1996). We call such grouping activities The Way/Process *techniques* and *tendencies.* The Way/Process techniques and tendencies are co-constructed in attempts to attain The Way/Process *process prizes* and to deal with The Way/Process *concomitants* (confusion, conformity, conflict, and consciousness: see chapter 6). All these co-constructed structuration processes manifest in potential The Way/Process pitfalls. You can employ the frameworks for Grouping and Group Direction and the Breakdown-Conducive Group to conceptualize and then create your own best communicative responses to these pitfalls.

❖ GROUPING TECHNIQUES

The Way/Process techniques range from any informal processes to all formal procedures; all are ways to help grouping members address their exigencies for having or for co-creating some ordered and effective process for grouping. For example, some of The Way/Process techniques introduced in this book are broaching the subject (chapters 3–7); orienting the group, especially step one (chapter 4, Table 4.8); analyzing the Purgatory Puddle (chapter 4); use of reminders and of checks and balances (chapter 4); ideals of the *demos,* of consensus, of a discussional attitude, and for deliberation (chapter 5); effective co-constructions of grouping conflict (chapter 6); procedural expert, dialogic virtuoso, and devil's advocate role specializations (chapter 7); cranking up the mindfulness (chapter 8); and observing groups well (chapter 10). These techniques range from formal procedures to formal orientations or skill sets for effective grouping, and they are all The Way/Process techniques designed to help you to expect, detect, and correct pitfalls to effective group experiences.

In addition to such formal procedures, note the processes suggested in simple statements such as, "What is your name?" (let's do introductions; let's discuss personnel parameters to find out "who are we?"; let's break the ice); "You go first" (taking turns; suggesting communication norms); "How shall we proceed?" (requesting a process; perhaps a call to set an agenda or to divide the work); and so forth. If a group is confused or struggling in any way, it may need a The Way/Process technique or it may need to change its current The Way/Process technique. Rhetorical responses to grouping needs and also to grouping pitfalls are typically constructed into a The

Way/Process technique, a process or procedure that helps the group co-construct its way to approach future grouping attempts.

When people perceive exigencies to group, they tend to employ the most basic The Way/Process technique in response: they talk, they begin to communicate with others about the exigencies that concern them. When talk becomes sufficiently complicated, people tend to employ the second basic The Way/Process technique in order to structure the time for their talk so that all can participate: they call a meeting. Having a meeting typically initiates a whole new set of issues including the need for procedures to make meetings work well. The Way/Process techniques consist of communication, meetings, and any other grouping procedures.

❖ TECHNIQUE PITFALLS

Communication Pitfalls

Communication pitfalls specific to grouping are discussed throughout this book. Beyond such grouping-specific communication pitfalls, the following brief list details some of the communication pitfalls you can expect will affect any communication attempt, including all grouping activity. For example, sometimes we make mistakes constructing a message because we think the people who will hear it will process the information the same way that we did or, perhaps, already share our view. *Assumed cognitive similarity* means "I think you think like I think." When we are not correct in assuming support for an argument or assuming that others will understand us, we do not explain

Table 5.1   Summary of The Way/Process Technique Pitfalls

Technique Pitfall	*Examples*
Communication as The Way/Process Technique Pitfalls	Assumed cognitive similarity; channel problems; message confusions; reception issues; feedback activities.
Meetings as The Way/Process Technique Pitfalls	Inappropriate number or length of meetings; poorly run meetings; poor meeting format or facilities.
The Way/Process Procedure Pitfalls	No process; faulty process; hurtful process; pitfalls in good process.

ourselves well enough. Sometimes *channel pitfalls* stymie our intentions. For example, sending ideas by e-mail is okay for some messages but not for personal information. Asking a third party to carry a message may be upsetting to a person who wants to hear directly from "the horse's mouth." Channel capacities are *overloaded* if too much information is put in one message. Messages passed through multiple people will be changed by a *serial transmission effect* as each person in the series changes the message a bit. *Physical noise* can affect the sending and receiving of messages. *Message pitfalls* result from the verbal or nonverbal symbols employed, most of which have some level of abstraction or ambiguity involved: two people using the same word or nonverbal gesture with different meanings in mind. When the message is received, *reception pitfalls* include the tendency we all have to *sharpen* some parts of a message, placing greater weight than intended on those parts; to *level* parts of the message, dropping important aspects out because we do not know they are important; and to *assimilate* the whole of the message into our own context and concerns, putting our own "spin" on what is said. The solution to many communication pitfalls is feedback, but *feedback pitfalls* are all too common as well. We restrict feedback, if we are high self-monitors or rhetorically sensitive, and we forget our obligations to provide accurate feedback in usable "doses," which are designed to help the co-construction of meaning rather than to impress or punish those with whom we speak. All such general communication pitfalls affect the potential for grouping effectiveness.

Potential communication pitfalls are faced by any individual attempting to communicate. You should expect communication to be a struggle in the same sense that grouping can be. *You should expect miscommunication to be possible and that you might be part of the problem, even when certain you are not. You should prepare yourself to detect and overcome such pitfalls when they are experienced. Think through important messages in advance, perhaps even preconstructing phrases to express key ideas and finding evidence in advance that your ideas merit consideration. Solicit feedback about what you are saying from the person you are talking to. Create questions you can ask about what he or she thinks. Attempt to paraphrase what you think he or she is trying to tell you to help improve the co-construction of meanings by double-checking your understanding against the intended meanings. Throughout important communication episodes, try to focus your energies on avoiding or correcting problems, not on casting blame or on finding fault for any communication pitfall.*

Meeting Pitfalls

The second basic The Way/Process technique is to call a meeting. The most basic meeting pitfall involves frequency of meetings and includes the failure to meet when grouping requires a meeting, or meeting too often when grouping activities or tasks do not require so many meetings. Some people seek to structure their grouping experiences to decrease the opportunities for interactions, and they may err toward too few meetings. Others may call too many meetings, perhaps because they like the social aspects of the team. Remember that grouping uses up member resources. *There should be enough meetings to best serve group functions.*

The second set of pitfalls involves how meetings unfold. A basic issue is meeting length: meetings that are either too long or too short given the circumstances. The lack of an agenda can keep a meeting from being as productive as might be anticipated. Too extensive an agenda can make a meeting uncomfortably long. *The appropriate length of a meeting is determined by the group's agenda, time line, norms, and supragroup pressures. Members should co-construct their ideas and expectations in this regard.* Meetings can be poorly managed. Unequal participation opportunities for members may influence their commitment and contributions to the group (Gastil, 1993). Such uneven contributions have two potential negative effects. First, there is a loss when problem solving is done without utilizing all the resources available in grouping members. Second, there is a potential diminution of climate and group cohesion as members feel relatively good or bad about their personal contributions to grouping processes and outcomes and to those of their compadres (see boxed text titled Focus on Scholarship). *The solution to poor group meetings is found in the ideals of the demos, of consensus, of a discussional attitude, and for deliberation* (see Tables 5.2 and 5.3).

A third set of issues involves the format and facilities for meetings. The format for conducting business in a group must change to fit the task and the size of the group. If the group gets too large or requires a "legal" process, *parliamentary procedure* may be implemented to allow everyone to be able to participate in a specified manner, strictly governed by a formal and rigid set of rules that are outlined in a book called *Robert's Rules of Order.* Parliamentary procedure changes grouping dynamics so much that group meetings may become a less valuable technique in the struggle to attain the process prizes of group work unless subcommittees or other informal grouping opportunities are made available, in which freely interactive dynamics can flourish.

Finally, meetings can also be held in facilities or using seating arrangements that are not conducive to member interaction. Seating can contribute to a member's tendencies to communicate with the group and also to the orientation of a group member toward task or relational aspects of grouping. The facilities may distract members' attention, may be uncomfortable or too comfortable, and may have any number of other effects. *Both format and facilities can and should be modified as members perceive exigencies for improving their effectiveness on those fronts. No format or facility should be tolerated for long if it diminishes the group's ability to serve its functions well.*

Focus on Scholarship:
The Democratic Group Meeting

Gastil (1993) describes the following pitfalls as ubiquitous and significant in attempts to attain the ideals of democratic deliberations: (a) *long meetings* result in an increase in relational talk and a decrease in the equality of participation, (b) *unequal power* results as less committed members are outweighed by high power members, (c) *formation of cliques* of grouping members who interact outside of meetings results in members coming to meetings with established opinions, (d) *different communication skills and styles* afford higher levels of participation for some members, and (e) *interpersonal conflicts* result from an inability to speak or having one's views ignored.

We are going to take some time here to outline four concepts that can enhance your tactical efforts to communicate effectively in groups and also provide a strategic orienting philosophy for your interactions with others as you group: *demos* (a self-governing group), *consensus, discussional attitude, and deliberation.* These concepts are as fundamental to effective grouping experiences as is understanding the frameworks for Grouping and Group Direction and for the Breakdown-Conducive Group.

The ideals of the *demos* include group meetings that involve everyone in group decisions, sharing power and authority, developing relationships that enhance deliberations, and free and open communication (see Table 5.2). Gastil (1992) synthesized arguments that have been made over the centuries about the nature and merits of democracy

Table 5.2   Orientation to Effective Group Meetings: The Ideals of the *demos*

Component of Democracy	Description of What Our Grouping Must Strive to Attain to Achieve the Ideal
A Democratic Group (*demos*): Has Power	Democratic groups have the power to get things done and sovereignty or jurisdiction to encompass the ideas on their agenda. Power is shared by group members, who have equal authority and responsibility for outcomes.
A *demos*: Is Inclusive	All affected by group have access to power, relationships, and deliberations.
A *demos*: Is Committed to the Democratic Process	Members internalize *demos* values: all participate; all respect group choice and go along with it, or accept the penalty, or withdraw from the group.
A *demos*: Is Committed to Democratic Relationships	Members acknowledge individuality (do not subvert the individual to the interest of the group), affirm competence (all have faith in the competence of others—to help make decisions for me, to not force decisions on them), recognition of mutuality (all move beyond my individual perspective to include a sense of what the group needs), and congeniality (what we consider to be amicable ways of working together).
A *demos*: Is Committed to Democratic Deliberations	(a) Members have equal and adequate opportunities *to speak*, represented by agenda setting; reformulation of issues already on the agenda; articulation of one's perspective for purpose of clarification and thinking matters through, not just for persuasion; persuasion (honest, forthright, critical thinking-enhancing efforts); voting (a simple expression of preference); and dissent (reminding others that we disagreed, though bound by the decision). (b) Members have equal and adequate opportunities *to listen*, represented by comprehension (if I can't understand the whole of what is said, I am deprived) and consideration (careful, quiet reflection).

into a single definition, which tells us how we should behave if we wish to co-construct democracy (it is much more than just the right to vote; see Table 5.2). Gastil argues that democracy is an unattainable ideal. However, groups should strive for the ideal because that effort improves grouping quality. We call such an orientation striving to attain the ideals of the *demos*. Your ability to co-construct effective group experiences is severely limited unless you strive to attain the ideals of the *demos*. Read the column on the left of Table 5.2 to see the components of Gastil's definition of a democratic group; the column on the right is what we must strive to attain, though in many cases we can only approximate the ideal and its values in our co-constructions.

Consensus is a carefully co-constructed agreement among group members about their grouping. For example, members may develop a consensus that x is the best way for us to interpret our Purgatory Puddle, or that y is the best The Way/Process for us to employ, or that z is the best Vision/Outcome we can develop. Consensus is not a quick agreement, born of inadequate consideration or haste to proceed, nor is it attained by voting or compromise, both of which have their place but are employed to speed the group along. The time spent and the inclusive processes employed to achieve consensus help the group develop a common understanding and rationale for what they are doing. They can then agree that their choice is better than one based in another form of decision making. Further, achieving consensus means that they all understand and can articulate reasons why their choice is the best one for the group. That high standard for agreement enhances the possibility of a process prize. A false sense of agreement, when members merely go along with the group without having achieved a consensus regarding why, is much less likely to fully serve the three group functions. Consensus is better than if one or two members manage to get their own way, or if members must compromise on what they want, or if members vote so that those who disagree have to go along, though they do not fully support the choice.

Consensus is important in interpreting and framing a group's Purgatory Puddle, The Way/Process, and Vision/Outcome. When a group works toward consensus, efforts to do so heighten opportunities for effective critical or creative work and the possibility of member acceptance of group outcomes (even if the group eventually fails to achieve a consensus).

People reared in a democracy tend to want to vote[3] to make group decisions. *Small groups, however, should avoid voting because that can stop the deliberations necessary for achieving a consensus.* There are five aspects of consensus that have been tested in research (DeStephen & Hirokawa, 1988). We translate these into levels of consensus quality, with the ideal of consensus represented by the co-construction of as much as possible of all five levels through grouping (see Table 5.3). You can get a sense of how rushing to a quick agreement or vote can diminish group outcomes by considering the five levels of consensus that might have been accomplished through harder work.

Individuals may lack subject matter expertise but still be able to add value to a group because of their grouping communication skills. Grouping skills begin with the orientation that *grouping is a learning co-construction*: a way to interact in order to sort through ideas and information. To do that requires placing a value in putting on a *discussional attitude* (Bormann, 1975) in order to enhance *group deliberations*. These are keys to any group that seeks to attain the ideals of the *demos* and of consensus (see Table 5.3). Both a discussional attitude and deliberation skills enhance the group's ability to achieve its process prizes.

A strategic approach to grouping and group meetings should breathe life into the ideals of the *demos*, consensus, discussional attitude, and deliberation. Those ideals should manifest in group meetings but are more important to effective group life than most grouping tactics or procedures because they represent a philosophy of grouping that can serve as a framework for addressing most of the pitfalls in this book. *Every group member should help make a meeting more effective. All should prepare to actively help try to provide group direction, at least as an effective follower, doer, or guide.*

Lack of Appropriate Procedures Pitfalls

Grouping requires process; grouping is process. The lack of appropriate process is a pitfall until group co-construction begins, at which point potential pitfalls with the process can manifest, both in flawed procedures and even in the misuse of an effective procedure. Even if all else appears in order, the lack of talk about what process to employ and whether it is working well presents a pitfall potential because such talk is the one significant distinction between effective and ineffective group communication (Hirokawa, 1980). *All groups should discuss and describe the process they plan to use. As their work unfolds, all groups should discuss how well their process is serving them, making changes as needed.*

Over time, one can expect that effective group processes and procedures will sometimes "go bad" if they begin to be employed in a mindless or "autopilot" sort of way by grouping members. An extreme version of this involves what Hoffman (2002) describes as *reification*, which is continued use of once-good procedures that have become inadequate or have otherwise gone bad over time. Reification results in

Table 5.3   Orienting Effective Groups: Ideals of Discussional Attitude,
Deliberation, and Consensus

Discussional Attitude

Keep an open mind to the ideas of others; listen carefully and follow up until
you understand.

Work hard to articulate your own ideas; do not just give up, especially on a
minority view.

Encourage contributions from all grouping members.

Seeks ways to adjust and improve your own ideas and opinions. Make
suggestions to others about how their ideas and opinions fit together with
others expressed in the group.

Develop a desire to talk about ideas instead of rushing to finish. Be
determined to allow the time that inevitably must pass before uncertainty
can manifest, then sort uncertainties out.

Deliberation Skills.

Try to expand the boundaries of the material considered by the group. Set as
a goal the creation of new ideas through group interaction and the
consideration of new sources of data.

Try to test all key ideas and information considered by the group. Seek out
and test group assumptions.

Try to use the testing of ideas and evidence to stimulate new ideas and
needs for evidence.

Be recursive. Keep track of ideas that need more thought. Return to key
topics as many times as necessary to resolve them and to reconcile them
with other group ideas and activities.

Consensus

When you have completed your grouping, will all the members of your
group be able to say,

"I agree with the group's decision."

"I am committed to the group's decision."

"I am satisfied with the group's decision."

"I am satisfied with my individual participation in the group's decision
making."

"I am satisfied with our decision-making process, including how others were
involved."

---

doing what is familiar and comfortable out of inertia, not because it is
best for the group. When we reify a process, we give the process more
credit than it deserves, continuing to use the process "because that is
how we do things" rather than because it is the right thing to do in this
case. In sum, if the means employed by a group do not serve the purposes for grouping, a change is in order. *Effective group members know*

that they will need to co-construct The Way/Process techniques: the commu-nication, group meetings, and procedures that help them address whatever pit-falls arise as they seek process prizes on their journey to Vision/Outcome. They understand that grouping techniques need to be monitored, discussed, and probably changed over time.

❖ GROUPING TENDENCIES: NORMS AND ROLES

All groups tend to develop norms and roles, which is why we call them The Way/Process tendencies. These tendencies are clusters of co-constructed meanings grouping members create for themselves: ideas about how the group should interact, about how members should behave, and about individual member responsibilities. *Norms* are co-constructed and negotiated expectations for appropriate behavior (Bormann, 1996). Most or all grouping members must share an expec-tation for it to be normative. Kelman (1961) says people conform for one of three reasons: because they perceive pressure to *comply,* which means doing something because the group expects it of them; because their *identification* with the group means doing something to show they are part of the group; or because of their *internalization* of the behav-ioral value. Norms tend to result from grouping, whether individuals are aware of them or not, whether they are helpful to the group's goals or not, and whether the group tries to make them explicit or not.

As perception of exigencies continues to stimulate grouping activ-ity, the need for specialization of member responses becomes evident and the formation of roles begins. *Roles* are co-constructed and negoti-ated expectations for a particular job or for a particular member who does the job (Bargal & Bar, 1990). Roles evolve as members attempt to specialize in serving functions required by the group. Their attempts are responded to favorably (allowed or supported) or unfavorably (contested or ignored) by others in the group: a response that either encourages or discourages further such attempts.

The absence of roles and norms early in any grouping attempt means confusion reigns until ongoing "negotiations" are used to co-construct The Way/Process tendencies. The first day of kindergarten, children do not know the norms or their role. The first day home with a first baby, parents must develop new norms and role responsibilities in their family. At the first meeting of a new group, primary tension provides evidence of the lack of clear norms and roles. Groups cannot

Table 5.4   Summary of The Way/Process Tendency Pitfalls: Norms and Roles

Norm Pitfalls	
Absence of Group Norms	Confusion: primary tension because expectations are not yet set.
Faulty or Inadequate Norms	Partially mature group; norms that hinder progress.
Bad Enforcement of Norms	Enforcement of a bad norm or bad enforcement of an appropriate norm.
Network Pitfalls	Centralization issues; saturation; excluded members.

Role Pitfalls	
Role Ambiguity	Confusion: primary tension because roles not yet set or clear.
Role Competition	"I wanna play the doctor." "No, I getta be the doctor!"
Role Collision and Conflict	"There's too little of me." "If I think this, how can I do that?"
Role Representation	"Does your group agree?" "You're a man; why do men do that?"
Role Favoritism	"I'll vacuum after I make sure the TV doesn't get stolen."
Constructing Bad Roles	Demagogue; tyrant; passive member; spy; saboteur.

function well until they have reduced those aspects of their confusion (see Table 5.4).

❖ NORM PITFALLS

Absence of Group Norms

When a group first meets, there is *primary tension* (Bormann, 1996) because individuals do not yet know what is expected in this group (norms) and how they should respond (role). That basic confusion provides an exigency for grouping action, for trying to fit in, and for trying to find one's place. Without norms, grouping members may be overly cautious or make mistakes. This early condition is an *immature group*. Uncertainty will motivate action, but rhetorical co-constructions of normative activity take time. Even *mature groups*, which have developed norms and roles that help them efficiently and effectively serve their three group functions, can experience the pitfalls that result from the absence of necessary norms if a new grouping contingency or a new set of perceived exigencies makes it evident that new processes need to be developed and employed. *Time spent grouping is the only remedy for the absence of necessary norms; being patient with an immature group is as reasonable as waiting for a tomato to ripen before you bite into it.*

Faulty or Inadequate Norms

Partially mature groups may develop faulty or inadequate norms, which help move the group along but perhaps not quickly enough or perhaps too quickly. These limit the group's ability to address grouping exigencies. When members in such circumstances interpret their Purgatory Puddle, they may observe, "we are not getting enough done" or "we only have a few days left," or they may fail to analyze some key aspect of their Purgatory Puddle, choosing instead to *jump to solution* without adequate consideration of the problem that faces them. In such circumstances, what has been co-constructed into normative behavior may need revision for the group to eventually succeed. Norms and grouping are dynamic processes. It is a difficult issue to know whether current norms are sufficient. In some cases, the group just needs more time to become successful and, in others, continuing with the same behaviors becomes more and more problematic. *Continued conversations are in order regarding grouping processes and normative behavior, especially how well they are serving the group.*

Included in the assessment of group norms should be consideration of the enforcement of healthy norms. Many of us have learned to avoid unpleasant tasks. To "take flight" from such activities may include the failure to sanction deviant behavior or underperformance. Sometimes such "comfort-seeking" orientations can allow the group to avoid activities with sufficient rigor to improve the quality of their interaction or task-related grouping outcomes. The life of a group requires a certain level of conformity to group norms. Enforcing healthy norms lends vigor to group activity. *Ongoing discussions of group norms provides the potential for improving them and the efforts to make them serve the group.*

Enforcement of Inappropriate Group Norms

The most obvious example of norm pitfalls is when a group develops a hurtful norm or overenforces a generally appropriate practice ("too much of a good thing"). These tendencies create disadvantages for the group. Examples include when teasing starts out in good fun but ends up traumatizing a group member or when creativity is squashed because "we don't do things that way here." *When a norm is hurtful, it is a pitfall to grouping. Someone in the group must notice and cause the group to think about possible negative effects: to point them out and help the group co-construct a change in behavior.* That is uncomfortable work because it involves rocking the boat and risks the bad feelings that can accompany criticism. *Each of us can help by orienting toward seeking criticism as a fundamental process for improving performance. We probably need to give our permission to other grouping members to be critical of us or they may just stay "polite." Some hire external observers or consultants for exactly that reason.*

Communication Network Pitfalls

All groups develop patterns to their communication, which are called communication networks. Informal communication networks are really nothing more than manifestations of norms and roles observable in who speaks to whom, how often, and about what. Network pitfall potential can involve *saturation* of information flow if one person tries to handle too much of the information flow, perhaps exceeding her or his channel capacity or leaving other members out of the loop. A related problem is *centralization* of the information flow, indicating more authority in one member than in others. This may be more appropriate when autocratic processes are in order, which, by definition, should not be too often in groups where participatory and democratic processes are needed. Greater centralization means diminished process prize potential. Other network pitfalls are evident in tendencies people have to create factions, including *cliques* (a small, exclusive group), *alliances* (agreements to cooperate), or *coalitions* (alliances for political action). It is generally a pitfall if lines of communication are not both open to and used by all group members. Open and active talk among all the group members cocreates an *all-channel network*, which typically characterizes effective group communication.

❖ ROLE PITFALLS

Role Ambiguity

Role pitfalls begin with the confusion of each new grouping member about "what is my job, my place in this group." Uncertainty precedes role formation. Once roles are being "tried on," *role ambiguity* is the uncertainty about whether one is playing an appropriate role and whether one is meeting the expectations of other grouping members (Kahn & Quinn, 1970). Until you know what your role is, how to play it, and whether others like the way you are playing it, you are an *immature grouping member*, not yet ready to group well. Regardless of group communication skills or subject matter expertise, all new group members and all new groups are immature in each new grouping enterprise because every system is somewhat unique. *Immaturity* is not a pejorative or negative term in this case, anymore than a baby, because immature is somehow bad. The individual or group that is immature is not yet fully able to perform. Uncertainty regarding roles can also manifest in a mature group whenever new members join, experienced members leave, or new exigencies are perceived and acted upon, which require shifting of roles among current members. Fruits, ideas, and groups all need time and energy to mature.

Role Competition

When more than one group member attempts to play a particular role, the group co-constructs a role competition. Especially as key direction givers emerge, a *process of residues* is used by grouping members to eliminate role contenders until only one, who is acceptable to the group, remains. Members may compete openly for the role they want to play, or they may defer when others indicate an interest. Deference does not last long when members become dissatisfied with how the group is progressing. When grouping members decide they want you to play a role, there will be pressure to conform to their wishes. Pitfall potential pervades this process and, in some cases, afterwards, depending on how a rejected member gets reintegrated into the group (Bormann & Bormann, 1996). Roles must be co-constructed and negotiated through a process of emergence. *Even assigned roles get co-constructed as the group and the person playing the role interact. Open discussion of the process and explicit willingness to adjust roles and to assess how well they are serving the group can aid this potentially bumpy process.*

Role Collision and Conflict

Role collision is when two roles an individual plays collide, creating a resource problem that makes it difficult for the person to fulfill the requirements of both roles. There is just not enough of the person (time, energy, interest) to play both roles. If you have a job to support yourself, are trying to raise a family, and are trying to get a college degree, your job gets in the way of being a student, which takes time away from being with your family. The roles are all important to you and consistent with each other; there is just not enough of you to go around. *Role conflict* is when two roles you play are in fundamental tension with one another; the values and beliefs basic to one are in conflict with the values of another. This is not a resource problem; with all the time in the world, this combination still results in conflict for you. As a manager, it is sometimes difficult to be a friend to an employee. As a parent, there is sometimes a tradeoff between encouraging your child and critiquing what he or she is doing. Constructing your own processes for dealing with your own roles, once your groups have finished co-constructing those roles with you, becomes one of the keys to a happy and effective life, including how your group work will help serve its individual function for you. *Do not despair alone when you let your roles get out of hand. It is better to say no than to grind yourself up. It is better to seek help from the group than to let them down.*

Role Representation in Boundary Spanning

Role representation is when you have to carry a role you play within a group to a setting outside the group. It is a pitfall if this role transfer makes it difficult for you outside the group or within. For example, a supragroup entity may ask your group's opinion on a subject or that you negotiate for your group. Unless the group has given you the charge to communicate on its behalf, it is a problem if you comply. Even if the group has given you the charge, pitfall potential is obvious. Another version is when you are stereotyped as a member of one of your groups: "You are a girl; will my mom like this?" or "Give me the male perspective" or "Tell me what African Americans think about this subject" or "You're a soldier; how do you justify this war?" *You must draw the lines around your own behavior by figuring out what is appropriate. Discussing the issue with your group can help, but if that opportunity is not available, communicate outside the group in a manner that pretends your group members are listening in so that you will be less likely to try to speak on their behalf without authority to do so.*

Role Favoritism

When you dislike one of your roles, or when you shift an inappropriate amount of your energy toward a role you really like, you demonstrate *role favoritism*. One obvious pitfall is when favoritism keeps you focused on a role you most enjoy playing to the extent that it creates a resource collision, which limits your ability to fulfill your other role obligations. It is not unusual for group members to claim they have too little time for a responsibility because, by the time they make the claim, they have constructed the condition. It is not role collision if a proper balance of energies does not produce the resource problem. As group members, we need to keep in mind that people change and their interest in playing a role may change. *Discuss roles in your group. Make it a norm to show interest in how other members play their roles. Make it a norm to solicit and to gently offer advice on how performance can be improved. Discuss ways to be flexible enough to allow some shifting of roles to take place, at least enough to create an informed membership so that the illness or loss of one member does not undermine the group.* When an individual is constantly called on to play a role she or he does not like, it represents a failure of the group to serve its individual function. When one individual keeps a desirable role from others, that selfish behavior serves similar ends and, further, limits group capacity in case of an unforeseen problem.

Co-constructing Some Bad Role Outcomes

It is counterintuitive that any set of grouping individuals would intentionally develop roles that do not serve them well or would intentionally allow one person to play an important role when another member is obviously better suited to that role. But it does happen, at least unintentionally, and because of interpersonal dynamics involved in grouping interactions (such as the tendency to make friends with some individuals and not with others), it might even happen intentionally. Bad role outcomes are the wrong person getting group approval to do a role or the wrong role getting co-constructed by the group given its needs. The former problem occurs when there is a better person in the group to play a role than the person the group has playing it (though that should not justify limiting the attempts of someone to learn a new role or allowing one member to dominate a desirable role). Even harmful roles are co-constructed through member consent. Consider the following metaphors, which obviously represent roles that should be reconstructed:

1. Harmful direction-giver roles include the *demagogue* who appeals to the base emotions of mob instincts; the *tyrant* who uses arbitrary, capricious, or cruel tactics to orient the group; the *cult of personality*, which uses favoritism and friendships to cultivate cliques; and the *windmill charger*, who sacrifices the group for the good of a lost cause.

2. Harmful direction-receiver roles include the *passive member*, who acts as though there is virtue in letting others decide what the group should do; the irate or *confrontational member*, who has a "bone to pick," and uses that bone to justify withdrawing or dominating behavior; the *saboteur*, who attempts to do harm to the group; the *ineffective member*, who has not been involved as a group resource; and the *spy*, who serves a hidden agenda.

Note that playing a harmful role over time is a different issue than any single, interaction-appropriate display. For example, there may be a time to show irritation and to confront inappropriate behavior. In contrast, the irate or confrontational member plays that role in most grouping circumstances, and, in all these cases, *the group must not tolerate the behavior if efforts to reconstruct the role do not succeed after a reasonable amount of time and number of attempts. Sanctions in such an extreme include a change in group membership or drawing a line between the offending member and group benefits.*

❖ PROCESS PRIZES

Process prizes are value added by doing work as a grouping entity rather than in some other way. Grouping should only be selected as a tool for a job if it offers potential for a process prize: increased critical or creative work or quality, or increased group member acceptance of group outcomes. Creative thinking is divergent: creativity is coming up with new thoughts, creating new associations between already existing thoughts, or developing new perspectives. To test the quality and value of new ideas, however, involves critical thinking. Critical thinking is convergent, trying to focus one's analysis of each idea. Critical thinking requires the ability to critique: to analyze and assess available options in order to note the merits and problems of each, and then to pick the best option. Grouping members must identify which of the options developed by their creative processes are actually best. Critical and creative thinking are processes in tension with one another but are also, at some point in the process, necessary to each other. Further, there are dynamics involved in grouping that can make it difficult for groups of people to think either critically or creatively.

❖ PROCESS PRIZE PITFALLS

Because group acceptance is won or lost in gradual degrees throughout grouping activity and involves grouping processes discussed throughout this book, the remainder of this section regards potential process pitfalls to critical or to creative thinking.

Deliberation process pitfalls (see Table 5.5) manifest in three related ways. *Mindlessness* is faulty cognitive processing in which grouping members work below their capacities (Elmes & Gemmill, 1990; McGarty, Haslem, Hutchinson, & Turner, 1994; Timmerman, 2002.). Grouping members get mentally lazy or disengage so much that they do low-quality or careless work (see Table 5.6).

Table 5.5   Summary of The Way/Process: Process Prize Pitfalls

Process Prize Pitfall	Examples
Deliberation Process Pitfalls	Mindlessness; fallacious reasoning; groupthink.
Deliberation Outcome Pitfalls	Insufficient deliberation or jumping to solution; tension-relieving decision-making tool.

Even when one is fully engaged or mindful, *fallacious reasoning* can still flaw the deliberative process. Deductive and inductive reasoning must follow valid processes in order to be trusted. Fallacious reasoning is specious; it is a flawed process, which seems to draw a compelling conclusion. People tend to select what their emotions tell them is true and then try to use logic to support their choice. Deliberations should be used to test such conclusions and attempts. For example, *overgeneralization* is when we use insufficient data to draw a conclusion. The *post hoc fallacy* is when we explain what is happening now by assuming it was caused by something that happened earlier (after this, therefore because of this). When your group makes arguments or accepts evidence without testing them, regardless of how "obvious" they appear

Table 5.6   Mindless Member and Interaction Characteristics

Characteristic	Description
Sluggish Information Processing	Members behave as if they are brain dead or paralyzed; appear as if they are just not "sharp."
Adherence to Rigid Frame of Reference	Members blindly follow a formula for group activities; "autopilot."
De-skill Self	Members are unable to express intellectual or emotional differences
Subjugated Self	Members act as though they are of one mind with others in the group.

to be, the group is diminishing potential insight and process prize quality. Remember that some argumentation is required. *Claims should be clearly articulated with solid reasons provided for accepting them.* Testing the strength and merits of an idea is not a personal attack; it is an effort to attain a process prize. *Seek possible alternative explanations and evidence. Make critical or creative thinking the norms to be valued, not the comfort and ease of the obvious.*

The final deliberative process pitfall involves a conglomeration of grouping phenomena Janis (1972, 1982) calls *groupthink,* which is a mode of harmful co-construction typified by the *illusions of unanimity* and of *invulnerability;* treatment of the *group as moral* and of those who oppose it as misguided, even evil; *self-imposed ignorance* about key information (*self-censorship* and *mind-guards*); and *miscalculation of risks.* Though each of these unfortunate dynamics may manifest in any group, including immature groups, groupthink is defined as a co-construction *only* when all these phenomena infect the efforts of a mature and highly cohesive group (cf. Welch-Cline, 1994). Others disagree with the Janis formulation, especially that a cohesive group could exhibit such undesirable grouping activities (Bormann, 1996), but the concept has a life of its own, is certainly an evocative and provocative metaphor, and does represent a list of undesirable activities for any group that seeks to attain a process prize.

❖ DELIBERATION OUTCOME PITFALLS

Deliberation outcome pitfalls keep a group from attaining its process prizes because the group prematurely stops one aspect of its work and

Table 5.7   Possible Jumping to Solution Activities

- Someone suggests a conclusion before the group has sorted out their Purgatory Puddle.
- Someone suggests how to proceed on the task before group goals are discussed.
- Someone frames the problem before key terms are defined.
- Someone suggests a vision/outcome before the problem is analyzed and criteria are set for outcomes.
- Someone advocates a particular vision/outcome before additional vision/outcome alternatives are identified.
- Someone asks for a decision before weighing pros and cons of choices under consideration.
- Someone asks for a decision before testing if the choice meets the group's goals and criteria.

moves on to another (cf. Schultz, Ketrow, & Urban, 1995). These pitfalls manifest from an *insufficiency of deliberation*, not from flawed deliberation. An example is inadequate understanding of the group's charge before trying to address it. Inadequate understanding of a charge makes all subsequent deliberations a potential waste of time and energy exploring a route that may not serve the group well. *Jumping to a solution* may be one of the most common pitfalls faced by groups (see Figure 5.7). This general psychological tendency for individuals and groups (Bormann, 1996; Janis, 1989) manifests as people try to "cut to the chase."

People are not always linear in their thinking processes, so jumping about among topics is to be expected. A benefit can even result from allowing the group to move back and forth between problems until they work their way through difficult issues. For example, more time spent from initial consideration to final determination allows incubation time in which confusions, uncertainties, and problems can become apparent. But the group must find its way back to the subject it has jumped through; it must find ways to *be recursive,* to reconsider an issue or idea until a strong consensus forms. If it does not, the jump to solution ensures diminished potential for attaining process prizes. *When such a jump occurs, be on guard. Note the diversion and make certain your group, at some point, goes back to finish their deliberations* before they get committed to a particular process or solution. Almost all of the strategic and tactical advice in this book can be applied to attempting to overcome the effects of jumping to solution. This is one pitfall your group is probably going to step into, regardless of your efforts to avoid it. Consequently, *being recursive is always required in a group, and making that need part of the conversation early and often is essential. Special efforts need to be made by effective group members to see that recurring consideration of key ideas is co-constructed into a group norm.*

The second deliberation outcome pitfall manifests whenever a group uses a conflict or tension-reducing decision-making device to end group discussion. Examples include letting members vote or flip a coin. "Objective" tools for deciding pick a "winning idea" without first developing a consensus for how and why the idea is the best. Groups may also tend to avoid topics entirely if they are too "hot" or difficult to address because of differences (conflict) among members. *The solution to both tendencies is conversation about the issues at hand from the perspective of a skilled group practitioner.*

Additional Ways to Expect, Detect, and Correct These Pitfalls

Effective group members find ways to co-construct healthy processes and orientations for grouping and for creating group direction. The Breakdown-Conducive Group Framework argues that part of each group's work is the co-construction of ways around or through the pitfalls they face: expect, detect, and correct grouping pitfalls. Because The Way/Process is at the heart of grouping activity and success, determined efforts to *talk about process, the group's way of doing things, is vital to the co-construction of effective group experiences.* What follows is a set of conversational prompts that can help you raise these issues: to broach the subject in a way that helps your group co-construct its way around or through the pitfalls in this chapter (see Table 5.8).

❖ CHAPTER SUMMARY

The Way/Process is grouping activity involved in attempts to create the means for changing a Purgatory Puddle. The Way/Process techniques and tendencies manifest during any attempt to group. Pitfall potential is evident in all aspects of The Way/Process grouping. Pitfalls manifest in the absence of effective grouping or structuration efforts. Pitfall potential manifests in any attempts at structuration found in

Table 5.8   Broaching the Subject on The Way/Process: Techniques,
Tendencies, and Process Prize Pitfalls

Getting started: Who are we?

1. *Get acquainted.* Break the ice; small talk; personal information; what's up?
2. *How do we contact each other?*

Getting to work: Why are we here?

3. *What should happen before our next meeting?* What should happen at our next meeting? How do we add ideas to our agenda? What is our contingency plan if the next meeting falls through? Should someone be responsible for anything we need for the next meeting?

Time out: We need some perspective taking.

4. *Identify possible exigencies for the charge.* What exigencies do we and our stakeholders have for our grouping? How should we take those exigencies into consideration as we set group goals and procedures?
5. *Identify possible stakeholders.* Are others outside the group going to be affected by our actions? How should we take these people into consideration in our processes?

How do we ensure that we do an effective job of grouping?

6. *How do we hold each other responsible?* Should we set up a process now in case someone stops attending meetings or does not meet their obligations to the group?
7. *Should we assign any roles* (such as devil's advocate, secretary, procedural expert, manager) to particular group members? How do we suggest changes in roles just for the sake of variety and so everyone gets a chance to play roles they want to? What about if a role is not being filled well or if it turns out that someone else in the group could fill it better?

8. *Do we have enough time available to us?* Can we develop a time line?

How do we want to do this: What do we want to get out of this?

9. *Discuss grouping goals.*
   a. What group goals should we have for this charge in particular?
      i. What kind of process should we use (for example, should we use the Orienting the Group technique in chapter 4?)
         a. As we are attempting to do general discussions or problem solving?
         b. As we are attempting to make decisions? (Be wary of voting; work instead for consensus.)
      ii. How do we give each other constructive criticism instead of just trying to be supportive and nice to each other?
   b. What sanctions are we willing to use against ourselves if we are failing to meet these goals, either individually or as a group?

---

grouping techniques (communication, meetings, and procedures), grouping tendencies (norms, roles, and communication network), and the process prizes (group member acceptance of group outcomes, and critical and creative work) that justify grouping as a human tool in response to a Purgatory Puddle. The Way/Process concomitants of grouping (confusion, conformity, conflict, and consciousness) will be unpacked for their pitfall potential in chapter 6.

6

Pitfalls in Confusion, Conformity, Conflict, and Group Consciousness

Grouping Concomitants

❖　❖　❖

I t is necessary for the success of any group that grouping members co-construct and employ grouping techniques and tendencies that help them attain a process prize from their grouping. Grouping concomitants always accompany such grouping activities. Grouping concomitants are dynamics that exist because of responses to grouping exigencies; they are even co-constructions of grouping activity. However, a grouping concomitant is not the purpose of grouping. Confusion, conformity, conflict, and group consciousness are grouping concomitants. They accompany grouping and are caused to exist by grouping, and they must be dealt with for grouping to be effective.

An analogy is that friction is a concomitant of movement, because it always accompanies and is created by the movement of a physical object, though it is not the process of movement and nor is it the purpose of the movement. Grouping concomitants always accompany grouping activity. Though the object of grouping is never to create these concomitants, they have to be dealt with every time you are in a group. The concomitants themselves result in a number of exigencies that must be dealt with for any grouping to be effective. In short, one must find appropriate ways to deal with friction between objects (e.g., using oil to lubricate moving parts) and one must find a way to deal with grouping concomitants in order for grouping activities to succeed. Grouping techniques, tendencies, and process prize pitfalls are The Way/Process dynamics we discuss in chapter 5. We now complete our discussion of The Way/Process pitfalls with a description of the concomitants of grouping and of the pitfall potential in each of these additional dynamics: confusion, conformity, conflict, and group consciousness.

The first concomitant of any grouping is *confusion*, because any perception of an exigency for grouping and ideas about how to respond to it immediately require the rhetorical responses of interpretation and framing: How should we interpret our exigency for grouping and how should we frame it? Early The Way/Process activities are accompanied by confusion, as a group tries to work out what it should do and how. As The Way/Process techniques and tendencies are co-constructed and as the other grouping concomitants begin to manifest, additional confusion is one consequence. *Conformity* is the second concomitant because there is no joint action, there is no grouping, until two or more people bend their efforts (conform) to blend their efforts (agree). When they agree, conform to some of the demands of working together, that conformity is a response to confusion.

Pressure to conform begins with the first attempted grouping. So does the potential perception of exigencies toward acting differently (conflict). If a different interpretation or framing is proposed, that would perpetuate some level of confusion about which choice of direction to accept. *Conflict* begins when perceptions are different regarding exigencies for grouping, or when grouping members perceive that different responses to their exigencies are appropriate, or when the members react differently to a grouping attempt. Confusion, conformity, and conflict are an amalgam of concomitants to rhetorical responses to exigencies for grouping. Working to co-construct grouping activities and to deal with the first three grouping concomitants results in the individuals involved beginning to develop a group *consciousness;* through their experiences they co-construct a sense of who they are and what they are all about. Coping with and co-constructing all of these grouping concomitants directly affect the group's ability to attain a process prize from grouping.

❖ CONFUSION PITFALLS

Confusion is uncertainty about what is going on or how to proceed. The first concomitant of grouping activity is confusion, because making sense of any exigency for grouping and of how to respond to it requires framing and clarification to bring the Purgatory Puddle, and possible responses to it, into focus for grouping members. "What's up?" "What is that?" "What are you doing?" "Can I help?" "What do I do next?" "What should we do about this?" "Hey, I'm not comfortable with that." "How can we do that?" "No, the other one instead." "Okay, I'll try." "Who will help me?" "I like this." "Don't do that!" "What am I doing here?" "Why are we doing this?" "Now what?" "You know what, we are just a lousy group, that's what!" The list could be endless.

Confusion precedes, accompanies, and *results from* attempts to co-construct and employ grouping techniques and tendencies. Confusion also results whenever one of the other concomitants presents new dynamics for the group to work through. Though unpleasant, *confusion provides a vital continuity of exigency for action. Confusion indicates attention.* Consequently, confusion is a dialectical tension for a group. That means confusion is both necessary and potentially problematic in every group. The absence of any confusion at the beginning of an attempt to group probably means the task does not require a coordinated inter-action-based, interdependent response. Too much confusion and the group may fail. When confusion is an exigency for grouping activity, both the failure to address the confusion and how the group addresses the confusion provide pitfall potential.

Confusion pitfalls are based in each of the Quadrad dynamics (see Table 6.1). Grouping is the response to confusion, either in interpreting and framing the Purgatory Puddle or in responding to it. Specific types of confusions tend to recur. First, uncertainty about whether to group or to proceed with grouping is evidence that the Purgatory Puddle is not yet interpreted and framed, and that the desire for grouping has not yet been sufficiently focused. Purgatory Puddle confusion is a pitfall until addressed by answering (a) who might be interested in group-ing, (b) what task is involved, and (c) what supragroup contingencies are involved, including who is trying to get us to group. Second, uncertainty about how to proceed is evidence that The Way/Process is not yet that of a mature group. The Way/Process confusions are pitfalls until we decide (a) what techniques to employ (because none are in place, or they are not working well enough, or because some of us are new to the group); (b) what tendencies orient us (because none are in place, or they are not working well enough, or because some of us are new here); (c) how we/I ought to behave when there is confusion, a need or pressure to conform, or a need for or problem with conflict; and (d) just who do we think we are as a unique group? Third, uncertainty about where to go about the purpose for our grouping is evidence the Vision/Outcome is not yet framed and worked through. Finally, uncertainty about who will give and who will receive direction and how is evidence that the Savior Complex is not yet framed and functioning well enough to manifest in successful direction for our group. Any confusion concomitant to grouping can be located and anticipated within one or more Quadrad bases.

Table 6.1   Summary of The Way/Process Grouping Concomitants: Confusion Pitfalls

Confusion Pitfall	Examples
Purgatory Puddle Confusion	Who might be interested? In what task are we interested? Who/what is doing this to us?
The Way/Process Confusion	What techniques should we employ: who are we and how should we talk, how should we meet, what procedures should we use? What tendencies orient us: how shall we behave; what shall each of us do; who talks to whom, how often, and about what? How do we respond to confusion, conformity, and conflict, and who are we as a group?
Vision/Outcome Confusion	How well do our outcomes solve the problem that started our grouping: how well do our outcomes serve our goals? How many new costs or disadvantages must we pay because of our outcomes? How well is our vision matched by our outcome?
Savior Complex Confusion	How will we give and receive direction: who will give and receive it; how well does our evolving Savior Complex serve us?

For the most part, the details for the confusion concomitant are addressed as pitfalls and appropriate rhetorical responses thereto in our discussions throughout the book because all grouping is integrated with confusion. *The solution to confusion is effective grouping activity; interactions that co-construct interpretations and frames for the group's work, processes, and outcomes. Treat confusion as a resource for working harder, for developing a better process, for working back through why you are doing what you are doing as a group. Treat confusion as a normal aspect of grouping, to be dealt with, not as a reason to give up on joint action. Use confusion to stimulate the conversations that can enhance grouping efforts. Seek out potential points of confusion as places where group attention to the confusion can add value to and from the group's efforts.*

❖ CONFORMITY PITFALLS

Conformity is any adjustment a grouping member makes in his or her thoughts or behavior to try to make them fit in with the grouping attempts of others; conformity is necessary to any effective grouping. With all grouping activity, members either try to provide group direction themselves, or they influence group direction by their responses to the efforts of others. The possible responses to a grouping attempt are to support it, remain neutral to it, ignore it, or contest it (conflict). Supporting and contesting are clear responses; remaining neutral and ignoring are not. Some people ignore grouping action by attempting to change the subject; that response is conflict, not conformity. When the choice to ignore grouping is silence, that silence can be construed as conformity: it allows group direction to continue. Each response is a manifestation of either conformity or conflict. Conformity is necessary for grouping; conflict is necessary for grouping quality.

There is a dialectical tension at work with conformity as there is with each of the other concomitants. Joint action, norms, and roles are all necessary for grouping and all require conformity. Conformity can also cut against the process prizes, which are the very rationale for grouping. When group members conform, they do not think new thoughts and creativity is not possible. When group members conform, they do not carefully criticize group work and critical thinking is not possible. *Grouping members need to ask themselves two questions. Am I doing enough to help the group with my conformity to the basic responsibilities*

Table 6.2   Summary of The Way/Process Grouping Concomitants:
Conformity Pitfalls

Conformity Pitfall	Examples
Too Little Conformity	Inability to coordinate or converge around grouping choices.
Maladaptive Conformity	Self-censorship; risky shift, mind guards; deindividuation.
Sanctions	Sanctioning group deviance; idiosyncrasy credits.

of grouping members? Am I conforming so much that I am not helping the group do its critical or creative work? Striking the wrong balance results in maladaptive conformity (see Table 6.2). Both insufficient and maladaptive conformity are grouping pitfalls.

Maladaptive Conformity

Minor Maladaptive Conformity. To conform does not have to involve doing something you think is wrong. Minor conformity is a change that is consistent with what one believes is acceptable behavior. Self-censorship, or keeping quiet about a potential idea, concern, or objection, is an example. Self-censorship is necessary conformity when it allows people to each get their turn to talk. It is maladaptive when a group member censors a thought or action that the group needs to receive. Grouping works because of deliberation, the exchange and testing of ideas. When important ideas do not get expressed, grouping is diminished and self-censorship is involved if someone knowingly withholds the idea. Self-censorship can be rationalized as serving a social function for the group, not "making waves" when everyone else seems to agree. It can seem to be appropriate if the group has a norm not to work too hard on a particular subject. If a group develops a norm not to test ideas carefully, its members learn to rationalize keeping to themselves any additional considerations they may have. At some point, members may just stop having critical thoughts altogether, devolving to a form of mindlessness. People can get to the point where they do not realize they are self-censoring.

We sometimes go along with processes or ideas that the group is employing just because it has become easy and familiar to do so. *An active and alert grouping member is best equipped by knowing that self-censorship can hurt a group, even though it feels comfortable to keep quiet. Help each other out. Ask other members what is concerning to them. Ask what is on their minds. If nobody seems willing to express concerns, consider playing the role of devil's advocate, suggesting potential concerns not because you believe they are true but rather for the sake of the quality of group deliberations. You might also consider asking your group to use the nominal group technique for part of its work. The nominal group technique is a noninteractive process designed to circumvent grouping dynamics, such as conformity, in order to get the best thoughts from all group members. Members each get several opportunities to contribute their ideas on a subject one at a time, with no feedback from the rest of the group, until everyone has expressed all that they can think of on the subject at hand.*

Moderate Maladaptive Conformity. Moderate conformity is making changes that go beyond what one thinks appropriate. For example, have you ever done something one night with a group of friends that you regretted the next day? At times, we each tend to adjust our behaviors to match those of others we are with, and sometimes it gets out of hand and we find ourselves doing something we feel we should not be doing. *Risky shift* behavior is the tendency group members sometimes have to behave in a manner more consistent with the group's values than their own. If a group appears to value risk taking, members will tend to be more risky in the decisions they make, the actions they may try, or the lines of thinking they may employ than they would if they were alone. Sometimes it can turn out well when you take a risk. Sometimes it can be disastrous. The same sort of problem results when groups develop norms that are overly cautious and group members shift toward becoming too risk aversive.

A second example of moderate conformity is when one develops *mind guards* to keep from having to pay attention to the dissonance or discomfort felt when behaving in an inappropriate or inauthentic manner. Because people tend to want to be consistent in their thoughts and actions, knowingly behaving in a manner inconsistent with what one believes can be unpleasant. A possible response is to change one's beliefs; another is to develop a way not to think about the disparity. A mind guard allows an inconsistency to be livable. Examples are evident from phrases such as "Everyone else is doing it" and "I wouldn't normally do this, I must be drunk" and "I don't want to look stupid, do I?" Each of us has ways of encouraging ourselves in difficult times, and when these techniques involve protecting ourselves from thinking about and making a rational choice regarding our conformity, a mind guard is being used.

A third example is *not rocking the boat*. This is a specialized version of conformity that probably involves all of the dynamics we have discussed up to this point, from mind guarding and risky shift to self-censorship. Once grouping activities develop inertia, members sometimes behave as though the group has become fragile. This can make the subject of potential change difficult to broach, especially change based in criticism or in rocking the boat, which involves pointing out something that the group is doing wrong. It is sometimes hard to say to grouping members, "this is not right," because saying so also means "we are wrong; we are at fault because we are doing this thing that is not right." Conforming in order to not rock the boat is a choice that favors grouping momentum, inertia, and comfort over the process prizes grouping is supposed to provide.

Strong Maladaptive Conformity. The strongest maladaptive conformity is when one disregards her or his own values and behaviors to such an extent that she or he turns personal decision-making processes over to the group. The individual does what the group does, thinks what the group thinks, and believes what the group believes. When one goes along with whatever the group is doing, one's complicity in such conformity may tend to get lost in a feeling that one is just a cog in the grouping entity. This is a rationalization that claims one is no longer personally responsible as a grouping member for making basic choices regarding reasonable actions and about the basic difference between right and wrong. *Rationalizations* are excuses for bad choices. In this case, both the cog-person and the group may become dangerous to the point that ugly phrases like "mob rule" may begin to describe the group and that ugly actions like riots, lynchings, and looting have been known to occur. Ideas and emotions are no longer tested: instead, they are just acted out. Grouping members may suffer from what Buys (1978) describes as *deindividuation,* which is the sense that one's actions in a group are really the actions of the group, and not the fault of the individual. One feels safely anonymous in the group. It is a tricky distinction to draw between being a loyal grouping member and losing yourself in the group. To correct this pitfall, *focus on behaviors and beliefs you believe are authentic representations of you personally. Say, "This action represents me and my choices." Ask, "Am I happy that it does? Would I be comfortable if this thought or behavior was attributed to me in the community newspaper where I live with my family and friends?"*

For moderate and extreme maladaptive conformity, there is one general rule for overcoming pitfall potential: *the more inauthentic group behavior and thinking feels to you as an individual, the more you need to give yourself permission to deviate.* Group dynamics will make it hard to do so. *You must make certain that you build some "alone time" from grouping activity into your life. Get away from the group at least long enough to let your head clear of the group's influence. If they try to stop you from being alone, flee!* Once you have taken the time to assess how you personally really feel about the grouping you had been helping to co-construct, you can act with a clear conscience. *Never lose sight of the fact that you are responsible for group processes and outcomes. Do not buy into a conspiracy of collective innocence; do not think that anyone other than you is responsible for what the group does. Do not sacrifice your integrity for the group;* doing so destroys who you are and it also hurts the group by denying it your best thinking and actions.

One final point on maladaptive conformity: The difference between minor, moderate, and the strongest forms of maladaptive conformity is found in the level of personal adjustment involved, not in the consequences from the conformity. Beware rationalizations for maladaptive conformity based in the claim, "I didn't think my action would make much of a difference; it was no big deal." Each form of conformity could potentially result in a range of consequences from small to large. Even a minor act of conformity—for example, going along with a friend who has been drinking and now wants to drive—can result in very bad consequences.

Sanctions and Idiosyncrasy Credits

Sanctions are punishments for inappropriate behavior. Sanctions are involved in encouraging expected and appropriate behavior and in discouraging inappropriate and punishable behavior. Too much sanctioning can lead to too much conformity, which hurts attempts to attain process prizes. Too little sanctioning can result in insufficient conformity, and the undoing of cooperative grouping. Maladaptive sanctions enforce necessary grouping activities in ways that are themselves inappropriate. If the punishment does not fit the crime, the whole system suffers.

Who will be sanctioned for inappropriate behavior and who will not is also a fundamental question. *Idiosyncrasy credits* allow higher-status members to deviate somewhat from group norms without being sanctioned by the group. If it gets to the point where some members are perceived as "above the law," legitimate questions should be raised about the appropriateness of such co-constructions. The opposite extreme is also a problem when the desire to treat all members equally means those who play high-status roles are punished for the differences in their behavior required by their role. *Interaction about whether there is an overreaction one way or the other should be used to clarify group values and processes regarding group sanctions and use of idiosyncrasy credits.*

Approach conformity as something that is natural and basic to grouping. It is another dialectical tension in every group because you cannot escape it; you should not want to escape it; and you should be wary of its dangers. *Try to co-construct a group's conformity wisely and well by talking explicitly about the issue in the group.*

❖ CONFLICT PITFALLS

Conflict is any difference in the grouping activities, orientations, or responses of grouping members regarding their grouping enterprise. Contesting an interpretation or activity, saying it is wrong, is obviously the strongest form of difference, but any difference can change the focus or nature of grouping activities. For example, the most subtle and mild form of response to the ideas of others may be to frown (conflict) or smile and nod (conform) at what they say. Another mild form is to stick to the same topic discussed by the previous speaker (conform) or to try changing the subject (conflict). We think you should approach *conflict* as another dialectical tension in all groups: something that is so basic to grouping that you cannot escape it and you should not want to escape it, though, if poorly co-constructed, members can use it to undo a group. *You should learn how to co-construct your conflicts wisely and well if you are to be a successful grouping member.*

If you have a negative connotation for conflict, you may be put off by our definition that conflict is any difference among grouping activities or orientations. (That is okay; such a difference or conflict among opinions can be useful.) Perhaps you have a connotation that conflict is a serious disagreement—maybe even a fight. But, human conflict has no objectifiable or consistent existence beyond some basic difference. People view the same difference differently. Consider a paraphrase of what the football player, played by Cuba Gooding, Jr., in the movie

Jerry Maguire, said to his manager: "That's the problem with you, Jerry. You think we are fighting, and I think we are finally beginning to talk."

Conflict manifests in perceptions of grouping members about their interactions. The smallest deviance may create a perception of conflict on the part of one individual. Others may say he or she is "making a mountain out of a molehill," that he or she "blows the situation all out of proportion." Both statements assume some specific quality and quantity of difference before there can "be a conflict." Such an objective standard is not meaningful to any grouping member who disagrees.

Conflict is a dialectical tension in all grouping because it is a necessary co-construction that helps test the quality of framings for and of responses to grouping exigencies. Further, conflict can stimulate additional grouping energy, as members direct their attention to the source of their differences. But some co-constructed conflicts get in the way of effective grouping (see Table 6.3).

Too Little Conflict for the Group

A lack of differences among grouping members means that both critical and creative thinking processes are inadequate. By definition, grouping without any differences cannot attain those two process prizes. It is healthy grouping activity to note some differences and to discuss them, and the absence of such activity is a grouping pitfall. Indeed, it is a strong sign of a potential pitfall when nobody in the group is noting any differences among grouping members. It is an even stronger sign of potential pitfalling when there really are no differences

Table 6.3   Summary of The Way/Process Grouping Concomitants: Conflict Pitfalls

Conflict Pitfall	Examples
Too Little Conflict	Inability or unwillingness to note group differences.
Too Much Conflict	Lose grouping objectives in all the differences.
Maladaptive Conflict	Conflict is personalized, competitive, or undifferentiated.
Inappropriate Responses	Force conformity; fight or flight; scapegoat or mortify.
Bad Conflict Outcomes	Conflict is not addressed; irresolvable conflict.

to note among grouping members. At such times, there is probably too much conformity, too much mindlessness, too much emphasis placed on the comfort derived from seeming to get along well with each other by not disagreeing. *Be alert for potential differences; note them, discuss them, and value them for their potential to improve grouping quality. Make use of them when you can and work through them together when you cannot.*

Too Much Conflict for the Group

Having too many differences, or one difference that is so strong it dominates grouping resources, can overwhelm the group: overwhelm their abilities to stay focused on their grouping objectives. Obsessing about a conflict that should be manageable can result in members becoming convinced that their differences are endless and that there can be no resolution of their differences. Such obsessing can be a sign of general dissatisfaction with the group. Relationships that are coming apart go through a phase called *differentiating* (Knapp, 1984), in which relational members focus only on their differences, where once all they could see were their common interests. Picking nits (head lice babies— they are really small!) can be as much a grouping pitfall as the inability to note any differences at all. Sometimes grouping members *take flight* from their grouping, using the rationalization that there is too much conflict for them to work through. When they do so, it is at the expense of developing and exercising grouping processes that could be used to address the conflict and that could be useful to their future efforts.

Maladaptive Conflict

Maladaptive conflict involves differences that become distorted or destructive as they are co-constructed by the group. Conflict that is *personalized* is a poor grouping co-construction because it embeds the conflict in interpersonal relationships, emotions, and personality, which are not easily changed. Depersonalized conflict is the preferred form of co-construction because it locates the conflict in issues and ideas (Pace, 1990). Issues and ideas are phenomena that grouping members are more likely to be able to work together to address. Conflict that is *competitive* is an unfortunate co-construction. It creates a *win-lose* mentality where, at best, only one side in the conflict can win and often both sides lose (*lose-lose*). Such a *zero-sum* mentality is characterized by defensiveness, hostility, and escalation (Pace, 1990).

The preferred form is using conflict as a source of energy for exploring a difference as a *win-win* proposition in which *value added* to both sides becomes the hallmark of their cooperative enterprise. They create a mutually beneficial consensus about how to resolve the difference in a manner that serves group functions. Conflict that is *undifferentiated* is an ineffective approach to grouping because it means the co-constructors of the conflict do not understand the nature and nuance of the differences that have started to bedevil them. Differentiated conflict (Pace, 1990) is the preferred co-construction and involves working to understand the perceptual and substantive nuances of differences across and among grouping members. Undifferentiated conflict represents a likely pitfall for those who do not know about the basic nature of and purpose for conflict or for those who are not willing to work to understand their differences with others in the group.

Inappropriate Responses to Conflict

Punishing deviation is coercion toward conformity. Inertia favors the tendency to punish differences rather than to attempt to understand and make use of them. Attempts to understand and to use differences require the effort needed to learn something new, but they also involve the potential benefits from learning.

Different responses to conflict can be useful, but each has pitfall potential as well. Some people tend to "lean into" conflict, wanting to address it head-on and forcefully. Others tend to "lean away" from conflict, wishing either that it was not so or that they were not involved. Either stance, in the extreme, may not be conducive to the deliberation necessary for effective grouping. However, aspects of both *fight* (the willingness and ability to engage difficult issues) and of *flight* (the willingness and ability to disengage from a difficult issue) can be helpful. Some people take personal comfort from attempts to *smooth over* a conflict rather than to understand and respond appropriately to the conflict. Others try to *avoid* conflict entirely, while still others *force focused attention* on conflict. *The basic issue is whether conflict is co-constructed in ways that enhance the effort to serve group functions.* If so, the co-construction is win-win and value is added. If not, the co-construction is win-lose or lose-lose and someone or all will pay the price.

It is a common error to confuse one's preferred, comfort-based response to conflict with what is best for the grouping effort. It is also a mistake to "play the blame game," which involves using more grouping energy to determine who is at fault for the group's differences than to understand the nature of those differences and how best to address them. Whenever something goes wrong, there is an ego-defensive human tendency to blame the situation or another person first, before looking to oneself. *Scapegoating* (blaming and then sacrificing a grouping member or nonmember) someone else for the conflict allows grouping members to avoid their own responsibility for grouping differences. Some members may use *mortification* (take blame onto themselves whether they are justified in doing so or not) because they mistakenly believe that taking the blame for problems will resolve grouping differences. Any response to conflict is a pitfall if it does not result in a co-construction that helps serve the three group functions.

When faced with differences, try to develop a sense of perspective for yourself and for your group by keeping your focus on the use of healthy grouping techniques and tendencies and on the long-term consequences of conflict for the success or failure of grouping outcomes. When your group can learn how to become stronger by how it constructs conflict, you have done well. *Equifinality* means different systems (and people from different cultures) can have appropriate levels of grouping success using different approaches to conflict.

Bad Conflict Outcomes

If a conflict remains unaddressed throughout the life of the group, it can result in a hidden agenda type of exigency that distorts grouping processes and outcomes in response to the conflict, rather than in response to group goals. It can also diminish the willingness of members to accept the group's Vision/Outcome at the end of their work. When conflict is addressed but not resolved, it can be a sign that the group does not work hard enough or use the necessary means to sort through its differences. It can also be a sign that the differences could not be reconciled. In either case, grouping outcomes are diminished.

Some groups do everything "right" and still are undone by their differences. If grouping members lose hope of success, it may precipitate a decision to terminate their grouping activity or to "fire" one or more of their members. What differences can so divide grouping members? Possible answers include acts of conscience based in conflicting values, devotions to other groups or other obligations, and personal pathologies such as perceptual distortions and personal experiences that cannot be brought into perspective. Most other differences can be worked through and worked out. Figuring out which conflicts can be resolved and which need to be managed and lived with requires a sophisticated set of skills and judgments that a group can only manifest through concerned conversation about how they can co-construct a mutually acceptable response to such differences.

Grouping members should not accept a perpetual grinding up of themselves or of their grouping enterprise. It is not necessary to put up with steadily degrading and negative outcomes from a difference that is co-constructed into behaviors that are so extreme and inauthentic that they become constantly damaging. *Do not take a decision for drastic change lightly. Assume that most such decisions do not need to be made if grouping members will just work harder at sorting through differences that bedevil them. When necessary, however, implement a proper termination process*, defined as one that ends the negative co-constructions as amicably as possible while also minimizing additional unfortunate outcomes as much as possible. *When necessary, be willing to declare an end.*

In sum, general scholarly wisdom says that conflict can be beneficial, that conflict should not be avoided, and that conflict needs to be resolved before grouping can be effective. We suggest that these generalizations be treated as prescriptions; they may well be the best medicine for many conflicts, but not, we think, for every conflict. Remember that what groups do best (if they are functioning appropriately) is to co-construct critical and creative work beyond what an individual might accomplish working alone. That purpose for grouping, coupled with an understanding of the equifinality of systems, suggests to us a stance of general flexibility and alertness as you proceed to sort through your conflict co-constructions. Our advice is that you *make the noting and the discussing of any differences into a norm of operation in any group.* Then the activities involved become familiar to the group, and grouping members learn to become adept at dealing with their differences before having to face differences that are so extreme that they threaten the life of the group (see Table 6.4).

❖ CONSCIOUSNESS PITFALLS

Group *consciousness* is the grouping members' sense of their group as an entity. When you help co-construct a group, you begin to worry about the group itself, rather than just about the individuals in the

Table 6.4   Toward More Effective Co-constructions of Grouping
Differences/Conflict

Your chances of success are enhanced if you prepare yourself mentally to
cope with conflict:

Before conflict communication begins:
Pick your conflicts carefully—which differences ought I focus on?
Figure out "what is the worst that could happen" in advance, which can help
put differences into perspective. Practice getting a time-out: know how to
say, "That's it for me for right now."
View conflict as an exercise that can help your group and that you personally
can learn from, not as a source of your self-esteem.
Make certain to tell the others that you are interested. Allow lots of time.
Arrange an opportunity to co-construct difficult conflicts when and where
there is low chance of interruption. Work in private when appropriate and
respect privacy so as not to embarrass members.

When conflict communication begins:
Let the other person talk. Anger takes energy, so allow time for it to be
expressed and to wind down. Work on listening, not answering or
counterarguing, until you grasp the difference.
Sometimes it is helpful to write down objections others aim at you and ask if
they are satisfied with the summary you have made. Paraphrase what you
hear and also what others appear to you to feel, and then ask them if you
have it right. Make as many corrections in interpretation as necessary until
all agree you have your paraphrase of their concerns right. Ask, "Is there
anything else we need to talk about?" and "Anything else I should ask
about?"
Tell yourself that "this will end soon" and that there is no rush to finish. Try
to do the job well; ask yourself, "What else can I try?"
Try to keep focus on substantive issues, not personal ones. Look for common
ground on which to base continuing discussions. Reinforce group members
for any small gains.
Do not say yes to things you cannot do or accept just to end the session, but
indicate a willingness to listen and respond to all reasonable ideas. Do not
draw final conclusions while the conflict is still heated.
Be willing to admit the possibility you made mistakes and apologize when
you find any grounds for doing so. Plan any necessary future modifications
in response.

group. The dialectical tension is that group consciousness is necessary
but can tend toward becoming too strong or maladaptive given the
other groups and responsibilities in one's life. *Group consciousness includes
a sense of group climate, of cohesion, and of group culture. Group climate* is a
general feeling based in how well grouping members think their group

serves individual, relational, and task functions. *Cohesion* is a general feeling that it is good and desirable to have been and to continue to be a part of the group: it is the sum of forces that keep you a member. *Group culture* is the convergence of meanings and the shared experiences co-created by members of a group over the life of their grouping activity. Group consciousness affects all other aspects of grouping (cf. Carron & Spink, 1995; Evans & Dion, 1991).

Group consciousness is born of converging symbols and interpretations members have for their group experiences (Bormann, 1996). Grouping members co-construct consciousness as they interact (*consciousness creating*). To sustain their sense of group consciousness over time, they must remind themselves of their group saga, of why they started grouping in the first place, and of how they value their grouping enterprise (*consciousness sustaining*). If they wish to grow and to remain strong, they need to recruit new members and to get others to support their grouping activities (*consciousness raising*).

An effective group member pays attention to how well the group co-constructs and perpetuates its story—its group consciousness. Special activities that socialize group members, that help develop a sense of cohesion among newer and more experienced members, and that provide an opportunity to "sing the saga song" should all be part of such attention. Your own family probably does these things. Listen to the stories older members of your family tell during holidays or family reunions. When a new in-law joins your family, what special stories are told? Are there "inside" words or phrases that have been used for a long time by your family? Do you and your best friends like to share jokes and stories about situations that you managed to live through together? Grouping members tend to converge upon a small set of symbols and stories to represent who they are and to help them tell their story. Such symbols are part of their perceptual boundaries; they also document a sense of group consciousness.

Consider the following three metaphors used in group research to represent co-constructions that fundamentally change a group or its direction. *Critical incidents* (Cohen & Smith, 1976) in the life of a group are stories about when a key direction giver succeeded in co-constructing a significant change in group direction. They indicate a significant and fundamental *breakpoint* in the ongoing script of a grouping entity (Poole, 1981, 1983a, 1983b). They could be the basis for *memorable messages* (cf. Knapp, Stohl, & Reardon, 1981; Stohl, 1986), which "individuals remember for a long period of time that had a major influence on their

Table 6.5   Summary of The Way/Process Grouping Concomitants: Consciousness Pitfalls

Consciousness Pitfall	Examples
Lack of Group Maturity	Group is starting; insufficient time to mature; members never mature.
Too Little Sense of Consciousness	Too little cohesion or culture; inadequate consciousness raising or sustaining efforts in the group.
Maladaptive Consciousness	Bad group climate; too much emphasis placed on cohesion.

life . . . . [Messages] regarding the norms, values, expectations, rules, requirements, and rationality of the . . . [system] which provide . . . sense-making structures to understand and guide . . . behavior" (Barge & Schlueter, 2004, p. 238). All of these metaphors represent key co-constructions in the life of a group: They can be thought of as *teaching tales*, which can be used rhetorically as *strategic stories*, to help shape and perpetuate group consciousness. They are residual *nuggets of* the group's *special saga*. How such stories are framed and retold can play an important role in co-constructing group consciousness (see Table 6.5).

Lack of Group Maturity

A sense of consciousness can begin to develop very soon after grouping begins, yet it also evolves over the life of the group. We represent this time frame by using the concept of group maturity (cf. Krayer, 1988). *Maturity* is the ability to do the particular work required in a group in the particular way required by others in the group. Maturity has two components for members: *ability* to do a task (composed of knowledge, skill, and experience doing it) and *willingness to take responsibility* for doing a task (composed of motivation, confidence, and commitment to group and task). Group members and groups vary continuously in their maturity level. Groups and members all start immature. Immature members have limited ability and willingness to take responsibility for grouping. Immature groups have few, if any, mature grouping members. Mature members are both able and willing to do the hard work necessary for effective grouping. A mature group member in one group is an immature member in a new group or in an old group they have just joined. An individual brought in to be the "leader" or "manager" or "CEO" is an immature member in the new role for the new entity until he or she has a solid sense of the group. The evolving maturity of a group can stall if shared interpretations of the Purgatory Puddle and of appropriate The Way/Process techniques and tendencies are not co-constructed by grouping members. Maturity requires substantial effective structuration.

Immaturity has negative connotations because it is used to describe aberrant behavior individuals should "know better" than do. We prefer a definition that locates immaturity as a natural state in time and process. All group members need time co-constructing the group experience and clarity of grouping techniques and tendencies to mature. *Conceiving immaturity as a natural state for newly grouping members and for new groups puts focus on the activities that can help change that state and also on the pitfalls that can result if we assume maturity when it should not yet be expected.*

Too Little Sense of Group Consciousness

Too little cohesion means grouping members lack the sense that it is desirable to be part of their joint enterprise. This can result in group meetings that are tedious or subdued and inappropriately brief. Grouping efforts may be perfunctory. Alternate activities and Purgatory Puddles are perceived to be more important. Too little sense of group culture is normal in new groups, but over time an insufficient sense of group culture is a sign that the group has stayed somewhat immature and has done insufficient consciousness-creating structuration. Insufficiencies in group culture can also result from problems in consciousness raising. An example is when needed new members are not recruited or are not given adequate opportunity to fully engage in grouping co-construction by experienced grouping members. A second example is when others outside the group are needed to help support the group but are not brought "up to speed" with what the group is all about and why supporting it is important. Consciousness-raising activity is needed to help new members learn about the culture in the group they have joined. Consciousness sustaining is insufficient when experienced grouping members lose sight of the reasons they joined or enjoyed the group in the first place: they need grouping activities that celebrate their accomplishments or that provide rituals of membership to rekindle the excitement for being an accomplished member of the group.

Maladaptive Grouping Consciousness

A bad climate is co-constructed as members develop a negative sense of how well they are accomplishing their individual, relational, or task functions as a group. *A maladaptive climate signals the need for direct discussion of the problem and possibly for some change in The Way/ Process.* Such groups can also be expected to have some difficulties with cohesion, either having too little cohesiveness or a maladaptive orientation toward cohesion. Groups with high levels of cohesion are not bad entities unless too much priority is placed on protecting the climate or cohesion of the group. That means the hard work required for improving work on the task function may not be fully undertaken. Indeed, overprotectiveness of the group from necessary disagreements for testing grouping quality may be a sign that cohesion and climate are not actually a strong point for the group at all. At issue is whether a priority on member relationships unduly diminishes the ability of the group to reach its process prizes. When a group places too high a priority on the relational function, it constitutes a grouping pitfall. The pitfall is in the imbalance of focus, placing too high a priority on individual and social comfort.

Maladaptive grouping consciousness can be created if a culture is co-constructed that produces negative outcomes for the group or for others in its suprasystem. Imagine a group of alcoholics who share comradeship in the dysfunctionality of their disease or a group that develops a cultural sense of itself as a set of victims who must accept the negative effects they experience because they come to believe that is their fate. Such a culture of victimization or of other self-destructiveness requires grouping activity to perpetuate and is obviously a pitfall to effective grouping. Being a member of such a group is a dark, damaging, and harrowing experience, but there are still aspects of relationship involved and some people end up codependents with such sick grouping entities. *The solution, as with maladaptive conformity, is time away from the group that allows the clearing of one's head and reorientation toward life priorities.*

Other less destructive grouping cultures are nonetheless limiting for their members. When cultural techniques and tendencies guide grouping behavior in ways that set limits or blinders or artificial constraints on the group, that culture is maladaptive for accomplishing the process prizes that justify grouping. Some cultures become so entrenched and have such a residue of hurtful or failed grouping experience that their symbolic convergence is around a saga of historical failure that forever distorts any future grouping attempts. When a person considers himself or herself to be "damaged goods," he or she is describing a negative residual effect of the experience. Some groups become similarly damaged, scarred for the life of the grouping enterprise in ways that present pitfalls to any attempt to work outside of the group's scars. Even some extremely effective groups develop a consciousness that is so all-encompassing and consuming that members, though successful in the group, sacrifice important aspects of their lives outside the group. Becoming a "workaholic" or becoming a group member first and foremost can help make one much less of an individual with a life outside the group in the process.

Maladaptive consciousness-raising processes provide pitfalls that can discourage the willingness of new members to get involved in the recruitment process or that can hurt new members who agree to go through the process. An odd case in point is the hazing activity that "used to" accompany joining the military or pledging a sorority or fraternity. *Hazing* is a consciousness-raising process designed to test the will and merit of new members by subjecting them to unpleasant activities before they are allowed to join the group. Extreme forms of hazing are now strongly discouraged or illegal because there have been deaths and permanent disabilities resulting from some of the processes. You might be surprised to learn that hazing has actually been documented to increase the cohesiveness of a group in some cases. Pledges, or new recruits to the group, in paying the "price of admission" required during hazing, then become more proud of their membership if the price they paid was high than if the price they paid was lower. So, this pitfall to grouping can actually add energy to later grouping activities. As is often the case, many grouping pitfalls have the potential for diminishing effective grouping outcomes, but struggling against those pitfalls can help a group learn to be more potent over time.

Finally, maladaptive consciousness-sustaining pitfalls manifest whenever a group expends too much energy trying to sustain the consciousness of its senior membership and consequently reduces the effectiveness of its grouping enterprise or unduly burdens its other grouping members. An example is the overuse of idiosyncrasy credits for the more seasoned members based on seniority, not merit, which creates a sense of inequity among members. Even if inequity is not perceived, the costs to a grouping system can be enormous if it finds itself having to compete for the continued attentions and services of its more experienced membership. Yet, without consciousness-sustaining processes, the sense of sufficient group culture necessary to sustain effective grouping can become inadequate for the demands of the work.

❖ HOW TO EXPECT, DETECT,
    AND CORRECT THESE PITFALLS

This chapter provides an extensive set of grouping concomitants that will play out in every group and may play out in unfortunate ways. Understand that there is no avoiding these concomitants and the dialectical tension involved with each. Careful management of the co-construction of grouping concomitants is an essential aspect of any effective group. Avoiding confusion, conformity, conflict, or conciousness is not possible, and attempts to do so diminish the possibility of effective grouping. This is an opportunity to remind you of the need for building checks and balances into your grouping experience so that you can harvest the benefits of these concomitants even as you are protecting your group from negative aspects of them. *Begin, in early group meetings, to lay the foundation for future attempts to deal with the pitfall potential from grouping concomitants by co-constructing a conversational history and group norms conducive to such efforts.* What follows is a set of conversational prompts that can help you raise these issues (see Table 6.6).

Table 6.6   Broaching the Subject on The Way/Process Concomitant
           Pitfalls

Time out: We need some perspective taking.

1. *Identify possible exigencies for the charge.* Are we taking into consideration the exigencies others might perceive as we act?
2. *Identify possible stakeholders.* Are others outside the group going to be affected by our actions? Are we taking these stakeholders into consideration as we make our choices?

If so: How do we ensure that we do an effective job of grouping?

3. *How do we hold each other responsible?* Are we all treating group work as though it represents us? Are we behaving in a manner that will make us proud?
4. *Should we assign any roles* (such as devil's advocate or procedural expert; see chapter 7) to help protect us against negative aspects of our processes?

(Continued)

Table 6.6 (Continued)

Should we try the use of the nominal group technique to limit our interaction for a time, while working on a key aspect of our group charge, so that we limit the effects our opinions have on each other?

How do we want to do this: What do we want to get out of this?

5. *Discuss grouping goals.*
   a. What group goals should we have for our processes for co-constructing effective responses to group concomitants and our need for important aspects of each of them?
   b. What is going to be required of us individually and as a group if we are going to attain these goals?
   c. How will we know if we succeed in attaining our goals? What criteria will we use to measure our success on the above goals? How often should we check to see if we all feel that we are accomplishing our process goals?
   d. What sanctions are we willing to use against ourselves if we are failing to meet these goals, either individually or as a group?

❖ CHAPTER SUMMARY

Grouping techniques, tendencies, and their concomitants comprise The Way/Process because grouping activity or structuration necessarily involves all three. Confusion, conformity, conflict, and consciousness manifest as The Way/Process techniques and tendencies begin to be co-constructed. All these aspects are experienced through interactions among grouping members as they struggle toward the potential process prizes from grouping. Grouping members experience the absence of process and the absence of group-constructed meanings as salient exigencies for grouping. Pitfall potential is found in every aspect of these grouping co-constructions.

7

Pitfalls in Vision and Direction Giving

❖ ❖ ❖

The Framework for Grouping and Group Direction says energy for grouping comes from the perception of salient exigencies to group. The exigencies for grouping, the rhetorical resources for responding to those exigencies, and the potential for grouping pitfalls can all be organized using the Quadrad: four terms that represent the recurring forms of dramatic action (perceived exigencies, rhetorical responses, pitfalls) involved in any grouping. The first two Quadrad terms represent *fundamental components* of grouping activity: the Purgatory Puddle and The Way/Process. The last two Quadrad terms represent *dimensional manifestations* from grouping activity. The first of these dimensional manifestations is some sense of where the group might be headed, which is called the group's Vision/Outcome, and the second is some sense of who can be trusted to provide direction to the group, which is called the Savior Complex. These two dimensions run through all grouping activity. They are inherently necessary for, and manifest integrally throughout, any group. In this chapter, we discuss pitfalls found in these last two bases of the Quadrad.

❖ VISION/OUTCOME PITFALLS

A sense of Vision/Outcome begins to develop while grouping members learn to understand their task as they frame and address it during early grouping interaction. That sense may manifest in agenda items, goals, objectives, or a mission statement; it may also manifest in the first rough drafts of a solution to the group's problem or an early description of a desirable group outcome. Vision/Outcome is the product or result of group work: the fruit of the group's labors. Vision/Outcome includes anticipation of those fruits, and helps guide ongoing choices made regarding how to achieve those fruits. Vision/Outcome is not necessarily clear to group members at the start of their grouping activity. *Outcomes* of a grouping effort (a combination of what the group achieved serving its task, relational, and individual functions) may be easier to assess than a group's vision. A group's vision and its outcomes may not entirely coincide once grouping has ended. The group's vision may result in them being disappointed with the outcomes they actually achieve: their fruits dismay them when they are not what was envisioned. Even as the "ends" of group work, Vision/Outcome is dynamic, as members co-construct an evolving understanding of their purpose and product.

Vision/Outcome is a group's *Promised Land* and is composed of those two components: promise and land. Potential Vision/Outcome pitfalls manifest as *promise* pitfalls, *land* pitfalls, and as combinations of those two sets of problems, which result in several *finishing issues*. Our focus in this chapter is on pitfalls involving task outcomes because relational and individual functional outcomes are covered elsewhere.[4]

Promise pitfalls manifest in insufficient attractiveness or salience of the Promised Land toward which a group works. Promise pitfalls indicate an undesired destination. A Vision/Outcome that is not perceived to be important (not salient) or attractive is not sufficiently desired. Such a Vision/Outcome creates no exigency of attraction for group efforts to reach it as their destination. Promise pitfalls are perceptual, manifesting in the lack of enthusiasm of grouping members to get to a particular Vision/Outcome (as opposed to land pitfalls, which are substantive and flow from the qualities of the actual fruits of the Vision/Outcome). Working to get your body into shape can be motivated by what is unpleasant about being out of shape (a Purgatory Puddle–type exigency) or by what is desirable or attractive about being in shape (a Vision/Outcome–type exigency). If you are not attracted to either the aesthetic or health benefits of being in shape, that objective lacks sufficient promise or salience to stimulate your efforts.

A completed Vision/Outcome must continue to generate enthusiasm or finishing issues may result, such as poor implementation and follow-through. The lack of support for its fruits by the group members who produce them is a pitfall that eliminates the member acceptance of grouping outcomes. A promise pitfall also manifests if nobody outside the group values the group's outcomes enough to respond appropriately. *The solution to this last concern is an ongoing discussion of the exigencies perceived by stakeholders and how those play out in group processes and outcomes.* Such a discussion is part of what is meant when policy makers describe a process as transparent: that stakeholders are able to know what issues are being discussed and what processes are being employed by the group so that the stakeholders' concerns can be taken into consideration as the group works toward shaping its Vision/Outcome.

To address most promise pitfalls, try to be sensitive to group mood as they discuss possible outcomes. If there is a sense of excitement about the outcome, there is probably energy for the effort involved to get there. If you sense that energy, make the equation explicit: "Does this mean we are willing to put the effort into pulling this off? How shall we measure our progress toward that end and how shall we adjust if we are falling short?" If you sense a lack of such energy, raise that as an issue of concern and have group members discuss what it means and whether there is anything they can do about it. Talk explicitly about trying to co-construct a Vision/Outcome that excites group efforts. Explain that potential promise will make the load seem lighter. Find a way to implement the old "spoonful of sugar" orientation (to help the medicine go down).

Table 7.1   Summary of the Vision/Outcome Pitfalls

Vision/Outcome Pitfall	*Examples*
Promise Is Inadequate	An undesired destination.
Bad Land: Disadvantages	An undesirable destination: (un)anticipated and opportunity costs.
Don't Reach Land: Solvency	An unattained destination: unsolved problem; unmet goal.
Vision Nature Problems	Wrong test for task; mistreatment or distortion of vision (construct).
Finishing Issues	Failure to get feedback or to finish well: termination trauma.

Land pitfalls manifest in negative aspects of the substance or nature of the Promised Land a group works toward and then achieves. Something desired is not necessarily desirable. By analogy, an addictive drug may be desired by the addict but undesirable because of what it does to the addict. Land pitfalls indicate an undesirable destination. An undesirable Vision/Outcome has negative consequences either because of some *disadvantage* it has over the status quo or because it fails to *solve* or to address the exigency that started the group on its trip.

Disadvantages to the Vision/Outcome

Advantages and disadvantages are metaphors borrowed from economics and argumentation studies. The terms invite comparisons between alternative choices. If a group faces two choices, one way to compare them is to look for benefits of one choice that do not accrue from the other. An advantage that is salient to a grouping member becomes an exigency for trying to turn the group in the direction of attaining that advantage. A disadvantage, if it is perceived in advance of the final decision, becomes an exigency for trying to turn the group away from a Vision/Outcome that causes the disadvantage. Land pitfalls include disadvantages to the Vision/Outcome selected or developed by the group. *To make a reasoned choice about whether to accept a Vision/Outcome with a disadvantage to it, ask, "How much will this disadvantage diminish our overall benefits from the Vision/Outcome?"* There are three ways to look for these disadvantages.

Opportunity cost is what the group loses by directing its energy the way that it does; opportunity costs are the other things that the group could have accomplished had it been using its energy doing something else. Consider the star college athlete who has the choice to finish 2 more years of college or to leave college in order to get an early start at being a professional player. The rewards from being able to play 2 more years of pro ball are an opportunity cost to staying in college. In rare cases, the opportunity cost to staying in college can amount to millions of dollars. Any choice a group makes to go in a particular direction, to follow a particular direction giver, or to select a particular Vision/ Outcome will have opportunity costs: the benefits that could have been realized had different choices been made. *When your group is settling in on its Vision/ Outcome, ask, "What opportunities will we lose if we pick this Vision/Outcome?"* The second and third sources of disadvantages to a Vision/Outcome come in anticipated and in unanticipated costs.

Almost 100 years ago, towns across America and Europe were faced with a problem: whether to allow "horseless carriages" (cars) to operate within city limits. The *anticipated disadvantages* to cars were obvious: noise that scared the horses that were the preferred mode of transport at that time and tires that went flat or were easy to get stuck. But at least cars were clean, never leaving piles of manure in their wake. Examples of *unanticipated costs* are the disadvantages we had to invent new names to describe: urban sprawl, gridlock, smog, head-on collisions, and greenhouse gases. *No matter how good a Vision/Outcome seems to your group, without a healthy attempt to incorporate the ideas of experts and stakeholders, the chances of leaving possible disadvantages out of your calculations is significantly increased.*

The sooner you can get your group to broach the subject of potential problems with their Vision/Outcome, the more likely the group will start to treat the consideration of such negatives as a normative part of their efforts and to make it a point to fully consider more than one alternative Vision/Outcome. Those are healthy signs. They indicate that grouping members perceive "permission" to raise potential concerns, rather than to self-censor what might prove to be a vital point. Encouraging such a norm for critical thinking also makes it more likely that the group will actually identify problems in advance that they can adjust to and attempt to ameliorate.

Make testing every idea for its downside into a group norm. Make certain that several possible Vision/Outcomes are considered so that the group becomes aware, as they test various downsides, that they have choices to make among potential desirable and undesirable effects from their Vision/Outcome. *Try to keep your group from becoming overly pessimistic, or feeling burdened by descriptions of problems, for there are always disadvantages to any course of action.* Selection of a Vision/Outcome with eyes wide open for potential disadvantages is the healthiest approach to constructing an effective group experience. *Be recursive, willing to reengage discussions of such disadvantages and what to do about them over time. Encourage levelheaded anticipation of negative outcomes and encourage processes that allow adjustments to group plans in attempts to limit negative effects.*

Solvency Pitfalls

Solvency pitfalls manifest as failures of group outcomes to meet group needs or goals. Solvency pitfalls indicate an unattained destination.

A Vision/Outcome that relieves most of the problems within a Purgatory Puddle or that accomplishes most of the advantage it is designed to attain can be said to have a high level of *solvency*. If a group's goals are met, the Vision/Outcome has addressed their purposes for grouping. Consequently, the failure to anticipate solvency problems is a pitfall to effective grouping.

Early in group life and throughout group interactions, attention to framing and revising group goals is important, as is the development of criteria for assessing whether those goals are met. Criteria are descriptions, in advance, of ways the group will assess or measure whether a goal, idea, or solution is good or worthy. Ongoing conversations about goals and criteria can help guide group process and outcome co-construction, as the group hones in on its desired fruits.

Vision Nature Pitfalls

In our discussion of disadvantages and advantages, we focus on *policy tasks*, which require a group to decide what to do, or how to do something. Every time a policy task or claim is considered, you should test Vision/Outcome solvency and disadvantages. But those are the *wrong tests* for other kinds of claims groups consider. For example, juries sort through the evidence in a murder case, groups of politicians disagree about the most important community values, groups of scientists argue about the kinds of relationships there are between phenomena, and we argue with our friends about who will win the next national championship. These topics involve issues of guilt, values, facts, and conjecture (Bormann, 1969); such tasks require different tests to determine if they are done well (Gouran, 2003). However, because of limited space, our advice is also limited. *When faced with a nonpolicy task, consult expert opinion, engage a careful discussion of the issues involved until a consensus is developed, and seek to anticipate and correct any pitfalls you face, especially those that limit your critical thinking.* Gouran's (2003) description of how people tend to sort through such claims gives us reason to believe you can be successful if you follow the basic advice in this book, but you might also consult a basic textbook on argumentation as well if given a formal and extremely important charge to complete an alternative type of group task.

When talking about a "vision" for one's group, there can be a tendency to *mistreat vision* as a thing that can be written down, cemented, and adhered to for the remainder of the group's life. In fact, groups can write down what they think their vision is, but effective groups are open to modifications and learning. A pitfall arises when an early sense of group vision gets reified or treated as a warrant for rejecting excellent ideas because "they don't fit the vision." *Try to co-construct a living and dynamic sense of your Vision/Outcome, as something created by all and for which all are responsible. Like a bush needs pruning over time, so, too, should a Vision/Outcome receive care and be modified as the group learns more about itself and its task.*

Vision distortion can result when excitement about finishing obscures the group's need to test its Vision/Outcome against the criteria they should have built for themselves in early discussions of what they expect from their grouping processes and outcomes. The propensity for this pitfall increases if there are no trained group members because the group may fail to construct such filters in the first place or because they may fail to apply those early decisions as tests for the Vision/Outcome they eventually construct. A careful analysis of disadvantages and solvency issues can lead a group to conclude that they have performed adequate tests of their Vision/Outcome, but if they forget to ask, "Does this do what we originally said we wanted it to do?" they may accept a distortion of their vision. An additional distortion comes if the group tries to "tiptoe around an issue" so as not to disturb a sensitive member or stakeholder. Taking flight from the activities necessary to fully address a group goal distorts Vision/Outcome. The squeaky wheel that gets oiled, in this case, does so at the expense of other important issues. *Distortions of the vision construct can only be addressed through group conversations that detect when the pitfall is occurring and that resolve to work out ways to correct the problem.* There is motivation to do so if the group has developed a clear consensus about its goals and criteria. Here is a case where understanding the problem is 90% of the cure.

Finishing Pitfalls

Finishing pitfalls have to do with how a Vision/Outcome is implemented or with what happens after the group has finished grouping. *Failure to finish at all* is the most basic and self-explanatory of the finishing pitfalls and includes a group's inability to come to any conclusion or solution or outcome. Perhaps they are avoiding a conflict or there is a stalemate between alternative Vision/Outcomes within the group because of incompatible visions, values hierarchy, or personnel.

Additional finishing issues include the *failure to implement the Vision/Outcome, the failure to develop a mechanism for gathering feedback about the effectiveness of the Vision/Outcome, and the failure to gather the feedback.* If a Vision/Outcome is not implemented, if a group's report gathers dust on a shelf, grouping energy was wasted. If no (or a poor) feedback-gathering mechanism is developed, no data will be gathered that can help judge Vision/Outcome quality even if it is implemented.

Finally, insufficient closure for the group is a *poor termination process pitfall,* which many grouping members find an unsatisfactory end regardless of whether their grouping outcomes were otherwise acceptable to them. Humans tend to like to *debrief,* to share their stories of what just happened to them, and to celebrate their successes. Group members are no exception. *Have at least one meeting or celebratory gathering to help create a sense of closure and successful termination.*

The solution to finishing pitfalls is to anticipate them well in advance. People who work with horses know not to let their horse start to run in the direction of the barn (where food and water await) because damage can be done in the bolting that results. When groups sense they are getting close to the barn, close to home, close to finishing up, they may tend to bolt as well, leaving loose ends and unfinished ideas to dangle and wither. *Slow that process down. If you can, start to initiate talk about working through completion, feedback, and termination processes somewhere nearer the middle of group life than at the end. Talk about the tendency to bolt as the group nears its ends. When the group is about done, make certain someone is reminding the group of what it still wants to accomplish in order to finish well.*

❖ SAVIOR COMPLEX PITFALLS

How well grouping members respond to exigencies for providing and receiving direction is a sign of how well they operate as a system. The second dimensional manifestation of any dramatic action involving grouping activity is Savior Complex, which has its origins in system personnel. Savior Complex represents the myriad of activities involved in negotiating who will give and receive direction in a group, and how that direction will be given and received. Some direction is provided a group any time one of its members commits an act or makes a statement that commands the attention and/or resources of others in the group. Such acts may move a group in a negative or positive direction or may function to reinforce where the group is already headed.

When we interact, we try to appear to be individuals whom others can trust. In groups, such efforts are involved in the tacit and explicit dance used to sort out who has what to offer the group. Grouping members provide direction by framing the Purgatory Puddle, by suggesting The Way/Process, or by advocating a particular Vision/Outcome. Other members use those acts as cues to their author's competence as a potential direction giver. Some members may try explicitly to frame a direction-giving or -receiving role for themselves by indicating their availability, interest, or competence. Examples are found in statements such as, "I am really interested in this subject and want to try to take an active part in this group" or "I don't know much about this, so I am going to just watch and learn" or "I did a lot of work on this subject on my old job." Savior Complex–specific rhetoric is any attempt to become or to act successfully as a direction giver. Broadly conceived, Savior Complex rhetoric often makes a tacit argument such as, "Follow me because of who I am, or because of what my experiences have been, or because of what my competencies are." "Follow me because of what I have done to help the group or because of what I can do to help the group." "Follow me because of how well I personify who we are: what we value, our process, or our vision." Such acts provide a multitude of cues about who might be able to give and receive direction easily and well.

The Savior Complex encompasses a wide range of member activities as each person probably serves alternately as direction giver and direction receiver (doer, follower, guide), though longer held roles such as a long-term guide, manager, or leader (see chapter 2 for definitions) are probably more stable and member specific. All grouping members are involved in the complex dance of direction-giving type and style preferences, power base choices, task or relational orientations, and temporal and procedural changes that are represented by the *Savior* and *Complex* metaphors. Remember from chapter 2 that *complex* has connotations both of the complexity involved in this direction-giving and -receiving dance and of the potential pathologies involved as members struggle for status and power. Both connotations are useful in anticipating the pitfalls groups may co-construct as they seek to find those who can be trusted to save them (or to help them escape from their Purgatory Puddle).

Table 7.2   Summary of the Savior Complex Pitfalls

Savior Complex Pitfall	Examples
Conception Pitfalls	Failure to want direction giver; overreliance on direction giver; overattribution of credit.
Ascension Pitfalls	Appointed, not emerged; flawed selection outcomes.
Poor Direction Giver Choices	Direction giver type choice; style choice; power base choice; fail to properly balance group functions given contingencies of the situation.
Transition Pitfalls	Failure to finish; failure to cultivate new direction givers; failure to enculturate new direction giver or group.

Conception Pitfalls

Conception pitfalls involve how grouping members conceive of direction and of direction givers. These conceptions can manifest in pitfalls to effective grouping both as grouping gets started and as grouping activities unfold. In general, any flawed conceptions of direction giving and direction givers will result in grouping members having inappropriate assessment tools in play as roles are negotiated in their groups. Those same flawed assessment tools are in play as they experience their grouping enterprise and evaluate how well it is going and why. Conceptions of how grouping should be done and of how direction givers should give direction are probably held by each of us as our own personal implicit grouping and direction-giving theories.

Failure to Want a Direction Giver. The first conception pitfall occurs when grouping members fail to want a direction giver though one is necessary. For example, groups that resist the idea that any one of their members is their primary doer or their long-term guide or their leader may be pitfalling if what they mean is that they will not allow anyone to have a role that gives that individual more power or status in the group than anyone else has. Some groups and grouping members console themselves for lowered task quality with rationalizations that at least they all contribute equally to the task and are cohesive. It is reasonable to oppose a particular direction-giving type in a particular circumstance. Leadership and management, for example, are not always indicated by grouping exigencies (see chapter 2). Opposing any concentration of direction-giving activity, however, can damage grouping.

Failure to Want a Necessary Type of Direction Giver. The second conception pitfall manifests when grouping members want a particular type of direction giver (typically a leader or manager) because they believe that all groups require such centralized or formal roles. For example, some are not comfortable with grouping processes, even when they might succeed, if there is not a clear and explicit "organizational chart" of who fills which formal role because of the desire for the comfort that having a manager provides. Others want one person they can rally around even though no crisis precipitates the need for such a commitment to a leader. Still others want the status for themselves that comes from playing the role of long-term guide, manager, or leader. All such cases are fraught with pitfall potential.

The type of direction giver and the need a group has to share and to co-construct their group direction should be allowed to play out through the interactive, communicative processes involved in grouping. Ongoing, changing perceptions of exigencies give energy for grouping activity and they should also be used rhetorically to help shape the form and direction of that activity. Remember that different grouping exigencies require different direction-giving types at different times.

Another form of this pitfall occurs when grouping members make flawed judgments about who is and who is not an appropriate direction giver. An individual's implicit theory of direction giving may create a pitfall if it results in rejecting a potentially effective direction giver because she or he does not fit the preconception. It is better to *allow grouping members an opportunity to "walk the walk" before deciding they cannot help direct the group. The orientation that all group members can and should help provide direction to the group enhances the role played by the ideals of the demos, consensus, and discussional attitude and increases possibilities of process prizes from grouping.*

Overreliance on Direction Giver. Once direction-giving roles are fairly well set, there can still be conception pitfalls at work including any tendency to rely too heavily on a key direction giver. A system might have a manager or guide who decides too much on behalf of the group or a doer who does too much. There is a tendency for pathological overreliance on key direction givers even within the normal development of functional groups. As grouping tensions are experienced early in the life of a group, grouping members may "flee" from them by trying to place themselves under the care of a savior or powerful group leader (Bormann, 1996). A form of *mindlessness* suggested by Freud can manifest in efforts by grouping members to co-create a mother or father figure, who will save them from their own responsibility for grouping (Elmes & Gemmill, 1990). There can even be the "hero worship" characteristic of indoctrination groups, where a single individual starts to speak for god or even becomes god to those who follow (Simons, 2001).

Overattribution of Credit or Blame. There is a natural tendency for over-attribution of causality to someone who is personified as the group's key direction giver. More blame or success is given to the direction giver than to the rest of a system, which is probably more responsible (cf. romance of leadership theory: Meindl, Ehrlich, & Dukerich, 1985). Any misattribution of cause allows inaccuracy in attempts to understand grouping dynamics and unfairness as grouping members are wrongly credited with cause for group co-constructions. Feeling hurt or big-headed by inaccurate attributions can distort an individual's grouping efforts. Grouping members, trained by their experiences with misattributions, begin to practice jaded grouping activities. Their future efforts may change because they need to "look out for number one" or because "what really counts here is whose butt you kiss" or "of course we didn't get any of the credit" so "only a fool tries hard."

The Framework for Grouping and Group Direction can be used by you to avoid or overcome these conception pitfalls. *Discuss the obligations and capacities every group member has for helping to give and receive direction.*

❖ ASCENSION PITFALLS

The Minnesota Studies, directed by Bormann, constitute more than three decades of empirical research using hundreds of case studies of natural and of ongoing groups. Their research indicates that group members negotiate who will give direction to a group through a *process of residues* in which grouping members are eliminated from consideration for playing key roles based on their actions in the group. This *process of emergence* unfolds until only one member remains to serve a primary direction-giving role in the group (Bormann, 1996). Using their implicit direction-giving theories and their interactions with and observations of the actions of other grouping members, group members tend to make simple dichotomous distinctions between those who appear to be potentially effective direction givers and those who do not (Offerman, Kennedy, & Wirtz, 1994). That is the natural process of emergence.

Appointed Rather Than Emerged. The most common of the selection process pitfalls is when a direction giver is appointed instead of being allowed to emerge through grouping processes. Sometimes appointment is necessary as, for example, ongoing systems hire a formal manager. But, that may nonetheless result in tensions among grouping members (either when someone is "brought in from the outside" or when someone is "selected from the ranks"). Regardless of the need for making such an appointment, the potential increases in such cases for the group to end up with a formal direction giver, who is supposed to be in charge, and an informal direction giver, who has great influence in the group. The pitfall worsens if the informal direction giver engages in role competition with the appointed direction giver.

A couple of key aspects of grouping activity are left out when a group misses the process of emergence. During a natural process of emergence, a direction-giving candidate has the chance to woo followers to support his or her direction-giving attempts. A follower is someone who starts to accept direction effectively, thus affecting group direction. A *lieutenant* (Bormann, 1996) is someone who helps make the case to the group that the group should follow a particular direction giver. An appointed direction giver begins work without any followers or lieutenants having made their choice to support him or her and must find an alternative way to develop such support while already acting as the direction giver.

Inadequate *credentialling* opportunities (Olson, 1987) may also be part of the problem. During an emergence process, grouping members get to know what each of their compadres has to offer the group in the way of pertinent past experiences and skills germane to the task they all face. Such credentials are at best provided in a resume when a direction giver is appointed, and that falls short of the co-constructed meanings about an individual's competencies that an emergent Savior Complex process allows. Even in a group with an emergent direction giver, members who hold back their competencies from others in the group may cause a pitfall through their hesitant or constrained participation and credentialling. If, for whatever reason, the group jumps quickly into following someone before other grouping members have a chance to show what they have to offer a group, there is also inadequate credentialling opportunity.

Flawed Direction Giver Selection Outcomes. The most obvious pitfall from flawed selection process outcomes is when the wrong member plays too much of a particular direction-giving role. *In the case of any poor selection outcome, the best advice is that you attempt to respond to the pitfall by remembering that roles and norms are negotiated among grouping members.* Nobody remains a direction giver long when grouping members refuse to follow. *Adjustments in the direction-giving roles can happen and should be considered normal and even a sign of grouping health.* In some circumstances, they are even built into a system of formal "rotation" of officers or chairpersons so that everyone gets a chance to serve in key direction-giving positions, which can be a very educational experience.

There will be an emergence of direction-giving preference in a group, even if it is only informal. Finding ways for your group to make use of those it prefers as direction givers is key to making them a useful resource and the group a functional system. *Try to provide adequate discussion of direction-giving credentials and interests so that all can hear what each perceives as their strengths and potential resources for serving the group.* Effective groups do eventually co-construct a Savior Complex that works for them, but they do not always talk about it. Such explicit discussions can soften the often painful pinch of the process of residues, consequently diminishing the possibly distorted perceptions of unfair and unworthy processes on the part of the person pinched.

Pitfalls From Poor Direction-Giving Choices

A healthy ascension process will provide some answers about what constitutes appropriate direction-giving process for a particular group (which is a third aspect of normal grouping processes that is lost when a direction giver is appointed rather than allowed to emerge). Still, unfortunate direction-giving choices can manifest that may hurt the group as they receive and help co-construct group direction. Such choices manifest postascendancy, which means that the group has settled, for the moment, its key direction-giving roles and process norms. The issue then becomes the ongoing set of choices made by the direction giver regarding how to provide direction.

Wrong Direction Giver Types. The wrong type of direction giver pitfall manifests when the grouping exigencies are perceived by grouping members to suggest one kind of direction giver but, for example, a key group direction giver tries to play the role of a manager for the group instead. Another example is when a group faces a crisis that will end it or forever change its basic nature. Members who keep trying to just follow or guide or do or manage may be maligned for their inability to transform the group through effective leadership. Given crisis contingencies, status quo protocols and less intense types of direction giving may prove to be insufficient.

Wrong Direction-Giving Style. A variety of direction-giving styles have been identified over the years (e.g., autocratic, selling, consultative, democratic, laissez-faire). Each style has potential merits and problems that should be considered by grouping members and direction givers as their stylistic choices are made. See Table 7.3 for a brief listing of such styles in addition to their merits and potential problems (Fiedler, 1967; Hersey & Blanchard, 1988). Our focus is on getting you to realize that you and other grouping individuals have choices regarding what style will be employed by your direction givers or as you attempt to provide direction. Those choices can and should change according to the needs of the group. Each style is appropriate only when it works,

Table 7.3   Direction-Giving Style Choices

Type	Definition
Autocratic	Centers power and decision making in the direction giver; fastest; least likely to attain process prizes except perhaps acceptance during an emergency.
Selling	Direction giver tries to get others to think/behave as she or he desires or requires; may be necessary when supragroup announces fait accompli; manipulative.
Consultative	Direction giver consults with group then decides; tries to attain ideas and acceptance but not diffuse responsibility or authority; risks process prizes.
Democratic	Direction giver facilitates distributed power and decision making among members; slowest; most likely to attain all process prizes when time allows.
Laissez-faire	Direction giver takes a "hands off" approach to power and decision-making processes; some mature groups need direction giver to stay out of the way.

which will be affected by a combination of grouping contingencies and of any grouping exigencies that are perceived to be salient.

Strive to strike a balance between those members who advocate centralized authority for a direction giver (e.g., autocratic, selling, consultative styles) and those who oppose such centralizations as inherently flawed. Each style has its strengths as a process. *Explicit conversation about those strengths tends to increase the chance they will manifest even if the style of direction giving the group finally co-constructs might otherwise be unexpected to show those positive effects.* Flexibility of style choice skills and the ability to help others to adjust their direction-giving style choices are both worth-while objectives.

Direction Giver's Orientation Toward Power. Power is the ability to get things done within your group. Power is not a thing or a possession. Power is a co-construction that requires the give and take among inter-acting people. French and Raven (1968) argue that there are six bases for power (see Table 7.4). Direction givers need to be astute regarding which base of power they attempt to employ. They need to *understand*

Table 7.4   Bases of Power

Type	Definition
Referent	Influence others because you are liked by them or they find you attractive in some way (e.g., as a colleague).
Expert	Influence based in competence or credibility given the intricacies of the task or subject matter at hand.
Legitimate	Formal authority or position you occupy in the group provides power to you or to whomever else holds that formal position (e.g., supervisors, CEOs, presidents, teachers, parents, and police officers all have some legitimate power; when put in charge of grouping individuals they could play a manager role because of that formal authority).
Information	Influence because of resources you can access or make available to others. You do not have to understand the information, only know that it is of value.
Reward	Ability to provide something desirable to others or to stop something undesirable from happening to them. The key is control over what others find rewarding.
Coercive	Ability to provide a negative thing (e.g., a punishment) to others or to remove a positive thing from others (also punishing).

what each group member finds "rewarding" and how to emphasize positive aspects of power in a relationship co-construction whenever possible. If inappropriate choices are made, remembering that power only works as a co-construction is the basis for suggesting a change.

Failure to Serve or Appropriately Balance Group Functions. The final direction-giving choice pitfall emanates from the most basic aspects of grouping (the functions groups are designed to serve—task, relational, and individual). It is not a problem when a group loses its focus on the task for a time, as long as it regains that focus in time to get its work done. It is reasonable that a group is "all business" at times, as long as individual and relational functions also get served at other times. What can be inappropriate is basing your implicit or explicit theory of how grouping should unfold in a construction that is comfortable to you but that fails to serve all three grouping functions. *A skilled group member can watch for signs of imbalance in serving group functions and should certainly note if any one of the functions is not being addressed. Bringing such concerns to the attention of the group is the first and most important step toward correcting any imbalance.* All three functions must be well-served in an effective group.

Direction giving, even leadership and management, are co-constructed roles. Except where institutionalization of power creates physical forces to cement the tyrant's rule, grouping members can stop inappropriate direction-giving practices by refusing to follow or by co-constructing a more attractive alternative direction, direction giver, or direction-giving process. That is what makes the follower, doer, and guide such potentially powerful direction-giving roles. *When style preference, power base choice, or any other aspect of a direction giver's activities are a concern to grouping members, talking about the concern enhances the possibility of serving group functions well and of attaining process prizes. Keeping silent and bearing the burden of an ineffective direction giver does not. So, speak up.* If a direction giver behaves poorly, the group must sanction that behavior or face continued co-construction of unhealthy direction-giving practices as a consequence of their flaccid response.

❖ TRANSITION PITFALLS

Failure to Finish. Failure to finish something is most likely if a direction giver is somehow cut off from the group. An individual providing a short-term bit of guiding or following who is interrupted provides the easiest example, for they have not been allowed, because of the interruption, to finish addressing the exigency that helped call their work into action. Interruption can create significant difficulties when the individual interrupted has filled a role for an extended period of time on a particular topic or set of activities. Imagine that a key direction giver in your group dies on the way to the next meeting. What is your backup plan? What that person knows, including what has been done and what still needs to be done, may be lost in transition. One possible solution is *working to understand the roles played by your compadres and to co-construct the cultivation of the next set of direction givers for your group.*

Failure to Cultivate New Direction Givers. Failure to develop the next generation of direction givers has its origins in taking comfort from a group when it has finally worked through its role struggles. When all is well, few feel an exigency to look ahead to times when new direction givers may be required. The consequence is typical: not preparing all members to be ready to take on new direction-giving functions in the group. The pitfall is more likely in groups where role rotation is not regularized than it is in groups that have built some rotation of roles into their expectations.

One basis for this pitfall can be traced to when grouping first begins: failing to get all members to contribute. Groups sometimes leave a member or two behind during early meetings, relying instead on those most willing to speak up, while others are allowed to play more passive roles. Some members may never learn to help shape group direction. Any willingness of grouping members to fail to cultivate direction giving from all group members, regardless of the reason, heightens this pitfall potential. To some extent, this whole book is about giving direction to groups. *Building a consensus for ongoing change and evolution of direction-giving roles into your plans as a group should make it easier for you to share direction-giving responsibilities and to back up current direction givers.*

If members believe they will never need to take on more responsibility, they may get lazy in their current roles or chafe at the constraints of those roles. Some members work against passing the direction-giving baton on to new members. They like the comfort of the status quo or they do not personally want to give up a desirable direction-giving role they play. Imagine a relay race where group success requires the ability to pass the baton from one team member to the next.

A transition pitfall occurs when one direction giver refuses to pass the baton or drops the baton or passes it on so poorly that others are not ready or interested in picking it up. This set of pitfalls is probably most evident when a previously successful and vigorous group "loses" its key direction givers and rapidly dwindles. A truly outstanding group should try to anticipate what may come next, including the need for new direction givers. College coaches call this preparation of the next generation of performers, "reloading"—preferring that to "rebuilding."

Failure to Enculturate New Direction Givers and Grouping Members. The final transition pitfall is failure to adequately enculturate a new direction giver and group. Remember that the new direction giver is immature in the new role and in the new system, regardless of previous successes in other roles. Remember also that the group has a new key direction giver, and it, too, is somewhat immature in its new form. It takes time to work through these issues. Some structuration processes must begin again, though many grouping members have vivid memories of "how things used to be."

A version of the enculturation pitfall is when an ongoing group assumes that one of their own members who has become a new direction giver "already knows the ropes." However, the new direction giver's experience of the group has not been what it will soon be in the new direction-giving role. He or she must learn what the new role requires of him or her. When a member misses several meetings or when a member moves to another institution and then returns after several years, similar discontinuities may result. Yet grouping members may make assumptions that the recently returning member is already "up to speed," and they may "miss the boat" on that judgment. *Prepare for these possibilities, discuss them in your group, then raise the issue again during and after any transition, and again, several weeks into a transition. Give people involved the chance to discover the difficulties they face including any temporal or procedural changes that have occurred in their absence. Try to raise and to discuss such issues as natural aspects of transition, rather than as signs of anyone's personal weakness.*

Most Savior Complex transition pitfalls can be avoided if grouping members develop norms for the easy sharing and co-construction of direction so that it is easy for all grouping members to give or receive direction from other grouping members and also to comment freely on any differences grouping members feel regarding the type, style, power base, or functional orientation choices made by their direction givers.

Transition pitfalls share a feature with finishing pitfalls in the Vision/Outcome. Few ever focus their attention ahead enough to anticipate the need until the group is caught in a swirl of change and must react. Typically, it is only at the point that such exigencies become salient. It takes an experienced and skilled group member to begin to frame such issues as important exigencies for the group to consider in advance. *You personally can show an interest in learning about roles played by others and, in them, learning about the roles you play.* Such an orientation, coupled with a free and easy exchange and sharing of direction-giving responsibilities, can help the group learn how to address more difficult pitfalls as they arise. *Try to encourage your group to talk about the next generation. Talk about how individual members are growing in their capacities as a consequence of their grouping experiences. Help each member get a sense of their own potential for a future with different roles. Then, make certain that some role rotation occurs over time in order to reward the extra effort it takes to become prepared in anticipation of potential need.*

❖ HOW TO EXPECT, DETECT,
AND CORRECT THESE PITFALLS

The Breakdown-Conducive Group Framework argues that part of each group's work is the co-construction of ways around or through the pitfalls they face: expect, detect, and correct the pitfalls. Focus on how communication can co-construct a higher quality Vision/Outcome and Savior Complex. Vision/Outcome provides a place to test goals and criteria against actual desired outcomes. Savior Complex provides a focus on the personal responsibility of each member to help co-construct a vitality of group direction. You have the basic information you need in order to co-construct an effective group experience once the nature of potential pitfalls is clear to you and you become vigilant. Remember also to broach any important subject with your group in order to begin co-constructing a conversational history and group norms conducive to effective responses when pitfalls become evident (see Table 7.5).

An additional technique introduced in this chapter is to develop a grouping role specialization. You can develop a specialty as an effective group member by focusing the refinement of your own skills. See Table 7.6 if you are interested in specializing in effective grouping activities as a particularly astute type of guide: *procedural expert, dialogic virtuoso,* or *devil's advocate.* Consider these three direction-giving roles

Table 7.5   Broaching the Subject on Vision/Outcome and Savior
Complex Pitfalls

Focus on the task.

1. *Define key terms* in the charge or task or problem. What do our various
   stakeholders think that this charge is all about? What do experts on the
   subject think? How can we build criteria into our process for making sure
   we do quality work as measured by how outside experts and stakeholders
   might assess our work on this subject?
2. *Discuss constraints and resources.* What external issues might make our task
   more difficult? What might keep us from succeeding with the charge? What
   resources are there outside of the group that we might access to help us and
   in what ways are resources limited that might reduce the effectiveness of
   our Vision/Outcome?

Time out: We need some perspective taking.

3. *Identify possible exigencies for the charge.* Why did someone give us this
   assignment? What exigencies do you suppose he or she perceived that
   resulted in this charge? How do we build criteria into our process for
   making sure that we address the exigencies our stakeholders think are
   important in our Vision/Outcome?
4. *Identify possible stakeholders.* Are others outside the group going to be
   affected by our actions? How can we consult with these people to help test
   our Vision/Outcome?

Is grouping really the way to proceed?

5. *Is this the right group for this task?* What are our strengths and weaknesses as
   individuals given this task? What does each of us bring to the task in terms
   of knowledge, skills, insights, interests, and useful relationships with experts
   or others in the supragroup who might be helpful or provide access to
   resources? Are there any of us who should not be in this group? Is there
   anyone we need to try to add to this group to make certain we have the
   direction givers and receivers necessary to succeed?

If so: How do we ensure that we do an effective job of grouping?

6. *Should we assign any roles* (e.g., secretary, gatekeeper, manager, devil's advocate,
   dialogic virtuoso, process guide—see Figure 7.6) to particular group members?
   How do we suggest changes if a role is not being filled well or if it turns out
   that someone else in the group could fill it better?

How do we want to do this: What do we want to get out of this?

7. *Discuss grouping goals.*
   a. What group goals should we have for this charge? How do we want to
      address it and how well do we want to address it? What quality of
      Vision/Outcome do we want to come up with? What criteria can we
      develop for the general kind and quality of outcome we want to
      attain? Note: Criteria are descriptions in advance of ways to measure

(Continued)

Table 7.5 (Continued)

important aspects of something, such as of a goal, of a strong idea or piece of evidence, or of a Vision/Outcome. Talk together about the important aspects of the thing (goal, evidence, or Vision/Outcome) and what are the keys to making it desirable versus just mediocre or even unacceptable. Those become your criteria for testing that aspect of the thing (e.g., of your goal, of the evidence you collect, or of your Vision/Outcome). Use your criteria to test every Vision/Outcome possibility you develop against group goals. Also, see if the evidence from experts supports your assessment and that of your stakeholders.

  b. What is going to be required of us individually and as a group if we are going to attain these goals?

  c. How will we know if we succeed in attaining our goals? What criteria will we use to measure our level of success in approaching and in reaching our goals? How often should we check to see if we all feel we are accomplishing our goals?

  d. What sanctions are we willing to use against ourselves if we are failing to meet these goals, either individually or as a group?

Table 7.6   Direction-Giving Skill Specializations or Role Clusters

Procedural Expert (function as a discussion-type guide)

Know, and be able to suggest, useful grouping *techniques* (necessary processes and helpful procedures) and *tendencies* (healthy norms, roles, communication network, and orientation that values the ideals of the *demos*, consensus, and a discussional attitude) for dealing with the concomitants of grouping (confusion, conformity, conflict, consciousness) and for working through common grouping pitfalls. Be able to describe the worthwhile *process prizes* (critical or creative productivity, member acceptance) attainable from optimized or synergized grouping.

Encourage your group to *discuss* their grouping *processes:* In advance, what kind of processes does the group set for themselves as a goal to use while they work; as grouping unfolds, are whatever processes the group is using working well for the group; after meetings, debrief how the meeting went and how the next can be better.

Make *use of reminders:* of generally understood standards for everyone doing their share of the work and for trying to do quality work; of specifically agreed-on goals for processes and outcomes grouping members claimed to want (the sooner desirable processes and outcomes are identified by the group, the better).

Encourage reflexiveness among grouping members, so they can revisit issues comfortably rather than forgetting or fleeing from them.

Dialogic Virtuoso (function as a dialogue-type guide)

Articulate the values and practices of dialogue and the importance of eliciting, sharing, and hearing stories about what really matters to grouping members.

In other words, the virtuoso has a passion for dialogue and for its role in human experience, can make keen judgments from small nuances in dialogue about what is going on, and is skilled in accomplishing the kind of facilitation of dialogue that makes others feel invited to participate.

Dialogic virtuosity involves *speaking "so that others can and will listen, and [listening] so that others can and will speak . . .* ; being profoundly open to others who are unlike you, and enabling others to act similarly. . . . Respond to another's invitation to engage in dialogue. . . . Extend an invitation to another to engage in dialogue. . . . Construct contexts that are conducive to dialogue" (Pearce & Pearce, 2000, p. 162; emphasis added).

Devil's Advocate (function as a debate-type guide)

Know and be able to explain how to *test ideas* and *evidence* for their merits and potential weaknesses. Do so with great care to minimize ego-defensiveness. This requires choosing your points of critical attack with discretion: (a) selecting only the targets that will most help the group and (b) accomplishing the criticism with a clear focus on the idea and not on any specific grouping member. Make certain that key assumptions and ideas get tested, especially your own (make a point of doing that openly), regardless of whether you agree with them or not. Do *not* use this tool to unduly advance your own cause or position.

Explain the role of devil's advocate so others may be less put off by your efforts. Encourage others to take on the role of devil's advocate to help take the sting out of the process and to enhance the quality of general group deliberations.

carefully and focus most of your efforts on the one you think is most conducive to your catching on easily and well given your own current skills, tendencies, and interests. Each of the three role specializations, once you have developed the capacity to play it well, provides a specific base for your claim to a group or to a potential employer that "I am an effective group member; I can help groups I am in to do better work."

❖ CHAPTER SUMMARY

In sum, once Purgatory Puddle exigencies are perceived and responded to rhetorically, The Way/Process grouping activities begin. Task, in particular, begins to be framed as potential Vision/Outcome. Personnel begin to transition through interaction into the Savior Complex. These four Quadrad bases for grouping exigencies, rhetorical activities, and pitfalling represent the recurring aspects of dramatic action in any grouping system.

8

(Un)Intended Group Outcomes

❖ ❖ ❖

The space shuttle Challenger exploded upon takeoff, killing seven crew members when vital O-rings failed and allowed fuel to leak from its booster rockets. In spite of warnings in advance that the weather conditions were dangerous enough to result in O-ring failure, six communication-based factors involving NASA officials and engineers led to the decision to launch, which resulted in the explosion. Faulty shared beliefs, questionable reasoning practices, perceived pressure to conform, a shift of presumption toward risk, ineffective persuasion attempts, and the use of ambiguous language are among the culprits (Hirokawa, Gouran, & Martz, 1988). Seventeen years later, the space shuttle Columbia burned up upon reentry to the earth's atmosphere. Research findings point to similar breakdowns in communication as contributing factors. Each situation involved pitfalls that personnel either co-constructed with their interactions or failed to overcome by necessary communication: pitfalls by commission or by omission. The pitfalls probably seemed minor in the moment, during the interactions that involved them; the results, however, were entirely unacceptable and the outcomes were awful.

Groups can be categorized according to the fruits of their labors: their outcomes. Every group has the potential to break down. Most groups have the potential to succeed. The propensity for group success changes with the activities of group members. In this book, potential group pitfalls were defined as anything that could result in diminished group outcomes, and group breakdown represents the actual diminution of group outcomes. Pitfalls are discussed as natural aspects of any grouping processes or activities. Breakdown is discussed only as an outcome. Most of this book is focused on group processes and pitfalls; this chapter is the only one focused entirely on group outcomes. In this chapter, recurring aspects of the dramatic action involved in attempts to group are condensed into a Set of Potential Group Outcomes (Burtis & Turman, 2005) that result from varying levels of effective or problematic grouping activities.

Assessing group outcomes is a useful tool. Group outcomes are the final products from serving task, relational, and/or personal group functions. The quality of those outcomes ranges from successful to breakdown. The outcomes can be short-lived, moderate in duration, or enduring (even lifelong in some rare cases). We describe a simple category system that depicts eight potential group outcomes (four successful, four breakdown). The category system is a tool that serves us in two ways. First, it allows an overall, or gestalt, assessment of how well a group did once it has completed its work. Such an assessment can provide a basis for comparison to other possible outcomes the group might have attained or to how well other groups do with their outcomes. Second, it provides a basis for a group member to attempt to orient his or her group toward achieving a particular level of group outcome while they are still in the process of grouping. As such, it can help group members to frame a goal for their time together, to discuss the importance that potential pitfalls can play in diminishing their capacity to achieve their goal, and to anticipate a standard for success against which they can measure their progress toward achieving their goal. The Set of Potential Group Outcomes provides us that useful tool.

Catastrophic outcomes, such as shuttle disasters, are not necessarily the result of grouping communication that is itself catastrophic in any immediately observable way. Instead, as is the case with most grouping activities, small differences in interaction content or dynamics can later be associated with drastically different group outcomes. An orientation that pitfalls should be expected, detected, and corrected is perhaps the best basic remedy. It puts grouping members on alert: *be on the lookout for potentially negative aspects of your grouping co-constructions.* To focus on how grouping pitfalls might be affecting potential group outcomes increases the possibility that group members can make intentional and appropriate choices when minor efforts to improve the quality of discourse might be made to matter the most.

❖ DYNAMICS INVOLVED
    IN POTENTIAL GROUP OUTCOMES

Our small Set of Potential Group Outcomes is informed by extant research indicating four different dynamics involved in grouping. We use these four key differences in interaction dynamics to discriminate among the outcomes that can result: (a) satisficing versus (b) optimizing, (c) positive or negative synergy, and (d) positive or negative aspects of enduring change or spin-off effects. These dynamics in grouping activity can result in substantial differences among group outcomes.

Satisficing and Optimizing

Grouping members employ different quality processes as they attempt to reach desired outcomes. For a number of years, economists described human decision making as *optimizing* behavior. The idea is that, when faced with a problem, individuals will search for the best or optimal solution for the problem. Individuals, and presumably groups, use their access to information to achieve the highest probability for a successful outcome. Simon (1955) suggests flaws in this thinking and offers *satisficing* as an alternative. He argues that individuals are more likely to strive for "simple pay-off functions"; they only work hard enough to achieve what they think is an acceptable choice given the task at hand. Our sense is that satisficing is more typical of group action because it is quicker and easier; optimizing may only be used in special circumstances, and then only if the individuals involved are properly motivated and capable of effective group communication skills.

Satisficing, optimizing, and the possibility of group breakdown provide the most basic outcomes because groups must either succeed or fail, and any success must either be satisficed or optimized. Failure is to be avoided, and among the remaining alternatives, satisficing rather than optimizing is the human response to most problem-solving situations. Pavitt and Johnson (2002) explain that people are generally less motivated in struggling to uncover the best solution to a problem than in efficiently finding one that is good enough to get by. These notions are exhibited in [Simon's] satisficing model; that people choose the first option they think of that meets some predetermined level of aspiration. (pp. 20–21)

Synergy

Some group experiences include an unusual sense of momentum and intensity from the process of working interactively with other people. Such intensity is called *synergy* or a synergistic effect from grouping activities. Henman (2003, p. 5–6) explains:

Synergy can take either physical or mental forms. The physical presence of others is often arousing, so more work is accomplished. In the mental sense, synergy emerges when a type of collective intelligence and shared memory begins to develop as the group matures. Also, synergy can play an important role for those group members who are energized through interactions with others. Instead of a scattering of energy, there is commonality of purpose, a shared vision, and understanding of how to complement one another's efforts.

In some cases, group members working together accomplish much more or much less than the combination of their individual talents and resources would suggest. *Positive synergy* is when joint action by grouping members results in a performance that greatly exceeds what is expected of them based on their abilities or resources. For instance, there are times when players with limited experience are able to perform far above the expectations set for them. The 2003 Minnesota Twins baseball team is an example. They had one of the lowest team salaries in major league baseball and few All-Star-caliber players. Commentators expected the team to be sold at the end of the season and to be moved to a city with a larger television market. Despite the odds, the players won their division.

On the other hand, *negative synergy* may occur when joint action produces group performance that falls well below expectations. Teams loaded with top talent can, at times, perform worse than teams with less talent but more "chemistry." Sometimes the talented group devolves into self-defeating behaviors and a cycle of ever worsening performances that can best be explained as a negative synergy. A short-term example might be found in a *fantastic failure* that is co-constructed near the end of a game when a team seemingly self-destructs, allowing what appeared to be an insurmountable advantage to be turned into a humiliating defeat. On the other hand, positive synergy might result in a *fantastic finish* when, in the final few minutes of a game, a team roars from behind to unexpectedly win a contest. Such memorable sporting events may be evidence of short-term bursts of positive synergy among the members of the winning team or negative synergy among the losers.

Intensity and Duration of Fundamental Change

Gemmill and Wyukoop (1991) describe fundamental levels of change that grouping members can experience through the dynamics of small group transformation. Applying their concepts to problem-solving group processes, we argue that the range of any group-wrought change can vary in intensity and duration. In addition, some grouping activities produce unforeseen outcomes (positive or negative spin-off effects), which can continue to manifest over long periods of time after the grouping has ended. We use *baggage* as a metaphor to represent any such changes or any such spin-off effects with a very long life after grouping.

In sum, it is useful to combine these dynamics into a small Set of Potential Group Outcomes. The dynamics are (a) the possibility of breakdown after any group action, (b) attempts to satisfice versus optimize and the different process qualities and effects involved with each, (c) synergy that creates extreme intensities of experience and quality of outcomes, and (d) the duration of change or of spin-off effects from grouping activities. Organizing group outcomes using the relationships among these variables provides us a useful tool for extending our frameworks for understanding grouping and breakdown-conducive groups.

❖   A SET OF POTENTIAL GROUP OUTCOMES

The following Set of Potential Group Outcomes (see Figure 8.1) can be used to describe the fruits of any grouping enterprise. The design logic of the set is to use the dynamics previously described to create a mirrored set of outcomes: for each dynamic, the mirror reflects either a desirable or a breakdown version of the group outcome.

Type I Group Outcomes: The Satisficed Group

We use the satisficing dynamic to begin the design logic for our set of outcomes. Both *Type I outcomes* are *Satisficed Groups* (see Figure 8.1) They mirror each other, one as a desirable outcome and the other as an outcome with some level of breakdown involved. These outcomes are the products of groups that use satisficing when analyzing their Purgatory Puddle, in their primary The Way/Process activities, and/or in their Vision/ Outcome testing. Type I outcomes can be good or bad because satisficing can be an appropriate choice (resulting in a Good Satisficed Group) or it can be a foolish choice (resulting in a Bad Satisficed Group).

A Satisficed Group serves all three group functions (task, relational, and individual) but does not do so as well as can be expected given the resources that are tied up by the group. Most observers or involved group members could point to ways that the Satisficed Group could have improved its performance. Type I outcomes involved risky behavior. Examples of satisficing activity can manifest as the group failing to properly analyze its situation, failing to discuss and develop good group processes, failing to identify possible reasonable alternatives

Figure 8.1   Model for Potential Group Outcomes

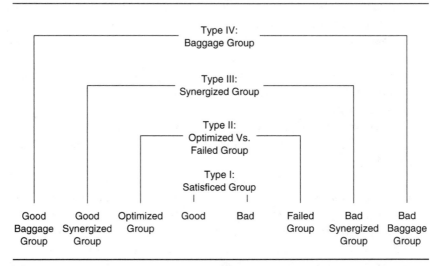

WARNING: This set of outcomes is *not* a phasic or linear sequence of possible outcomes.[5]

to their Vision/Outcome, or failing to apply sufficient quality control to adequately test their co-constructed Vision/Outcome. Satisficing involves cutting corners by not carefully testing such key assumptions, ideas, evidence, or processes. That is why Satisficed Groups risk breakdown, even in cases where the decision to satisfice is intentional and appropriate.

Satisficed outcomes are typically average, mediocre, or adequate results that groups co-construct when not motivated to do the hard work necessary to optimize their grouping. This can be contrasted to Type II success, which is full accomplishment of all three group functions to an extent that allows everyone to agree that there was little room for improvement in how the group did their grouping. The members of a Satisficed Group may be satisfied by their work but they should not be pleased or impressed by it unless they are rationalizing the experience. For example, the following are generic versions of common group rationalizations for their satisficing: (a) "our work does not need to be very effective because the task is not very important" or "our task is boring"; (b) "we do not have to get along very well because we are almost done"; (c) "the only thing that matters is how well we did," which is used to justify bad behavior (see common metaphors against worrying about relational and individual group functions— e.g., "You gotta break a few eggs to make an omelet" or "Winning isn't everything, it is the only thing") or to claim that work, which is not strong, is strong because it was given a stamp of approval, as in, "we got an A, didn't we?"; and (d) a non sequitur such as "our work must be strong because we all like each other so much and are a cohesive group" or "we must be cohesive because the work we do together is so strong." Such rationalizations may be used by groups to allow grouping members to feel comfortable with their satisficing. Such rationalizations provide a version of a mind guard because they allow the group to perpetuate a conspiracy of false belief that their basic satisficing behavior is acceptable, when in fact it may be the source of potential breakdown.

Is it a group breakdown if the group does not actually fail? If a group somewhat serves its three functions, why should we care if it does not perform up to its potential? If everyone in the group appears to be happy and they seem to have gotten by okay, isn't that enough? A Satisficed Group is a breakdown group when fewer individuals could have accomplished the same outcome, thus reducing the resources tied up in grouping. For instance, could one, two, or three optimizing people outperform five people satisficing and, consequently, let the additional two or more group members attend to something else? Further, the Satisficed Group can never know what they have lost because they never explored their potential. Satisficing also risks setting problematic norms of underproducing, which may well be perpetuated in future grouping activity. Finally, cutting corners risks mistakes and further weakened outcomes. Satisficing behavior results in diminished group outcomes, which is the definition of group breakdown.

The Good Satisficed Group. In spite of these costs and risks, satisficing is sometimes justified, providing the possibility of the *Good Satisficed Group.* Satisficing activity can be time- or energy-saving behavior, though it is not necessarily so. Group members may need to satisfice because their priorities and resources are such that they cannot or should not work any harder or longer on a particular task than is necessary to get to a minimal level of acceptable outcome. When circumstances warrant satisficing activity, and if the decision to satisfice is made *intentionally* by the group after careful *deliberation* in which there is open-minded consideration of the potential costs involved, the Satisficed Group that results can be an acceptable group outcome. Only when the intentionality and deliberation criteria are met can the choice for the group to satisfice be appropriate, though even in such cases a group accepts some level of group breakdown and risks wasting member resources. In short, any Satisficed Group is a risky outcome, but sometimes the risk is justified.

The Bad Satisficed Group. The *Bad Satisficed Group* carries the same risk as the Good Satisficed Group and more because it is an *unintentional* and *untested* use of satisficing behavior, without due consideration for the risks involved. Satisficing activity can easily become normative; it can become a default orientation or level of engagement, letting inertia continue existing grouping practices (the group is on autopilot) without determining whether status quo approaches are appropriate given the current problem. Over time, satisficing can manifest in the inability of grouping members to focus sufficient cognitive energy on their grouping activities in order to do them well when circumstances become more difficult or important. The tests to determine whether a choice to satisfice is an appropriate one include explicitly determining whether satisficing fits the group's needs and goals given the circumstances and whether the decision to satisfice is an intentional choice made only after careful consideration of the possible ramifications from satisficing.

Table 8.1   Reasons for the Frequency of Satisficing as a Primary
                  Grouping Mode

- First, satisficing is what individual humans tend to do when responding to problem-solving situations because it is easier than optimizing.
- Second, satisficing becomes more likely in groups where any kind of effort is made more difficult by the increased number and complexity of dynamics involved in group settings.
- Third, the next most likely group outcomes (optimizing or failing) have stronger exigencies at work against groups accomplishing them, which makes satisficing more attractive.
- Fourth, it is typically more acceptable socially to satisfice. For example, one need not point out problems if others do not seem to notice them. One need not work hard if others are not working hard. One need not change one's own priorities in order to do the hard, constrained work to optimize the group's processes if nobody else appears willing to make a sacrifice.
  - Satisficing reduces the risk of being perceived as someone who is trying to cultivate favor with those higher up in the supragroup.
  - Satisficing reduces the risk that another group member's poor performance will become an issue.
  - Satisficing reduces the risk of being perceived as critical. Signs of this tendency are claims that, "Everyone is entitled to their own opinions" and "If you can't find something nice to say, don't say anything at all."

Type I group outcomes, the Satisficed Groups, are at the heart of our set because they are the most likely group outcomes. There are several reasons for this relatively high frequency (see Table 8.1), but it is the basic fact that satisficing is the natural human response to most problems that results in our using it as the basis for our design logic. However natural the many reasons for satisficing may feel, all of the exigencies for satisficing are at cross-purposes with grouping as a useful tool because grouping is justified by the improved creative and critical work it allows us to do. Satisficing limits or eliminates the possibility of such process prizes from grouping. Regardless, the combination of exigencies to satisfice (and the exigencies against optimizing or failing) places satisficed groups at the heart of our design logic.

Type II Group Outcomes: The
Optimized Group Versus the Failed Group

The *Type II outcome* (see Figure 8.1) is based in the dynamic of optimized success versus failure. It includes the difference between a successful outcome (the *Optimized Group*) and a poor or unacceptable outcome (the *Failed Group*).

The Optimized Group. The Optimized Group has served all aspects of its task, relational, and individual functions as well as can be expected given the resources brought to the grouping activity. It is different than a Satisficed Group in degree of success. That difference manifests from the quality and effort involved in interpreting and framing the Purgatory Puddle, in co-constructing The Way/Process, and in testing Vision/Outcome alternatives. Though a knowledgeable observer of a Satisficed Group will easily identify ways its members could improve the quality of their work, neither knowledgeable observers nor group members can think of easy ways to improve the processes or outcomes of the Optimized Group.

The Failed Group. In contrast, the Failed Group failed to serve one or more of the three functions all groups must serve. A Failed Group has not maintained itself or it has failed to serve its individual members or it has failed to accomplish its task. Failure is more than some diminution of group outcome, which is the definition of group breakdown. Failure is an unsuccessful attempt to serve a group function. Although group breakdown is involved in any Failed Groups, group breakdown also manifests in Satisficed Groups, Bad Synergized Groups, and Bad Baggage Groups, which are diminished, but not necessarily failed, group outcomes.

There are three distinctions between Type I and Type II group outcomes. The first is that they are different in quality, the second is that they are different in amount of quality, and the third is that they are different in the exigencies involved, which tend toward Type I and against Type II outcomes. The difference in quality between Type I and Type II outcomes is represented by Simon's two original metaphors *satisficing* (the basis for Type I outcomes) and *optimizing* (the basis for the Optimized Group).

Optimizing behavior involves a consistent and coherent effort to find the best solution to a problem. Satisficing does not. Optimizing is exemplified in the assumptions and propositions laid out in Gouran and Hirokawa's (2003) functional theory (see Table 8.2) for how grouping members ought to behave when they are doing their best work. A second distinction between Type I and Type II outcomes is the amount of quality that separates them. The Failed Group is worse than the Bad

Satisficed Group. The Optimized Group is better than the Good Satisficed Group. The final distinction is represented by the relationship the Type II outcomes share; there tend to be strong exigencies *against* Type II outcomes. Just as there are natural human tendencies *toward* satisficing, there are natural human tendencies *against* optimizing (too much work) and against failing (too painful or noxious a state; nobody but a saboteur would strive toward failure). The negative exigencies associated with failure and with the hard work involved in the efforts to find the best possible solution, result in the relative

Table 8.2   The Functional Perspective to Group Decision-Making Effectiveness

Assumptions	Members want to make an appropriate choice.
	Members want to understand their task and its requirements.
	Members have access to necessary resources like information and time.
	Members possess capabilities and skills needed to deal with various facets of the task and the process required for successfully completing the task.
Production Propositions	Members must attempt to satisfy five fundamental task requirements.
	1. Show a correct understanding of the issue to be resolved.
	2. Determine the minimal characteristics for acceptable alternatives.
	3. Identify a relevant and realistic set of alternatives.
	4. Examine alternatives in relation to the minimal characteristics for acceptable choices.
	5. Select the alternative most likely to have desired characteristics.
	Members must employ appropriate interventions for overcoming constraints (which would include the pitfalls described in chapters 3–7 of this book) that interfere with satisfaction of task requirements.
	Members must review processes by which the group comes to a decision and, if necessary, reconsider judgments reached (even to the point of starting over).

infrequency of Failed and Optimized Groups when compared to satisficed group outcomes.

Type III Outcomes: Synergized Groups

The possibility of good or bad synergistic effects from grouping activity adds the third dynamic. *Type III outcomes* (see Figure 8.1) result from intensified grouping experiences that manifest as either acceptable (Good Synergized Group) or unacceptable (Bad Synergized Group) synergistic effects from grouping. Synergized Groups are stronger versions of the kinds of success or breakdown found in Type II outcomes. Type III success (the Good Synergized Group) and failure (the Bad Synergized Group) come from grouping that creates a synergy of interaction and resource, which results in group outcomes beyond reasonable expectations. The resources available to the group determine reasonable expectations. Synergy changes the basic equation, adding energy to the system beyond that indicated in its basic resources.

The Good Synergized Group. The *Good Synergized Group* is a better outcome on one or more group functions than grouping members or critics expect or even imagine possible. Our earlier description of synergy includes the details of what is involved. Bormann (1996) exemplifies the distinction between the Optimized and the Good Synergized Group and notes the relative infrequency of the latter:

> Ken Kesey, in his novel *Sometimes a Great Notion,* describes three men cutting timber, a scene that captures the spirit common to all task-oriented small groups when they are functioning at peak efficiency. "The three of them meshed, dovetailed . . . into one of the rare and beautiful units of effort sometimes seen when a jazz group is . . . swinging together completely, or when a home town basketball squad, already playing over its head, begins to rally to overtake a superior opponent in a game's last minute . . . and the home boys can't miss, because everything . . . is clicking perfectly. When this happens everyone watching *knows* . . . that, be it five guys playing basketball, or four blowing jazz, or three cutting timber, that *this bunch*—right now, right *this moment*—is the best of its kind in the world! But to become this kind of perfect group a team must use all its components, and use them in the slots best suited, and use them all with the pitiless dedication to victory that drives them up to their absolute peak and past it." Of course, even highly

cohesive groups working efficiently achieve such moments only rarely, but they do achieve them, and they are among the most gratifying experiences of people who work with and participate in groups. (pp. 249–250)

The Bad Synergized Group. The *Bad Synergized Group* begins with the same diminution of success in serving a task, relational, or individual function found in the Type I or II group breakdowns, but synergy adds additional "badness" to the effect. In other words, things may not be working out and then they start to go from bad to worse because of how the group co-constructs its continuing problem. An intensification of negative effects can manifest when relational processes worsen because of the nature of grouping dynamics. They can manifest in the sting felt by individual members from the public aspects of group failure. They can manifest in the products of the group being somehow made worse. Grouping members might feel less inclined to support the group's work once it is made public. Grouping members may feel a heightened desire to scapegoat to cover their failure. Such intensifications of unfortunate outcomes can be considered products of negative synergy. Some people, as they struggle with group demons, might be strengthened by the struggle, possibly leading to better group outcomes as a consequence. Others tend to weaken and may potentially become undone by the struggle, leading to the Bad Synergized Group.

Public displays of failure and the effects of grouping synergy both help heighten the effects of failure and are two paths to a Bad Synergized Group outcome. The *public* aspect of failure has two meanings. First, group failure is public because others in the group see each grouping member involved in the failure. For some, there is comfort in sharing such trials, but for others, failure in a group is particularly gruesome, even when it is not a personal failure. Second, *public* can mean that others outside the group get some glimpse of the group's failure. That type of discomfort is represented in phrases such as, "We should keep our dirty laundry to ourselves" and "Don't let others see the skeletons in our closets." Finally, synergistic effects from interaction around deteriorating or negative outcomes can create a sort of *snowballing*. In such cases, breakdowns are exacerbated, failings are actually made worse (not just made to feel worse) because people who continue to interact do more and more damage to themselves, to their ability to maintain their group, or to the group's task outcomes.

Both synergy and any perception of being a public failure are co-constructions by grouping members. The Type III Bad Synergized Group can be an especially onerous co-construction. Bad synergy can create the kind of grouping dynamics that do damage beyond even the Failed Group. Doing such damage often involves grouping concomitants such as a destructive co-construction of conflict, of competition, of conformity, or of group consciousness. It can also involve the process prizes as group activities squelch creative or critical work or member acceptance of grouping processes and outcomes. Both the Type I Bad Satisficed Group and the Type II Failed Group are basic potential group outcomes: neither requires unusual grouping activity. The Type III Bad Synergized Group is different. It requires grouping activity that exacerbates bad choices or failure (and that runs counter to the logic for grouping in the first place) and heightens the negative effects from such grouping. In some such cases, groups of people are capable of co-constructing incredibly unfortunate outcomes for themselves!

Type IV Outcomes: Good and Bad Baggage Groups

Type IV outcomes (see Figure 8.1) are based in enduring aspects of the change or of the spin-off effects that result from some grouping experiences: what we call a Good Baggage Group or a Bad Baggage Group. These come from the possibility that any group may create long-term, even lifelong changes or other spin-off effects from its grouping activity. And, these long-term effects can be either desirable or negative.

The Good Baggage Group. The *Good Baggage Group* is when there is positive "lifelong baggage" that was co-constructed as a concomitant of grouping. Concomitant means that these effects of grouping are probably not a direct or intentional result of one of the three functions the group was created to serve. An example is any individual group member's personal strengths gained from grouping that enhance his or her future capacity to succeed in relationships or groups. Bormann (1996) argues that "each individual ought to have the opportunity to grow and develop his or her potential within the group" and when this is achieved, strong mental health becomes an unintentional byproduct of the group experience (p. 280). Additional examples are when there are worthwhile and enduring spin-offs or byproducts to the group's work (e.g., the orange drink Tang is such a spin-off from NASA's work) or when group members develop lifelong friendships that can be traced back to their work in a group. Because they are not intended group outcomes, a Good Baggage Group is an especially delightful serendipity.

The Bad Baggage Group. The *Bad Baggage Group* results from any unforeseen and enduring negative effects from grouping. Several examples help clarify the point. When someone has her or his abilities to work well with others in future groups permanently and adversely affected by an earlier group experience, such hurtful baggage is one of the outcomes from that earlier group. Producing inexpensive internal combustion engines helped serve humankind but also began a cycle of air pollution that threatens unexpected consequences and is certainly a negative concomitant of the completed project. If someone in a group dies or is permanently disabled because of what the group did, that is awful baggage. Because they are not intended group outcomes, a Bad Baggage Group is an especially unfortunate breakdown.

In sum, (a) the tendency to satisfice, (b) the option to optimize and the potential to fail, (c) the potential for synergy, and (d) any long-term baggage provide the dynamics for four basic types of potential group outcomes, each of which can be either good or bad. The practical application for this set of outcomes is that you have some basic choices to make about potential outcomes when you are involved in any grouping enterprise.

Using the Set of Potential Group Outcomes to Expect, Detect, and Correct Group Pitfalls

Presented with an exigency toward grouping, group members will tend to satisfice, but they have a choice to work harder and to try to optimize. Small group communication books typically focus on helping grouping members improve their performance by orienting toward trying to achieve the Optimized Group outcome. This book has a different orientation. It is designed to help you understand the distinctions between group outcomes and then to make a reasoned choice as to the quality of grouping activity you wish to pursue given the nature of the task and circumstances involved. We argue that you should learn how to make an intentional choice whether to satisfice or to optimize.

When the group's work is sufficiently important, a reasoned choice can be made to optimize. We represent that choice and the effort it involves with the metaphor *crank up the mindfulness,* which is intended to represent the potential for optimizing, the effort involved in making such an effort, and that there is a reasonable choice to be made about whether or not to satisfice. When it is not important, a reasoned choice can be made to satisfice: a Good Satisficed Group becomes the goal. That leads us to a framework for making choices regarding group outcomes: the Good-Enough-Group argument (Burtis & Turman, 2005). This argument constitutes our advice to you regarding group outcomes (though the following section is too long to put its entirety into italics).

The Good-Enough-Group argument puts intentionality into play. Intentionality requires the group to gather sufficient focus to do an effective job discussing how important various aspects of their grouping activity are to them: "Can we make an appropriate decision to satisfice?" The choice about how hard to work at a particular grouping enterprise is the basis of our Good-Enough-Group argument. The Good-Enough-Group employs several ideas we have already developed in this book.

1. The importance of grouping exigencies and of group work varies from one grouping enterprise to the next.

2. Potential group outcomes vary.

3. The effort put into grouping should reflect the importance of the group's work and the outcomes desired by grouping members.

4. For important work, groups should try to crank up their mindfulness to optimize their outcomes.

5. For less important work, groups should explicitly consider well-reasoned, careful choices to satisfice.

Cranking up the mindfulness involves working hard to *ensure that appropriate grouping processes and problem-solving practices are used in your group.* Good-Enough-Grouping argues for intentional focus on the question of whether satisficing or optimizing is an appropriate idea in this particular group for this particular issue. This involves discussing two of three potential questions. "Should we generally try to optimize on this task?" If so, "Is satisficing a reasonable option for at least some aspects of the task?" When a general decision is made to satisfice on a given group task, "Are there parts of the task where we need to optimize?" Cranking up the mindfulness may be more important on some aspects of group work than on others. And, when deemed to be necessary, cranking up the mindfulness is easier in some circumstances than in others. *Intentionality involves explicit discussion of grouping circumstances, group and personal goals, grouping processes, desired outcomes, and personal contributions to be made to the group.* Because the decision to crank up the mindfulness involves the effort necessary to optimize, and because the exigencies for optimizing need to be perceived as strong enough to sustain the effort, *the group should carefully and explicitly co-construct its reasons for any effort to crank up the mindfulness.*

When should you try to crank up the mindfulness? Functional perspective theorists Gouran and Hirokawa (2003) summarize the answer: *in grouping circumstances that are consequential or uncertain.* Table 8.3 begins with a row that unpacks their advice by providing several recurring points in grouping experiences when it is an appropriate idea to consider cranking up the mindfulness, at least to the point of explicit discussion regarding whether to satisfice or to optimize. The center row provides a summary of the advice provided elsewhere in this book that could help you crank up the mindfulness. The third row lists circumstances where mindfulness may tend to be high without much additional effort required. You can use this knowledge strategically to approach your group when it is in a direction-conducive mode: when it is most likely to listen.

Though the choice to optimize does not guarantee success in achieving that difficult goal, there can still be a reason for celebrating the attempt. It is a desirable thing if Good-Enough-Grouping results in intentional, explicit, and careful discussion of these issues in your group regardless of whether group members are actually effective in bringing to life their choice to optimize. That is because being intentional about grouping involves a discussion of group processes, and such discussions themselves enhance the potential for a group to be effective. Consequently, Good-Enough-Group processes are justified as a prescription even when the effort to optimize is not fully realized or even when the choice is eventually made to satisfice.

When might satisficing be a reasonable choice? First, satisficing is appropriate *when grouping members are too busy, yet the work must get done.* Sometimes there are no excellent choices available. As pressures mount, a better choice than failure can mean that satisficing must occur on jobs that need, but cannot get, an optimizing grouping effort. If limited time or other resource constraints cannot be overcome, satisficing at least allows projects to get done that might otherwise languish and bring even worse outcomes than the satisficed. *Warning: Do not be too*

Table 8.3   Cranking Up the Mindfulness

When to Try to Crank Up the Mindfulness	When the group is getting started.
	When the task is important or difficult.
	When the group operates in a dynamic supragroup environment.
	When the group is considering (or not) a process for proceeding.
	When the group is failing to make progress, you should consider forcing a choice: crank it up or quit.
	When the group is trying to create options.
	When the group is about to make a major decision.
	When limited time forces coming quickly to a resolution.
How to Crank Up Mindfulness	Employ values of the *demos* and consensus.
	Learn processes for a discussional attitude and deliberation.
	Learn critical and creative thinking techniques.
	Employ the Orienting the Group technique.
	Learn techniques to encourage dialogue.
	Learn techniques for testing ideas: devil's advocacy and debate.
	Learn communication skills.
	Engage competition with self or others.
	Discourage discussion-reducing decision-making techniques.
	Search for joy in doing the work—some form of importance.
	Search for fear in not doing the work—potential guilt or shame.
Times Naturally High in Mindfulness	When the group likes the task.
	When the group wants to succeed.
	When the people are competing.
	When group norms require mindfulness.
	When vicarious learning and the excitement that goes with it produce mindfulness.
	When you can stimulate anticipatory regret: See boxed text titled Focus on Scholarship.

quick to decide that optimizing is impossible. The desire not to work so hard provides a ready-made exigency for such a rationalization that may not stand the test of time. Groups have enormous capacity for doing tasks that might daunt the individual and, when necessary, can sometimes accomplish what seems to be impossible. When grouping members co-construct a commitment to success, they often find a way to succeed even in times of seemingly inevitable failure and despair. Do not bet against a group in such circumstances.

Second, satisficing is appropriate *when optimizing is too expensive.* Sometimes the difference between satisficed and optimized outcomes is small and unimportant and the additional energy required to optimize does not justify the additional value that it may provide. Sometimes satisficing can allow a group to continue to make progress rather than getting bogged down in endless minutia or in perfectionist ideals for quality outcomes. Of course, you can only know that these are the case after careful consideration of the circumstances.

Third, satisficing is appropriate *when the grouping activity is relatively unimportant.* Grouping members may not care about their task, even after a careful consideration of its possible merits. Groups sometimes "result" because of a cultural bias favoring use of groups to deal with problems instead of some other tool. Sometimes a group results simply because it is the preferred tool for a single involved individual, who puts social pressures on others to "keep me company." These biases can result in the use of a group in rhetorical situations that are not Purgatory Puddles. Such biases make it possible that some grouping enterprises are themselves mistakes. But circumstances are not always under the control of the group. For example, your job or other supragroup entity may require that grouping work be done. In any case, a decision that a particular grouping enterprise should not be given too much energy should only be made after a careful consideration of the facts of the case. And, if possible, do not continue grouping in circumstances that do not justify such a use of grouping energies. Regardless, do not allow your initial boredom or disinterest in an assigned task to determine your judgment regarding the importance of the task.

Focus on Scholarship: Anticipatory Regret and Satisficing Group Behavior

Janis and Mann (1977) define "anticipatory regret" as "the main psychological effects of the various worries that beset a decision-maker before any losses actually materialize" (p. 222). They argue that when confronted with making a decision, group members will consider the potential losses to self, losses to significant others, self-disapproval, and social disapproval that would occur in the event that the wrong decision is made. When group members worry about such losses, they are motivated to continue to search out additional information even though their tentative choice for the best solution has already been found. When do group members worry about such potential losses? Janis and Mann describe five circumstances that indicate the potential for anticipatory regret. First, when there is an "illusion of no real choice," members will struggle to find differences between the forced choice and a desired alternative. Second, when the consequences of an inappropriate choice will become public directly after the decision is made. Third, when a superior previews for the group the significant importance of their outcome. Fourth, when the group is aware that there is a potential that additional information exists or will emerge that will influence the success of the group's work. Fifth, when a superior expresses interest in the decision and a lack of concern about the amount of time a group takes to complete its task. When a group faces any of these circumstances, they are likely to find themselves experiencing higher levels of anticipatory regret as they make their decision. Consequently, the group will feel an increased sense of urgency for cranking up the mindfulness in order to attain a higher level of outcome quality.

Understanding the Set of Potential Group Outcomes

The set of outcomes can be applied two different ways. First, it can be used to assess a group according to how well it did on its worst of the three functional outcomes: task, relational, individual. So even if a group optimized its personal and relational functions, if it failed on its task function, the assessment would be that it was a Type II or Failed Group. Such a single measure ensures an assessment that considers the importance of all three functions to effective group experiences by giving the greatest weight to the function least well served by the group. The second way to apply the set is to indicate, for each of the three functions served by the group, which of the outcomes was achieved by the group. So, for example, a group could, in that sense, be a Type I success group on the task function, a Type IV breakdown group on the individual function, and a Type II breakdown group on its relational function. Our preference is for the first approach, because of the values it expresses for all grouping functions, but we note the potential benefits from the details provided by the alternative approach.

We suggest that you consider using the first approach when setting goals for your own group outcomes and for assessing the general progress you are making toward achieving them, and that you use the second approach to assess the final outcomes for your group. However, we warn you against using the second approach as an excuse to devalue the importance of any one of the three functions groups are supposed to serve. Doing so could limit the potential for attaining a process prize from your grouping and decrease the likelihood that you can overcome the barriers to effective group experiences.

Despite the usefulness of this set of outcomes as a tool, a word of warning is also in order. This set of outcomes does *not* serve as an appropriate assessment tool for microgrouping processes or episodes. It is a measure of outcomes, not of the pitfalls experienced during the daily grind of grouping activities. Grouping activities can be very messy, confusing, and difficult, which are not necessarily negative things for the overall success of the group. To use the set of potential group outcomes to label one's group a failure in a particular meeting is to overclaim, and perhaps perpetuate, the effects of what went wrong that day. It also underestimates the remarkable abilities individuals have to respond to a painful meeting in ways that help the group grow. You will know that the set of outcomes is being misapplied if you hear grouping members say such things as, "We were a Type II success today" or "I did not join the argument at the meeting because I didn't want to make us into a Bad Synergized Group." The Set of Potential Group Outcomes is detrimental if used as a tool that discourages members from innovating or from co-constructing responses to the exigencies they perceive for grouping. Do not use the set of outcomes to finalize any judgment about the quality of a single meeting, communicative exchange, or grouping episode.

❖ CHAPTER SUMMARY

The knowledge that group outcomes vary significantly in quality and duration of effects can help strengthen your attempts to overcome barriers to effective group experiences. The Set of Potential Group Outcomes depicts the range of quality and duration among four mirrored types of outcomes ranging from the exceptionally successful to the exceptionally negative. The Set of Potential Group Outcomes extends the nomenclature and grammar in the frameworks for Grouping and Group Direction and for the Breakdown-Conducive Group. Constellations of considerations are involved in rhetorical responses to direction-conducive and breakdown-conducive groups. The Set of Potential Group Outcomes allows individuals to make better choices regarding their grouping activities. Individuals who are aware of potential outcomes, and how they are associated with the four grouping dynamics described earlier in this chapter, can learn how their communicative attempts to help their group avoid or work through various pitfalls can bear fruit. It is then easier to make appropriate decisions regarding when to try to crank up the mindfulness.

9

To Group or Not to Group, That Is the Question

❖ ❖ ❖

Have you ever had "one of those days?" For example, do you know people who will not admit that they made a mistake or when they changed their position on something? Have you ever dreaded the prospect of having to go to a meeting? Do you know of people who grumble about their team? Do you feel your choice to do or say what you want is restricted because those you associate with might disapprove? Do you know anyone who tries to avoid meeting new people? Ever see people roll their eyes or sigh and look bored or chitchat with others during a meeting? Can you think of anyone who seems incapable of communicating effectively; she or he might be especially quiet or might fumble around enough that everyone else begins to ignore her or his contributions. Have you ever thought up excuses to avoid meetings? Do you know someone who seems to prefer working alone? Each of these cases can indicate an individual who perceives an exigency against grouping. Imagine that you have to work in a group where every one of these exigencies against grouping is in play. Pretty bad, huh? Now, imagine that all of these exigencies against grouping are in play but that you do not know who in your group is experiencing them. Even worse, huh? Now, imagine that they are all in play in your group but even the people who are experiencing them are not fully aware that the real issue they have is that they just do not want to work as part of a group. Welcome to reality. Welcome to "one of those days."

Grouping requires you to expend energy. Some people are predisposed against spending their energy working in a group. They may have nothing against the particular group; they just do not like any group. A general bias "not to group" affects their choices. They try to avoid group work and if they find themselves in a group in spite of their best efforts, they then try to get the group to end quickly or they display their dismay in some other way. In cases where grouping is appropriate, a general orientation against grouping can be a problem. It is difficult to co-construct an effective group with potential members who cannot overcome their preexisting notion that groups are a bad tool. Such exigencies can infect your own thoughts or the thoughts of others you must work with by keeping a group from getting started, or by distorting how grouping unfolds. If general exigencies perceived against grouping are more salient than those in favor of grouping, more energy may be spent avoiding group work or being upset by it than will be spent trying to construct an effective group experience.

People like different things, do different things well, and orient differently to working with others. Some like working in groups because they have group skills, because they like people, or because they feel they get the support they need from others in the group. Others do not like working in groups for a variety of reasons (to be discussed in a moment). Use yourself as a test case. When you have the choice, do you generally like to work alone or in a group? If the kind of work you do requires you to work in a group, do you look forward to that aspect of your job, or do you wish someone would invent a way that eliminates your need for having to depend on other people as you work? Now, consider the other people you work with. Do any of them have problems getting along with others on your team? Do you think any of them might prefer to do their work alone? If you prefer working alone, you may need to orient to the material in this chapter as you might to green vegetables or to some other type of essential food that you do not like. You avoid them at your own risk. And, if you love groups and can't imagine that anyone might prefer to work alone, the material in this chapter may be especially important for your efforts to understand your compadres who may disagree.

❖ GENERAL EXIGENCIES AGAINST GROUPING

Exigencies perceived as reasons for not involving oneself in grouping activity are exigencies against grouping. Exigencies against grouping act as constraints on effective attempts to group or to affect group direction. Bitzer (1968) describes "constraints" on rhetorical action as "persons, objects, events and relations which . . . have the power to constrain decision and action needed to modify the [rhetorical situation]. Standard sources of constraint include beliefs, attitudes, documents, facts, traditions, images, interests, motives and the like" (p. 8). Purgatory Puddle exigencies are perceived as reasons for grouping. Exigencies against grouping are in some way in opposition to, or ameliorate the effects of, Purgatory Puddle exigencies: they help constrain grouping action or attempts to change group direction.

Neither exigencies against nor exigencies toward grouping are inherently good or bad. You are not necessarily a good or bad person (or even a good or bad group member) because you tend to perceive exigencies against grouping whenever you consider a grouping possibility. Perception of exigencies against grouping is as much a part of the human experience as is the perception of exigencies toward grouping. The tendency for some of us to be more concerned with certain exigencies than with others is just part of what makes each of us unique. Sometimes exigencies against (or for) grouping are reasonable and valid: other times they are not. Sometimes exigencies against (or toward) grouping create problems if they are acted on; other times ignoring them creates problems. Sometimes an exigency is perceived by one person to favor grouping and by another person to favor some other sort of action in response. Describing potential exigencies against grouping in this chapter is done in order to make them part of your awareness and part of your calculus for understanding grouping activity.

When any exigency against grouping is perceived by a potential group member, it must somehow be overcome or worked through in the service of effective grouping activity. The general and specific exigencies against grouping we discuss in this chapter are in addition to the basic force of inertia, which also must be overcome in any successful grouping attempt. They are also in addition to all of the potential pitfalls that can be experienced during grouping activities, though those, too, can turn into disincentives for continuing to group. Our goal in this chapter is to make you aware of the potential for such exigencies, so that you can be vigilant. *Properly framed and discussed, exigencies against grouping can sometimes be used to test and improve the assumptions and processes involved in a grouping attempt.*

General exigencies against grouping manifest in three ways (see Figure 9.1). The first is as distrust of grouping as a tool, which is similar to Keyton's (1999) concept of *grouphate*. Distrust of grouping is a personal stance against the use of grouping as a human tool, favoring instead some other form of action in response to a rhetorical situation. The second manifests as distrust of oneself as a grouping member. The third cluster is distrust of any aspect of a particular grouping effort, which results in a general unwillingness to become involved. Such exigencies against grouping are general objections people have toward grouping *before* any grouping on their part even begins.

❖ DISTRUST OF GROUPING

The first cluster of general exigencies against grouping involve an individual's distrust of grouping as a tool. These exigencies flow from the belief that there are few, if any, Purgatory Puddles that warrant the need to group. Most of the Purgatory Puddles perceived by grouping members are instead perceived by these individuals as rhetorical situations that can and should be addressed in ways other than by grouping.

Groups Waste Time

Some people believe that groups are a waste of time. This rationale is used as a general condemnation of almost any grouping activity, not just of one's own involvement in a potential group. Certainly, when groups operate as they should, they will take more time, even a lot more time, than one person needs to make a decision alone. Indeed, one of the tenets of the Good-Enough-Group argument we make in chapter 8 and of the "wrong task for a group" pitfall we discuss in chapter 3 is that some tasks do not justify grouping. However, if grouping is required to do a job well (to attain one of the process prizes), then the expenditure of time is justified. If anyone raises this objection, *try to shift the perception of wasted time, which puts the focus on how long grouping takes (making groups always look bad), to consideration of the value that could be added by the group if it can be used to enhance the critical or creative effort brought to the task or member acceptance of group outcomes.*

Figure 9.1   General Exigencies Against Grouping

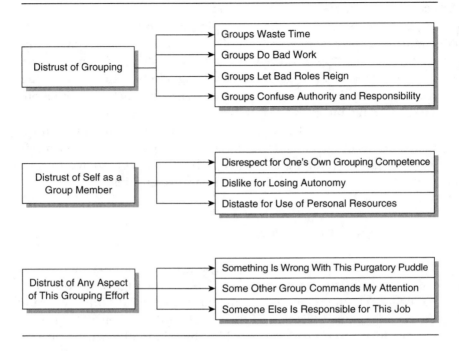

Groups Do Bad Work

Some people believe that groups are inherently flawed, co-constructions that by their very nature tend to result in low quality, even bad, work ("a camel is a horse designed by a group"). Unfortunately, there is some truth to this concern because some groups do create bad work processes and outcomes. One possibility in any group experience is that pitfalls to effective grouping might diminish the quality of work outcomes below what an individual might accomplish alone. Further, Satisficed Groups tend to cut corners in order to complete a task quickly rather than to put in the effort necessary to optimize group choices. When a group does poor work or wastes the time of its members, it perpetuates the bias against groups that some people perceive as an exigency against grouping. McMillan and Harriger (2002) note that this perception is particularly true among students whose "*Initial Attitudes Toward Deliberation are Ambivalent* [emphasis theirs]. . . . Students arrive at college with an opinion of group decision-making that is often both negative and distrustful. Despite their young ages and limited experience, students already have found groups to be slow, often ill-informed, and uneven in participation." (p. 244). Why would anyone be interested in that?

However, some groups do excellent work. That is the answer to this general exigency against grouping. One cannot know in advance whether a particular group will do poor work, but the answer lies in the efforts of the involved individuals. People with a general orientation against grouping based in the belief that groups always do bad work are part of the problem if they refuse to co-construct a better effort and outcome. If anyone raises this objection about groups, *try to shift the attention from a focus on stories about Failed or Bad Satisfied Groups,* which inevitably tend to get told when this subject is broached, *to your own favorite stories of Optimized Groups, Good Synergized Groups, or Good Baggage Groups.* These can become "memorable messages" that bring comfort and support to grouping members when times get tough.

Groups Let Bad Roles Reign

Some believe that groups are havens for slackers or other mal-adroits (e.g., social loafers, budding autocrats, or Machiavellian personalities who will ride roughshod over more reasonable or sensitive group members). This perception can be based in the reality that work in many groups is neither evenly divided nor even in quality across group membership. Once grouping begins, such dynamics are always possible. They are, however, a co-construction of the grouping members involved. Because most people are not inherently evil, efforts to focus interaction on more positive role constructions can often bear fruit. If anyone raises this objection about groups, *try to shift the attention from a focus on lazy members or on the evils done in past groups to the fact that each group co-constructs whatever roles it allows to reign. Participate in a general discussion of how effective group members should behave, a specific discussion of how members in the current group can hold each other accountable for their efforts, and then help co-construct a sense of responsibility for successful group outcomes, including the roles that each member will be encouraged to play. In sum, co-construct a sense that responsibility for any poor grouping co-construction rests squarely on all the members of the group.*

Groups Confuse Authority and Responsibility

Some believe that groups are "conspiracies of collective innocence" or "conspiracies of collective ignorance." And, there are certainly strong tendencies found in common rationalizations, mind guards, and typical grouping dynamics to construct such conspiracies. *Conspiracy* means that several people co-construct a common stance that gives them a secret advantage over others. Sometimes they may co-construct a common stance or idea that is a false or incomplete explanation about what has happened. *Collective innocence* means that grouping members act as though they are not responsible for what they did as a group. *Collective ignorance* means that members act as though they do not know the answers to key questions about what they are doing as a group, or what they did as a group, and especially they do not know why the group behaved as it did. A group is a conspiracy of collective innocence or ignorance when its members try to escape their own responsibility for what the group does by blaming their own ignorance or by blaming others. "It is not my fault," or "I was only following orders," or "we were set up to fail," are typical human reactions when joint action is difficult to undertake or when it goes awry.

Groups are co-constructions. If they do poorly, that is the co-construction, even of the social loafer. If they do evil, the responsibility includes those who did not co-create a different action. Ignorance does not mean innocence when one is a group member. It means the grouping one helps co-construct did not involve all members as it should have, which is both a pitfall and a sign that those doing the excluding and those excluded have constructed a flawed communication network, process, or outcome. Regardless of flaws, the co-construction is the responsibility of everyone in the group.

People can mortify (accept blame), scapegoat (blame others), or transcend guilt (claim that it does not apply). Some groups will scapegoat one of their members for negative outcomes. Other groups will scapegoat a supragroup entity or individual. And, some members will try to scapegoat their group as an entity, attempting to excuse the actions of any individual member. When these rationalizations are used, it tends to weaken grouping efforts and also to give group work a bad name. If anyone raises such an objection to groups, *try to shift the attention in the stories being told from a focus on failures of group members to take responsibility for their actions to a focus on how, in the current group, that does not have to happen. Use any horror story provided about an irresponsible group as a "teaching tale" for your own group: vowing to not let history repeat itself.*

In sum, any general orientation against groups or grouphate can become a potent impediment to grouping. *The best solution to any general orientation against groups and grouping is to become involved in a successful group. That requires a grouping attempt that is a reasoned response to strong, salient exigencies for grouping activities and that becomes evidently excellent in the eyes of the skeptical member.* Over time, enough such experiences may change a person's orientation toward groups. However, so many such experiences may be needed that any basic overhaul of this attitude is not reasonable to expect from a single group experience. Instead, *the focus of any single group attempt for such an individual needs to be on providing evidence from the get-go that "this group is different."* The people involved are different. The task is different. Their approach to the task is different. The outcomes that can be expected by working with them are different.

How can you create such a sense of difference? The anticipation and exploration of exigencies against grouping; the orientation toward expecting, detecting, and correcting any pitfalls that arise while grouping; and a reasonable and balanced sense of how to work well with others will all have to be involved as you work to co-construct an effective group experience. In short, *the hard work of effective grouping is the only antidote to these general exigencies against grouping.* Focus your attentions on effective grouping activities. Do not waste time or effort trying to convince someone who is not already a believer that "groups are good."

❖ DISTRUST OF SELF AS A GROUPING MEMBER

There are those of us who have learned through our experiences with groups that we are not to be trusted as an effective group member. Consider the following familiar statements. "I'm not a team player." "I don't like to go along with the crowd." "I do not suffer fools gladly." "I don't want to feel obligated to someone else." "Groups waste my time." "I don't do well in groups." People who say or who think such things probably have personal experiences that result in them drawing their conclusion. Distrust of self as an effective grouping member is a general exigency against grouping that manifests in one of three ways, including a disrespect for one's own competence as a member of a grouping enterprise, a dislike for losing one's personal sense of free choice or autonomy to the demands of the group, or a distaste for using one's resources up on the hard work required from grouping.

Disrespect for One's Own Grouping Competence

Some oppose grouping efforts because they do *not* feel *competent* or qualified to serve as a member of the group. A sense that one lacks competence is a sense of limitation, in extreme form, a sense of help-lessness. Sometimes it is warranted; often it is not, especially when it comes to being able to make a contribution to a group. Helplessness can become an excuse for inaction. "But, I don't know how," or "I don't know what you want from me," are phrases some use to suggest it is another person's job to provide what they lack. For some, this becomes a basic orientation to any new assignment or group task. What may actually be missing is a sense of personal responsibility and initiative.

Other people feel personally anxious or threatened by any circum-stance in which they have to work with others in a group. They experi-ence this exigency as a form of communication apprehension specific to group contexts: anxiety about working well in social circumstances. Trying to give direction to those who lack initiative can be like trying to herd a flock of chickens. Trying to direct those who fear group interaction can be like trying to get a stunned or unconscious person to play a game.

If anyone raises such an objection to grouping, *try to shift attention from a focus on inadequacy to a consideration of how any individual can find a way to help a group.* If the problem is a lack of initiative, you will find that out in this discussion as a never-ending stream of excuses or objec-tions are raised, which should be taken as a sign that the potential con-tributions to be made by such an individual are not worth further efforts to try to get him or her involved. If the problem is a real sense of lacked competence, you will find that out as the person demon-strates his or her interest in the group by trying to find other ways to make a contribution to the group. *You can encourage the discussion by admitting to any sense of insecurity about group work you may have, and you should try to help your group co-construct ways to turn a member's liabilities into group assets. For example, a member who is reticent about speaking up in the group may be willing to take notes for meeting minutes or to help members who must miss a meeting catch up on what was missed.*

Dislike for Losing Autonomy

Some people oppose grouping efforts because they do not want to *lose autonomy.* Autonomy means an individual's free choice: I get to do what I want to do, how I want to do it, when I want to do it. Dislike for loss of autonomy may manifest as, "I don't want others to tell me what is important or what I have to do" or "I don't want to be obligated." Group membership necessarily cuts into one's personal autonomy. Bormann (1996) explains: "When an individual joins a group and works for it, he or she must give up a certain amount of liberty. . . . The group may require individuals to do work that they do not enjoy, or it may demand discipline that they do not demand of themselves. Membership may require a distasteful compromise of principle, or restrict individual freedom of expression. A given group may exact all these costs, and a person may find the price too high" (p. 273). For some, the loss of autonomy involved in joining a group is generally too high a price to pay.

Focus on Scholarship:
Relational Dialectics at Work in Groups

Baxter and Montgomery (1996) explain the dialectical perspective, which suggests that relationships are composed of contradictions (the interplay between two opposing forces) and oppositions (forces that mutually negate each other). Relationship dialectics are tensions between perceived relational exigencies: (a) *connection-autonomy* is the tension between an individual's need for independence and his or her need for relationship; (b) *predictability-novelty* is a tension between the desire for stable and predictable behavior in one's relationships and the desire for change; and (c) *openness/closedness* is the need to disclose one's feelings and experiences, which is in tension with one's need to be protective and strategic about the use of such information. These same relational tensions may emerge as exigencies against and for grouping. For example, when individuals are faced with an exigency to group, their sense of autonomy may be threatened and they experience a sense of tension as they struggle with their need to connect with others who are similarly concerned by some salient aspect of a Purgatory Puddle. As grouping is co-constructed, members may continue to experience tensions regarding the amount of connection they are willing to maintain, which comes at the expense of their autonomy. *Relational dialectives suggest that there is no "correction" to this pitfall, in the sense that one could ever hope to make such an exigency against grouping "go away." Healthy groups and relationships require an appreciation of the dialectics involved and serviceable co-constructions for how to continue interaction.*

All of us have some sense of autonomy, or of individual choice, and we can appreciate individuals who are adept at accomplishing things all on their own. We admire individuals who work well with others, but we also admire rugged individualists, those who take care of themselves, who pull their own weight, and who are willing to stand alone against adversity. The competing values between individual and collective action parallel dialectical tensions humans feel in relationships between some need for personal autonomy and some need for connection with others (see boxed text titled Focus on Scholarship: Relational Dialectics). Some of us are more used to autonomy than others. Some of us prefer autonomy more than others (some seem to flee any situation that involves making their own choices). Those who prefer autonomy may manifest that preference as an exigency they perceive against grouping, regardless of the merits of a grouping project. Even those who do not generally prefer autonomy may find themselves at times feeling the need to be alone or to work without a group of people present.

Perceived loss of autonomy also occurs in instances when individuals oppose grouping efforts because they do not want to pay the potential price of risked failure that accompanies trusting a group. This exigency manifests as a sense that it is safer not to risk one's valued ideas or one's self-image to grouping dynamics that tend to reshape ideas and self-image. Artists, physicians, engineers, and professors are notorious for thinking that their art, their diagnoses, their processes, and their ideas are self-evidently appropriate. Such individuals may tend to chafe at group-developed restrictions or mandates. Many college students share such concerns. McMillan and Harriger (2002) note, "Students also fear that their individual interests will not be best served if left to the whims of collective decision-making. Repeatedly, students express a profound sense of distrust and the need for what Hofstede terms 'emotional independence' (1980, p. 221) from group decisions that might restrict their individual progress and success" (p. 244). A specific fear from lost autonomy is that it will dilute one's personal skill. If anyone raises this objection, *try to shift the attention from a focus on what the individual will lose in group membership to what might be gained, individually, relationally, or in work on the task. Here is an opportunity for the group to affirm its concern for providing a balance of service on all three of its functions.*

Distaste for Use of Personal Resources

Some oppose grouping efforts because they do not want to *expend* the *energy* to group. In particular, they do not want to use the resources they have available on what a group requires of them. It is hard work to group. Some want to conserve their resources for use on what they want to do, others do not want the hassle involved in co-constructing a process, not to mention having to deal with the conflict and conformity involved in any grouping attempt. Still others are just lazy (er, sorry; "cautious about expenditures of energy"). Even the most delightful of activities such as eating a wonderful meal, co-constructing sexual intercourse, or going to an amusement park have diminished appeal when one is too busy, too tired, or too sated to put the effort into eating, sexing, or walking. Sometimes it is just easier not to group. If anyone raises this objection, *try to shift the attention away from costs to what the benefits might be. In a good grouping experience, for instance, the joy and energy that comes from synergized group success is almost unparalleled in the human experience.*

In sum, distrust of self as a grouping member provides a general set of exigencies against grouping that are particularly thorny because they are born of the personal experience as an incompetent; or are integrally related in some way to one's sense of self, including one's opportunities to exercise free choice; or they involve the undesired expenditure of personal resources. If they are part of one's self-concept or involve use of one's personal resources, one might feel personally threatened by an attempt to group. Grouping efforts may feel like an attack on the individual's personal resources, personal freedoms, or beliefs about herself or himself. Ego-defensiveness can be the expected response if such a person is pushed too hard to "join the group." *The only solution to such pitfalls is to remove, to the extent possible, any sense of threat to involvement in the group. That can be accomplished if grouping members can co-construct opportunities within the grouping enterprise for the afflicted individual to feel she or he is making a reasonable contribution; others in the group must come to respect and appreciate that contribution as well.*

❖ DISTRUST OF ANY ASPECT OF THIS PARTICULAR GROUPING EFFORT

The final category of general exigencies against grouping involves individual distrust for some aspect of a particular grouping effort. This results in a general sense that "I do not want to be involved in this grouping attempt." You may have experienced times yourself when you can point to a particular aspect of a group that discourages any involvement on your part. This form of exigency is divided into three subsets that include the perception that something is wrong with this Purgatory Puddle, that an alternative group is commanding all of one's attentions or energies, or that there is a reason you should not have to do this particular grouping activity. Any of these may combine as a general stance against using a group as a tool in this particular case.

Something Is Wrong With This Purgatory Puddle

This exigency against grouping manifests when someone *does not want* to group as a response to *this particular Purgatory Puddle*. These exigencies against grouping have their rationales based in the circumstances of a particular proposed grouping enterprise, which necessarily involves a particular Purgatory Puddle. Subsets of this exigency are found in each of the basic components of any Purgatory Puddle, as in, "I know you, and I know that I don't want to work with you" (personnel component); "I know this subject, and I know that I do not want to work on it" (task component); and "I do not want to bend to these particular contingencies" (supragroup issues). In sum, any one or more Purgatory Puddle component can provide a general exigency against grouping in this particular case.

Some Other Group Commands My Attention

Some people feel that they have insufficient energy available for a new grouping effort because an alternative Purgatory Puddle, and the grouping that it involves, commands their attention and their energies. It is common for other supragroup obligations to demand the time, energy, and attention of grouping members. The bona fide group perspective describes how negotiating the boundaries between obligations and relationships to the group and outside the group is a central feature in explanations for why groups struggle (see Putnam & Stohl, 1990). An individual may be doing something else already, which has priority because it was first in line. In this case, people experience a general exigency against new grouping even though they might otherwise like the project.

Someone Else Is Responsible for This Job

Finally, some oppose grouping efforts because they do not feel a sense of duty for a particular grouping activity: it is *not my job*. If one feels that one's boss is assigning work that the boss should be doing, the thought "this is not my job!" will roll around in one's head throughout efforts to complete the task. One of the reasons college students cite for not wanting to have a class assignment that they complete some sort of community service is, "This is not my community" or "I'll wait until I have my own home and family before I worry about such things." If you have ever driven past an automobile accident or have walked by someone passed out on a sidewalk, it could be that you feel social services should handle the homeless or some other authority should handle an accident scene (it could also be that you do not feel competent to address the situation or that you do not want to get involved because it would take up too much of your own time or resources, which are both exigencies addressed earlier). The sense that something "is not my job" may be both true as well as problematic.

When the people of a community expect their government authorities to address their needs, their framing of problem situations invariably involves the need for some sort of government intervention. This may or may not be accompanied by a personal sense of their responsibility as part of the needed response to the problem. What happens to one's sense of citizenship when there is no sense of personal engagement or responsibility for one's community? Lack of obligations to the larger community, lack of involvement in any sort of service work or civic organizations, create personal experiences that are short on any sense of responsibility to "the commons" or for the "common good." Seeing oneself as passive or as a pedestrian or as an observer, rather than as a player or as a citizen or as an active member in society, may indicate the propensity to employ "that's not my problem" or "it's not my job" as a sort of personal motto.

A liberal arts education is supposed to help students learn to become better citizens, among other things. In the first half of the twentieth century, college campuses used classes in small group discussion to help enculturate the values of democracy and citizenship into a population swelled by immigrants after two world wars. In short, one must learn to take responsibility not only for one's own actions but also for problems that face our social groups, if we wish for those groups to continue to survive.

The three reasons for distrust of involvement in a particular grouping effort are the most focused set of general pitfalls against grouping. There may not be a solution to the issues raised in this final set of exigencies against grouping. If there are objections to who or what is involved in a grouping effort, those exigencies may well outweigh a desire to get involved. If there is a lack of energy remaining for grouping because all resources are used on some other Purgatory Puddle, even a well-intentioned grouping member brings little to the effort. If he or she gets involved, he or she will almost certainly let down one or another set of people who are depending on him or her. If there is no sense of responsibility for the grouping project, the salience of any perceived exigency for grouping is absent. *These exigencies against grouping, once identified, may indicate that a polite "thanks, anyway" is in order and then a shift in focus to recruit grouping partners somewhere else.*

All three of the general sets of exigencies against grouping create problems for those who need to co-construct effective group action. They are not the sole cause of problems for those who wish to group, however. We have already described a plethora of potential pitfalls once grouping begins. In addition to those and to the general exigencies against grouping, we remind you that there are always the forces of inertia to be added to the mix of concerns that must be addressed for any grouping action to be effective. And, there are some specific exigencies against grouping to be added as well. Those final issues add potential problems for an attempt to group.

❖ INERTIA AND SPECIFIC
    EXIGENCIES AGAINST GROUPING

To get a glimpse of the forces of inertia, we provide the following piece of advice. *Never underestimate the attraction some people have for continuing to do things the way they have always been done.* This may be as much based in their sense of tradition as it is in their desire to "not make any waves" or to "stay under the radar." We call such a mindset, "I like my rut." When I am in a rut, I know where I am going and how I am going to get there. My life is stable and comfortable, even if it is stale and contrived. If I am deep enough in my rut, I might not be able to see over the sides of it, which spares me the view of upsetting thoughts and actions outside my everyday experience. My status quo is familiar and comfortable. I like stability because . . . it is stable. "If it ain't broke, don't fix it." "Gimme that old time religion; it's good enough for me." "You can't teach an old dog new tricks." Such are not objections to grouping so much as they are objections to the change that grouping can wreak.

The basic equation that is always involved, if you want to try to motivate a grouping attempt, is that you must employ the rhetorical resources found in an exigency that is perceived as salient for grouping action in the mind of another individual. The rhetorical resources available to you are represented by the four Quadrad metaphors. In short, you must convince those individuals that something is wrong with their status quo (that their rut or Purgatory Puddle is filling with water that will drown them if they do not escape), or that something can be improved in how they go about doing things (there is a better way that provides them a short-cut from one end of their rut to another), or that some golden opportunity awaits them (they must look outside their rut to see the vision of a Promised Land), or that some individual whom they admire and respect is counting on their making a change (a savior commands them to stand up and to walk, in a new direction). The perception of salient action, born from one of those four general bases for grouping activity, is needed to overcome inertia.

Finally, there are specific exigencies against a specific approach being taken toward grouping. These exigencies do not oppose a grouping enterprise, but they result in a constraint to some aspect of that enterprise. These reasons are not the force of inertia or pitfalls from attempts to group. They are not generalized distrust of grouping, distrust of self as grouping, or distrust of any aspect of a particular grouping attempt. In fact, these reasons involve a desire for some sort of grouping action to be undertaken, but they create some sort of constraint on the proposed or current grouping attempt. These specific exigencies against grouping either manifest in opposition to a specific aspect of the grouping enterprise or as support for that enterprise that ends up putting a burden on the grouping that limits its effectiveness. This is the final set of issues that stand in the way of effective group experiences that will be discussed in this book.

Specific exigencies against grouping can manifest from opposition to the grouping as it is proposed or as it is currently unfolding. Figure 9.2 depicts reasons that people, who are not generally opposed to grouping or to activities within a Purgatory Puddle, might still oppose or otherwise hinder an attempt to group. Their reasons might include the following: Though they accept the need for group action in response to Purgatory Puddle exigencies, they may believe the particular change being advocated is wrong or the particular process being employed is wrong or that the particular direction givers who seem to be in charge are an unfortunate choice. They may rue the opportunity

Figure 9.2 Specific Exigencies or Activities That Constrain Specific Grouping Acts

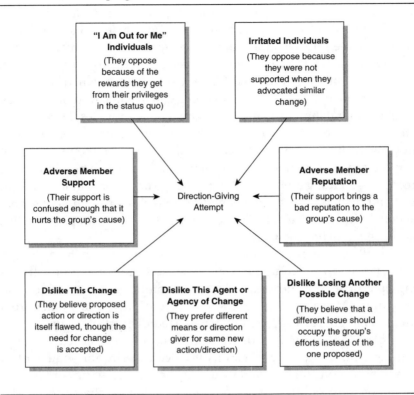

costs from not using the same group resources on another issue in the same Purgatory Puddle instead of on the issue or task that seems to command everyone else's attention. They might benefit from how the current system works and want to protect their turf and privilege from new grouping practices. They may be irritated because they advocated the same sort of change without support for some time before someone else proposed the same change and received support. Perhaps they wanted to be in charge of the effort to make the change. Each of these is a specific exigency for opposing particular aspects of a grouping attempt, not the whole of a grouping attempt.

Specific exigencies against grouping may also manifest as attempts to help the grouping process that turn out to actually be counterproductive. Some people may try to support a grouping action only to find that their help is not wanted or appreciated. Their support may even hurt the cause. For example, they may have a reputation that makes their presence an inducement to others to quit the scene or to withdraw their support of the action. They may misunderstand the grouping action enough that their help, instead of being helpful, actually creates sufficient confusion to confound the attempts and to exhaust the energies and interests of those involved. *The key to addressing these exigencies is to try to be effective in the co-construction of shared meanings that help the grouping process.* This final set of problems, added to the forces of inertia, in addition to the general exigencies against grouping, in addition to the potential pitfalls from grouping, are *finally* a complete list of all the barriers to constructing effective group experiences.

❖ HOW EXIGENCIES AGAINST GROUPING MAY MANIFEST

What can an individual do after being asked to group when she or he does not wish to group? She or he might (a) say no, (b) make an excuse, (c) put off or delay making a decision, or (d) agree to group in spite of his or her objections. It is the last case that has the greatest pitfall potential. What happens if someone groups when he or she perceived an exigency against grouping? Perhaps he or she will find it was a wonderful choice in spite of earlier concerns, but it is also possible that he or she might bring less energy to the effort, might be late or often absent from grouping events, might be easily distracted, might somehow be subversive to the grouping efforts, or might be quickest to bolt the affair at the first signs of trouble. *These are possibilities that the skilled group member must expect and strive to detect.*

How an exigency against grouping manifests is a concern for anyone who attempts to group. For example, the Purgatory Puddle–specific exigency against grouping ("I don't want to work in this particular group") may manifest directly or indirectly. For instance, the desire not to work with someone can manifest in a direct statement—"I just don't trust you enough to work with you"—or it can manifest in changing the subject. The desire not to work on a particular task can manifest as "that project is a waste of time" or as an attempt to appear to be very busy working on something else. This constitutes a sort of defrayed manifestation of the exigency against grouping. What are other group members to think?

To further complicate the matter, a person might not initially be aware that she or he has a reason to not want to group until she or he has carefully thought through the situation. Often, that requires more time than is available before the response to a request for grouping is required. By then, she or he might already be committed to group work. And, of course, an individual might just be blind to her or his reason for opposing grouping. That might appear to eliminate any exigency against grouping but it does not. There are times when general angst or uncertainty motivates a concern without any coherent framing for the concern. Lacking an ability to articulate one's angst or reticence, some people may just comply with a grouping request. In such circumstances, the exigency against grouping remains but the behavior in response to it will likely be indirect.

The simplest cases where an exigency against grouping manifests are those where an individual gives voice to a concern and refuses to group ("I don't want to do anything with anyone else right now; I just want some time to be alone and to do what I want to do"). Of course, even such a direct expression of exigency against grouping can be a problem if the involvement of that one individual is crucial to the grouping enterprise. *All* the other *cases* are more difficult and *should* also *be anticipated by individuals who want to be effective at* instigating *grouping or direction-changing activity.*

❖ EXPECTING, DETECTING, AND CORRECTING THESE PITFALLS: GENERAL ORIENTATIONAL ADVICE

Awareness of the potential for exigencies against grouping allows you to expect and to try to detect such issues when they become an aspect of a particular group experience. Trying to correct these particular pitfalls is a little more difficult because they are oriented outside of the grouping experience. Even the pitfalls in chapters 3 and 4, which include Purgatory Puddle considerations that may predate group inter-action are, nonetheless, encountered only as they manifest in grouping activity. That means that the possibility of using generally effective group communication strategies to avoid or to work your way through them is the best orientation to those potential pitfalls. Consequently, our advice in those earlier chapters centered on broaching the subject of potential pitfalls and finding ways in early meetings to prepare and orient the group for dealing with them.

To a limited extent, you can use a similar approach to exigencies against grouping. Some of the conversational prompts provided in those earlier chapters can help you with the issues raised in this chapter as well, especially the ones (a) that initiate telling stories about effective and poor group experiences, (b) that stimulate discussion of concerns members have about their obligations to the group, and (c) that focus discussion of which project tasks can be accomplished without group interaction. These are among the ways for trying to turn exigencies against grouping into tests of the assumptions and processes to be employed in a grouping attempt in a manner that improves grouping outcomes.

Exigencies against grouping may require additional work as well. We have indicated a number of possibilities throughout the chapter. To those we add the basic idea that you cannot expect to "correct" an exigency against grouping because it has probably been developed by a lifetime of experience. Further, there are probably ego-defensive aspects of general and specific exigencies against grouping, and such attitudes are especially difficult to change, whether or not they are supported by an extensive set of experiences. Consequently, trying to "correct" one of these exigencies is like trying to change a habit that has a particular attraction to it and is a sort of "trademark" characteristic of an individual: as a general rule, "that just ain't gonna happen."

What is done with those who oppose grouping can still have value for a grouping enterprise. *The response to exigencies against grouping should be a blend of creativity and serenity. Creativity should manifest in finding ways to integrate exigencies against grouping into grouping processes so that potential weakness brought on by objections to grouping are turned, somehow, into strengths of the group that managed to harness the creative energy of the objection. Serenity should manifest in accepting the fact that the inclusion of diverse perspectives on grouping will make the task a little bumpier.* The conversational prompt, that people tell their stories of especially poor and successful group experiences, can allow the topic to be broached.

Often the best you can hope for is that those who oppose grouping say so and include their reasons for concern, discuss the issue openly until there is a sense of mutual understanding among group members, discuss the issue of what circumstances do require grouping until grouping members can agree on at least a general set of those circumstances, and attempt to find a way that everyone can make a contribution toward the shared goal. Any or all aspects of such a conversation provide at least a possibility of improving the grouping experience. In the end, though, serenity is accepting the things you cannot change and working with what is left.

Other grouping members have obligations as well. *The rest of the group needs to agree on the importance of such a conversation and to work toward a shared sense of which activities require grouping and which do not. They should not require those who oppose grouping to be unduly happy about times when grouping is required. Further, there needs to be some effort made to protect the interests of those who wish to group as well as those who wish to work alone* whenever that can be done without diminution of group outcomes. *They need to engage the process of trying to help all members become not just contributors to group outcomes but actual resources to the group.* The members who like working in a group need to accept and try to understand the reservations of their colleagues, need to be especially careful not to violate individual autonomy and choice to deviate unless it is essential to grouping success, and need to be alert for opportunities to do some of the tasks (that may not be better done in a group) as individuals. Trying to help their recalcitrant compadres to be useful and valued resources, not in spite of, but because of, their reservations, is the ideal.

❖ CHAPTER SUMMARY

Potential exigencies against grouping can be expected to manifest as constraints to any group experience. Individuals will not succeed in starting a group or in changing the direction of a group if they cannot overcome exigencies against grouping. Different potential outcomes result from grouping motivated or constrained by perceptions of different exigencies for and against grouping. Expecting, detecting, and discussing exigencies against grouping can help you to co-construct them into resources for testing and improving group assumptions, processes, and outcome.

10

Observing Groups Well

❖ ❖ ❖

H ave you ever tried to show a sport or a game to people who do not know how to play it? No matter how smart they are, their ignorance about the game makes it hard for them to understand what is going on or to keep up with the action. They might not even be able to tell who is winning or who is playing well. They would certainly not be able to do an effective job playing the game themselves. Have you ever watched people playing a game or sport that you did not understand? Think back to what that was like, to how much you missed. We want to help you be able to watch and understand the game of grouping. To do that, we introduce you to methods you can use to observe groups well. These allow you to be more intelligent about what you see happening in a group. Some of the methods in this chapter are used by experts who study small groups. You can use them to improve your own group skills. To do so, you must become an effective observer of group interaction: you must learn to observe the group game well.

❖ OBSERVING GROUPS

One way to learn about groups is to watch groups and to try to figure out what is happening in them (be an observer). This is what a consultant does, using the results of their observations to provide advice to grouping members on how they can improve their processes and their outcomes. A second way to learn about groups is to participate in groups as a grouping member and to learn from that experience (be a participant). For the individual with strong group communication skills, the latter involves doing two things at once: trying to assess the quality of grouping as it unfolds and trying to use your understanding of groups to help your group improve (be a participant-observer). Don't trick yourself into believing that you can only learn through personal experiences in groups. You will learn faster if you become a student of all the groups to which you have access. That includes your own groups and any groups that allow you to visit their meetings to observe them. It includes groups you see depicted in movies, on the news, and in literature. Once you understand group communication pitfalls, for example, you should start to notice whenever you observe a group pitfalling.

You must learn how to observe groups well to be able to figure out what is really going on as people group. You must learn how to study groups, how to ask questions about them, and how to get useful answers through careful scrutiny of the data you collect. When you can see and understand what is really going on, you are better equipped *to offer meaningful advice to yourself or others* in the group *about how to behave* differently in order *to make the group better and more successful*. It is a skill to be able to tell what is really going on as people group. It is an additional skill to be able to improve your own grouping communication because of what you have observed in the group. Helping others enhance their own competence in groups is a third valuable skill. All three of these skills are aspects you can mention to a prospective employer. "I understand how groups work." "I have strong group communication skills." "I can help other people in groups be more effective."

Having read chapters 1–9, you are already fairly well equipped for observing groups well and for providing consultations that can help grouping members with their efforts. Your assessment tools include your ability to employ the Set of Potential Group Outcomes for telling the differences among failed, adequate, and successful groups. That includes being able to tell whether intentional choices were appropriately made according to the Good-Enough-Group argument. Your understanding of the Breakdown-Conducive Group Framework and of potential group pitfalls can be used to determine whether grouping members successfully expect, detect, and correct the pitfalls facing their group. The Framework for Grouping and Group Direction can be used to help describe what you observe in terms that capture the dramatic action involved in creating or changing group direction. In this chapter, we use the Quadrad terms to organize several additional tools that can help you observe groups well.

Observing a group well involves using tools that give insight into the group's situation, processes, and outcomes. All groups are hurt if their members fail to consider whether the group's processes are serving the group's purposes by helping to accomplish the group's desired outcomes. For the most part, such efforts involve analysis of the group's Purgatory Puddle and analysis of the group's The Way/Process. Consequently, all of the new tools we provide for you in this chapter are focused on one of those two Quadrad bases, though we also remind you of the resources available elsewhere in this book for observing the quality of a group's Vision/Outcome and Savior Complex. In short, any group can be helped if its members focus some of their attention on improving the processes by which the group orients itself, does its work, clarifies its goals, and assesses whether it is making sufficient progress to attain desired outcomes. Your ability to observe groups well enhances your capacities as a group member and also as a consultant to others as they struggle with their own groups.

❖ IMPROVING OBSERVATIONAL FOCUS AND QUALITY

To observe groups well, you must make choices regarding the focus and quality of your observations. You cannot do an effective job observing everything that is happening at any one time during grouping because it involves such a complicated set of interacting dynamics and processes. How do you limit your focus in order to make your observations high quality and worthwhile? Your own experience in groups can provide you with some insight about what is important enough to focus on. This book also provides a plethora of possibilities. For example, potential pitfalls to grouping and potential exigencies against grouping can be meaningful focal points for your observations. The most important factor in narrowing your focus is to figure out what matters to you. Why are you observing a group? The answer to that question should help you determine what you should be looking for.

Keyton (2003) argues that a group researcher must make a number of choices that help to narrow the focus for observation. She suggests four basic questions that we modify into two prompts for you to consider. First, you should ask, "Who are the members of the group and who are the rest of the group's stakeholders (individuals who will be affected by or are otherwise interested in group processes and outcomes)?" This seemingly simple question may be hard to answer. As the bona fide group perspective suggests, the identification of group boundaries can be a difficult task. For some groups, members may operate with boundaries that are fluid, allowing input from "nonmembers," or permitting individuals outside the group full access to grouping resources, materials, and assets. Other groups establish more protective boundaries that limit member exposure to outside agents: ultimately influencing the flow of information and access to resources outside the group. How groups negotiate their boundaries and communicate with their stakeholders are key dynamics in clarifying group membership and appropriate group processes. To observe a group well, you probably must focus part of your attention on who is involved in the group.

Second, you should ask, "What am I looking for as I observe this group?" Developing your answer to this question involves deciding the level of activity you need to focus on: the whole of the grouping enterprise as they interact with each other or some subset of the group, such as the activities of one or more individuals in the group. Are you interested in better understanding how group members work interdependently or are you more concerned about the contributions of individual group members? For instance, if you are interested in the group's sense of direction, you might look at the entire group of interacting individuals as they try to discuss their goals. If you are interested in figuring out how individual group members can improve their skills, you might focus your observations on measuring individual member activity. Making an appropriate choice among available observational tools requires you to first decide what it is you are looking for when you observe a group.

The answer to the second question also involves determining what your *unit of analysis* should be. The unit of analysis becomes the focus of your observations. It is the behavior you study or count or investigate. For example, you have a choice as to whether you will assess specific words or look at some aspect of nonverbal behavior during group interaction. A focus on specific words might be appropriate if you think one member frames everything from his own perspective. So you decide to count the number of times he uses a singular pronoun (*I*) instead of a plural or group-based reference (*we*). Those pronouns are your unit of analysis. Nonverbal behaviors can indicate relationships, power, and orientation to the group. You might study such dynamics by observing aspects of the group's use of time; use of space; the body movements of individuals as they interact; their facial expressions and eye contact; use of touch; and vocal cues such as volume, pitch, pace, and so forth. In short, your unit of analysis should provide a focus on the heart of what you are looking for.

Observations can focus on the smallest detail or the broadest of themes. From use of individual words, to entire phases in the decision-making process, the unit of analysis "turns up" the dramatic action of interest to you. Your unit of analysis could be attempts to maximize the use of individual members' resources by the group's direction givers; group tendencies when co-constructing conflict; the number of times discussion of ideas or themes recurs; the effects from use of a creativity-enhancing technique by the group; whether group members ever express disagreement or dissatisfaction with ideas before the group decides to accept them; the presence or absence of warrants and supporting evidence when group members argue for a position; what memorable messages and critical incidents are reported by grouping members after they are enculturated into the group; or the efficiency (in terms of time spent for each important point raised) of oral reports made by members to the group. The list is as endless as the possible questions you might have about a group. Your observational focus should be indicated by the questions you have about the group. In short, to observe groups well, you need to *narrow the focus of your observations so that you gather data that are useful for answering the questions you have about the group.*

The quality of your observations must begin with observational focus, but it is determined by how you proceed to gather and to analyze your data. As a general rule, you should cast as wide a net as possible when you look for data, once the focus for your observations is clear to you. Though you must narrow the focus of your observations, whenever possible, collect your information and observations from multiple sources before you draw any conclusions about your group or one of its members. *Triangulation* involves collecting various forms of data at various points in time using various research methods in order to develop more valid and reliable findings. For example, if you are interested in how well a group manager provides feedback to new group members, you should observe more than one interaction between the manager and a new member. You should also observe interactions with more than one new group member. You should also interview more than one of the new members after they have received their feedback. If possible, you might involve a colleague to also observe these interactions and to conduct her or his own interviews. Such activities provide triangulation, looking at a single issue from a variety of different perspectives in a variety of different ways. Having multiple sources of data and at least two interpretations of the data to compare increases the potential for better critical thinking. When possible, *triangulate your observations of any group before you draw final conclusions about what is going on and why things are going well or poorly. Until and unless triangulation is possible, do not draw any final conclusions.*

How do you proceed once you have figured out what to focus on? There are a variety of tools available for your use. For purposes of simplicity, we refer to all of these tools as ways to *observe a group well,* meaning that each can help provide insight into a group. All the tools for observing groups involve learning from groups, though not all of them involve actually watching a group in real time. Just as you need a variety of tools to cook, garden, or make mechanical repairs, you need the flexibility that having several basic observational tools can provide for understanding groups. Knowing about these tools helps you figure out ways to get answers to your questions about what is going well or poorly in a group.

❖ OBSERVING THE PURGATORY PUDDLE

We encourage you to consider beginning your observations with the group's Purgatory Puddle: specifically, with how well the group analyzes and frames its Purgatory Puddle. The Purgatory Puddle represents the sense of exigency and the rhetorical resources for beginning to group or for beginning to change the direction of the group: it is the bias toward dramatic action found in aspects of the group's scene. Analysis of their Purgatory Puddle gives a group the opportunity to consider and to co-construct frames for the nature of the *task* that faces them, the *personnel* resources they can bring to bear on the task, and the *supragroup* issues that will affect their work. Throughout the life of a group, their discussion and understanding of their evolving Purgatory

Puddle is an important consideration in effective grouping. Consequently, until the exigency for grouping, which spawns a Purgatory Puddle, is dissipated by completion of the group's project, ongoing analysis, by the group, of their Purgatory Puddle remains an issue for the grouping members and for the observer.

As an observer, you should ask yourself, "How well does this group of people orient themselves to their Purgatory Puddle?" When people experience an exigency to group, they need to try to understand their situation, including the other people and task involved. You can assess their orientational attempts by examining whether they work through the following issues. A group can be effective without dealing with all of these issues right at the start of their first meeting. They may need some time before getting to each of them, and each issue may be more important in some groups than in others. However, all of these issues will probably need to be addressed at some point, early in the life of the group, in order to have the most positive impact on grouping. Consequently, you will find these issues similar to some of the conversational prompts we provided throughout this book as advice for improving your own grouping efforts. They are also listed in short form in Table 4.8 (Orienting the Group in the first step, Analyze the Purgatory Puddle). As an observer, you need to note when a group pays attention to any or all of these issues. As a grouping participant or participant-observer, *try to get your own group to consider the following orientational issues.*

Defining and Discussing Key Terms

Even when a group discusses and develops shared goals, misunderstandings can still be obscured by the use of common words for which grouping members have different meanings. The co-construction of shared meaning is less likely without talking explicitly about the definition each member is using for key words in their "common group goal." The same is true for key words used over and over by grouping members to describe their task or the problem their group faces. Each recurring term may have several definitions and connotations. Grouping members need to talk explicitly about which definition they have in mind when they use the word. Asking for definitions of key terms is important, especially if the group is given a formal charge from someone outside the group. *Do group members explicitly discuss definitions of key terms? Do group members check how experts on the subject and how key stakeholders would define the problem, task, or charge?*

Analyzing the Group's Task, Problem, or Charge

Some grouping evolves out of a sense of exigency that a problem needs to be addressed or that a task needs to be done. Other groups are given a charge to act. A *charge* given a group is the job someone with authority tells the group to focus upon: their assigned task, issue, or problem. In some cases, a formal audit of the situation, conducted by experts external to the group, may be necessary to get a clear enough sense of the status quo and of the problem. In other cases, the group may just need to spend its own time trying to analyze the nature of their scene and of the problem they face. In all cases, grouping members need to spend time gathering information about and analyzing the issues they must address. *Do group members carefully gather information, including from outside sources, regarding the grouping situation and problem? Do they then analyze the nature of the problem they face, using the information collected?*

Identifying and Discussing Stakeholders

A stockholder is someone who owns part of a company. A *stakeholder* is anyone affected by that company including the stockholders, government agencies that regulate the company, the neighboring community dependent on the company for its prosperity, the employees and management of the company, and so forth. All group members are stakeholders but so are other people affected by the group. For example, if you are assigned to do a group project at work, the stakeholders include the other groups that must interface with yours, your supervisor, the family members who may be affected by group members working late or by the bonus grouping members receive for outstanding contribution, and so forth. Creative discussion that attempts to identify and understand potential stakeholders can be a sign that grouping members appreciate the nature of their bona fide group, their Purgatory Puddle, and especially their supragroup. *Do group members spend time trying to identify and discuss others who may be affected by their efforts, activities, processes, or outcomes?*

Identifying and Discussing Exigencies For and Against Grouping

The effort to identify grouping exigencies involves the reasons people perceive for their grouping actions. This effort should not be limited to those exigencies perceived by grouping members. In chapter 2, we describe the nature of grouping exigencies, and in chapter 9, we describe the bias some individuals carry against working in a group. It is useful for grouping members to discuss their perception of the exigencies that resulted in their grouping and also if they have any general or specific bias against their work in the group, which may constrain grouping activity. The group also needs to attempt to identify exigencies various stakeholders perceive regarding their grouping processes and goals. In particular, if there is a supervisor who has assigned the work to the group, what exigencies was he or she responding to and how well did the group charge reflect his or her exigencies for making the charge? *Does the group discuss why we are interested in this project? Which exigencies support and which constrain our desire to group? Why do you suppose our stakeholders might want us to do this? What is the boss trying to accomplish by giving us this assignment?*

Identifying Limitations on the Group and Grouping Resources

Closely related to an understanding of the exigencies for and against grouping is an exploration of the resources and nonexigency-based constraints and contingencies that can affect group work. What resource needs can be expected to slow grouping members down? What contingencies could arise that might impede the grouping enterprise? Where can the group turn for necessary support? *Does the group try to identify and to understand the limitations and resources that could affect their grouping effort?*

Once people begin to group, they often make a mistake by tending to focus most of their attention on the Vision/Outcome, without first spending time discussing the nature of their Purgatory Puddle and The Way/Process. Any discussion that helps understand and frame Purgatory Puddle issues can help group members orient themselves and their future efforts. As an observer or participant-observer, it is important to note any dearth or shortage of such discussion and, if so, to try to get the group to increase their efforts at such analysis. As grouping unfolds and contingencies arise, healthy groups continue to analyze their evolving Purgatory Puddle and to then try to adjust their The Way/Process accordingly. Analysis of the group's Purgatory Puddle should enhance efforts to refine their The Way/Process and Vision/Outcome. It allows them to figure out where they already are, which is important to know before shifting to focus on where they are going to go and on how they are going to get there.

Discussing and Setting Group Goals

Grouping members may have different goals for their seemingly-joint enterprise. Grouping members may disagree about what is important for the group to focus on. They may disagree about appropriate processes or about appropriate levels of individual participation in the process. Some members may be very concerned about doing well, having an orientation for high levels of effort and achievement that others do not share. Such potential problems can be addressed by discussing issues such as, "What is going on here?" and "How should we proceed?" and "What do we hope to accomplish?" Unfortunately, many groups fail to have such orienting conversations, relying on an assumption of shared goals. *Does the group discuss process and outcomes goals? Are they explicit about the meaning of each goal and of what it will take from each of them to accomplish that goal? Do they discuss why they have such goals and to what extent they share their goals?*

❖ OBSERVING THE WAY/PROCESS

The Way/Process represents the sense of exigency and the rhetorical resources for bringing a sense of order or coordination to grouping activities. The Way/Process represents the readiness to respond to grouping exigencies through dramatic action that orients the group and helps to organize its means for proceeding: its agency. Explicit analysis of their group's The Way/Process gives the group the opportunity to be intentional in its efforts to expect, detect, and correct the pitfalls they may face as well as its means for co-constructing its Vision/Outcome. We encourage you to pay particular attention to whether the group analyzes and makes explicit attempts to improve its The Way/Process. In any case, the group's activities will include ample evidence of their co-constructed The Way/Process, and your observations probably need to include careful consideration of those manifestations. Regardless of whether they pass the intentionality test, you can observe The Way/Process in one or more of the following recurring aspects of group activity:

- *grouping techniques* (grouping communication, meetings, and procedures such as brainstorming or use of a decision-making matrix such as Orienting the Group, see table 4.8);
- *grouping tendencies* (norms, roles, and communication network);

- *process prizes* desired from grouping (critical and creative thinking, and group member acceptance of grouping processes and outcomes);
- *grouping concomitants* (confusion, conformity, conflict, and group consciousness—climate, cohesion, and culture).

We describe only a very few of the many observational tools available to collect data on these phenomena. You may decide to develop your own tools in addition or to search out any of a number of other resources available for observing such The Way/Process dynamics.

Grouping Techniques

If you are interested in how a group goes about its work, the techniques its various members advocate and the ones the group eventually employs are of primary concern. The most basic grouping techniques are to *communicate,* to begin to talk about perceived exigencies for grouping; to call *meetings,* to provide an open opportunity for all to engage in discussion of key points; and to develop *procedures* for use in those meetings that can enhance grouping efforts. Several tools for analyzing communication as a grouping technique are provided throughout this chapter (e.g., see the IPA, Table 10.2 below). Tools for assessing the quality of meetings can be developed by you once your group has talked about what it expects, for the use of its members' time, from an effective meeting (e.g., should there be an agenda, what is the time frame for discussion, how will member contributions be balanced). Additional procedures require specialized tools for observation. If you research a particular group dynamic, you will find that others have probably already developed a tool for observing it.

You might also decide to develop your own tool, so that you can put its focus on units of analysis that most concern you. You can begin to do so by modifying an extant instrument (even one found in this chapter). You may want a tool that organizes what you see happening as you watch a group or one that allows you to interview group members. Table 10.1 provides a basic format to one such tool, called a Likert scale. You can insert whatever prompts get at the issue that concerns you and then use the tool to gather information from grouping members about their experiences.

Additional questions or focal points for your observations of techniques can include the following: What, if any, problem-solving

Table 10.1   Partial Likert Scale Instrument

This feedback instrument has been designed to assess our group's techniques. After reading each statement, please circle your response using the following scale:

1 = *Strongly Disagree*   2 = *Disagree*   3 = *Neutral*   4 = *Agree*   5 = *Strongly Agree*

1. A sufficient amount of information was collected before framing any solution.	1	2	3	4	5
2. Group members did not take the time to get to know each other.	1	2	3	4	5
3. The group discussed the merits of the problem-solving techniques we used.	1	2	3	4	5
4. We took the time to discuss the goals we had for the quality of our work.	1	2	3	4	5
5. Consensus was not reached because we just wanted to get done and quit early.	1	2	3	4	5
6. I felt my contributions were not given much consideration by the group.	1	2	3	4	5

---

process is in evidence? How are grouping concomitants and process prizes affected by use of the group's procedures (e.g., encouraged, punished)? Are democratic deliberation processes in evidence? Are levels of consensus stimulated through use of group procedures? The number of possible procedures a group might employ, and that you might have to observe, can be as high as the number of pitfalls there are to grouping processes, because it is those pitfalls that such techniques were invariably developed to address.

In sum, your observations about grouping techniques can be adapted according to which aspects of group behavior are of greatest concern to you. In general, you might ask, *Do grouping members make any formal attempt to start a process to help move their group along or do they just begin to work on their task? Does the group discuss what process, procedures, or techniques to use and why?* Once The Way/Process techniques are identified by the group or by your observations, *are there any signs that such techniques are working well or poorly,* in particular *whether or not they appear to be serving group needs* and goals. *Does the group ever discuss how well its processes are working for it?*

Symbiotically related to any observation of grouping *technique* is consideration of grouping *tendencies* (norms, roles, and communication networks), and grouping *concomitants* (confusion, conformity, conflict, consciousness).

Norms in Groups

In addition to grouping techniques, there are several grouping tendencies you can observe in any grouping enterprise. The first of these grouping tendencies is the development of group norms; every successful group establishes, maintains, and recreates norms. Norms are the typical ways grouping members develop for behaving and for interacting with each other. In your observation of any group, you need to ask, "How do they typically tend to behave?" and "Which of their norms are productive and which need modification?"

Structuration theory (Poole, 2003) suggests that identifying group norms can be a challenging assignment, but a number of the methods identified in this chapter can serve as valuable tools to help you. For instance, an Interaction Process Analysis (IPA) of your group (see description and Table 10.2 below) may signal group norms for dealing with conflict. If each utterance categorized as a disagreement is followed by a series of dramatizing or solidarity statements, you may begin to see a norm of avoiding conflict. Although this may appear to you to be good, it could play out in a detrimental manner if the time comes to encourage critical thinking and members are not willing to disagree with each other. A norm of "taking flight" from conflict can short-circuit talk before members fully understand their differences and begin to address them in a productive manner.

Another approach you can take to answer questions about group norms is to use a more open-ended approach. Open-ended interviews or questionnaires let participants use their own words and experiences when answering a question and "thereby, allow people to respond with what is on their mind" (Frey, Botan, & Kreps, 2000, p. 100). Open-ended questions can be direct: "What norms have been established by the group?" They can be indirect: "How well do you think our current group reflects the right way for doing things?" Grouping members are given more latitude in the way they respond to such questions, potentially producing more in-depth insight for you.

Roles in Groups

A second grouping tendency is for members to co-construct specialized roles for each other to play as they group. Key direction-giving types (chapters 2and 7) and roles (chapter 5) have already been discussed, but there are also a number of additional role specializations that may manifest. You can get at these roles by asking, "What kinds of

Table 10.2   The Interaction Process Analysis (IPA)

Behavior	IPA Categories	Definition
Socioemotional: Climate	Shows Solidarity (Seems Friendly)	Positive thought toward member
	Dramatizes (Tension Release)	Group/member anxiety reduction
	Agrees	Approval of member idea
Task: Attempted Answers	Gives Suggestions	Direction for engaging task
	Gives Opinions	Provide task-relevant belief/value
	Gives Orientation/ Information	Report factual observation/ experience
Task: Questions	Asks for Orientation/ Information	Appeal for observations/experiences
	Asks for Opinions	Request task-relevant belief/value
	Asks for Suggestions	Seek direction for task completion
Socioemotional: Relational	Disagrees	Rejection of member comment
	Shows Tension	Signify group/member anxiety
	Shows Antagonism (Seems Unfriendly)	Negative thought toward member

Note: Terms within parenthesis represent IPA category name prior to 1970.

communication are evident in the group and what role function do they serve for the group?" Robert Bales (1950, 1970) developed the IPA, which can be used to categorize any grouping communications and to understand the roles and functions they serve (see Table 10.2).

The IPA can help you identify which of the task or relational functions are being performed and by whom in the group. Patton and Downs (2003) suggest that you can assess the level of participation across the group and compare that with your own contributions. You can tabulate the relative frequency of each type of communication for each grouping member. That could provide you with a sense of who is attempting to emerge as a key direction giver (i.e., high amounts of information, opinion, or suggestion giving) or who serves as a harmonizer for the group (i.e., shows solidarity, dramatizes). Bales and Hare (1965) examine 24 studies that used the IPA as a coding procedure and produce a set of relative percentages for each of the 12 task and socioemotional categories (see Table 10.3). You can tabulate a percentage of the total for each of the 12 categories in your own group. Dividing the number of comments reflecting "shows solidarity" by the total number of comments allows you to compare your group's interaction with

Table 10.3   Observed Group Participation for IPA Categories

Behavior	Category	Percent	Estimated Norms
Socioemotional:	Shows Solidarity	3.5	2.6–4.8
Climate	Dramatizes	7.0	5.7–7.4
	Agrees	18.5	8.0–13.6
Task: Attempted	Gives Suggestions	3.8	3.0–7.0
Answers	Gives Opinions	24.5	15.0–22.7
	Gives Orientation/Information	8.3	20.7–31.2
Task: Questions	Asks for Orientation/Information	10.3	4.0–7.2
	Asks for Opinions	12.5	2.0–3.9
	Asks for Suggestions	2.3	0.6–1.4
Socioemotional:	Disagrees	1.0	3.1–5.3
Relational	Shows Tension	7.8	3.4–6.0
	Shows Antagonism	0.5	2.4–4.4
	Total	**100.0**	

estimated norms established for typical groups. Doing so may provide you with a sense of what is occurring in your group. A high percentage of time spent on climate-building behaviors may suggest that your group is having a difficult time focusing on its task.

Brilhart, Galanes, and Adams (2001) present a modified version of the IPA that is more complicated for coding grouping communications but that may be more helpful in sorting out the particular role functions served by that same communication. Their work informs our description of potential communicative attempts and the roles they play in the group (see Table 10.4). If you develop a coding sheet with each of the functions listed on the left-hand side of the page and each group member listed on the top, you can compile a running tally of the particular type of messages that interest you.

As you work through these role functions, keep in mind that communication is a co-construction of grouping activities and meanings. One communicative utterance may serve multiple role functions, and roles themselves are not discrete (e.g., serving a task function might also serve a relational or personal function, serving one task function might also serve another task function).

Network Analysis and Sociometric Indices

As grouping members communicate, another grouping tendency is for them to develop a communication network or pattern. One of the most established techniques for assessing this information is *network*

Table 10.4   The Modified IPA Classifications

Group Function	Definition
Task	
Orienting Efforts	Attempt to get group to discuss or frame its Purgatory Puddle.
Suggesting Procedure	Describe or attempt to employ technique or process for group work.
Initiating Ideas	Offer solutions or approaches for addressing group charge or task.
Coordinating	Organize and establish connection between ideas and suggestions.
Clarifying or Summarizing	Explain, recap, or restate perspective of grouping member or of group.
Information- or Opinion-Seeking	Search for clarification or ask for ideas or suggestions.
Information- or Opinion-Giving	Apply own experience to task; provide facts or view to group.
Elaborating	Develop suggestions or provide justification for ideas of others.
Evaluating	Provide critical reflection on ideas.
Consensus Testing	Measure the level of agreement across members in the group.
Recording	Take note of ideas, record decisions, or provide group memory.
Relational	
Establishing Roles	Attempt to provide or receive direction for the group.
Establishing Norms	Articulate standards for group; apply standards to group process.
Gatekeeping	Foster participation of others; open the channels for communication.
Supporting	Applaud contributions of others or offer acceptance for viewpoints.
Harmonizing	Attempt to resolve disagreements or encourage review of differences.
Tension-Relieving	Efforts to reduce conflict or discord between others.
Dramatizing	Shift of group from here-and-now to there-and-then.
Showing Solidarity	Attempts to build coalition across group members.

analysis. This method is used to discover structure or hierarchy that exists within a system by examining the connections between individuals in that system. One conducts a network analysis by observing members of the system as they interact to create a blueprint of the network (see Figure 10.1). When looking at the figure, envision a group discussion with five members. The arrows pointing to each of the members represent comments received from another member of the group. The dashes on each of the arrows signify the number of times interaction occurred between each of the members. For instance, the first time that Clee talks to Thane, you place an arrow to represent the interaction; when subsequent exchanges occur, you mark a dash on the arrow. This network analysis begins to show the interaction patterns for a group discussion. You may be able to discern who is a key direction giver for the group by determining who has the most comments directed to them by the other group members. You can also begin to determine the level of participation for group members and whose comments are not sought by the group. For example, you can see that Cher made several attempts to talk to group members, but none of them replied. This also demonstrates a limit to network analysis, the absence of context. Cher may have missed the meeting prior to this discussion without informing her grouping colleagues. Perhaps they want to reduce her role in the group by ignoring her. Without context we cannot know. Getting a sense of context is one of the justifications for always trying to triangulate.

Figure 10.1   Network Analysis for Group Discussion

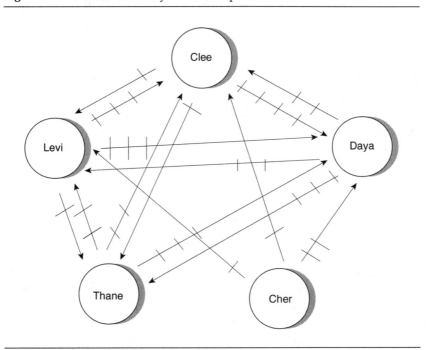

Sociometry is useful for assessing other meanings grouping members co-construct about themselves and their relationships (Moreno, 1953). Sociometry asks, "Whom in the group would you like to work with the most?" and "Whom do you like the least?" Using member responses to these questions allows you to develop a diagram reflecting the relationships among group members. Those members chosen frequently as "liked," are classified as *stars,* to signify their popularity in the group, and Moreno (1960) calls those chosen most infrequently, *isolates.* Group members who list each other as their first choices are called *pairs* and subgroups or cliques in a group are called *chains.* A sociometric index of your group could provide you with a view about The Way/Process and also the Savior Complex because you can get an idea of who has status in your group (who is the star; who is rejected as a direction giver), who displays deviant group behavior (refuses to conform or is involved in pernicious conflict), and the integration and orientation of grouping members (who is involved in a coalition). Grouping concomitants such as conflict, conformity, and group culture may also be evident in such sociometric ratings.

Group Consciousness: Climate, Cohesion, and Culture

Any group outcome depends on a variety of issues, dynamics, and circumstances. Some of the most complex outcomes manifest as a part of the grouping concomitant we call consciousness, which involves a sense of group climate, cohesion, and culture—all are interwoven with relational and individual functional outcomes. A positive sense of "group-ness" or of group consciousness can help grouping members develop synergy and attain results they never thought possible when they first perceived a sense of exigency to group. A method very useful for assessing and understanding the culture, cohesiveness, and climate of a group is fantasy theme analysis, which is part of symbolic convergence theory (Bormann, 1972, 1982, 1996).

Bormann extends the *dramatizing* category in Bales' IPA to focus our attention on grouping interactions that create recurring patterns or themes. *Dramatizing messages* manifest in a variety of *symbolic cues* ranging from something as simple as a series of words (i.e., puns, play on words, double entendre, figure of speech) or as complex as a narrative or story or rhetorical vision constructed by the entire group (i.e., parable, allegory, fable, etc.). Both Bales and Bormann call dramatizing messages *fantasy* and the sharing of such messages in a group *fantasy chains*. Fantasy is a "there-and-then" frame of focus for the group rather than the "here-and-now" focus in play when a group is at work directly on doing its task. Bormann argues that a group co-constructs its sense of itself through symbolic convergence to a few key symbols, stories, or inside references and jokes grouping members use to describe their group. They create this symbolic convergence by sharing group fantasies and recurring symbolic cues about those fantasies and about their group.

Have you ever had an experience where your group is working toward the completion of a task when one grouping member, let's call him Samson, begins to complain about how much time work is taking away from his other passions? Other passions do not involve the here-and-now task for the group but, as alternate Purgatory Puddles, they can still command the attention of grouping members. As a group, you have two choices regarding Samson's dramatizing message. You can reject it by politely listening and then moving back to a focus on the task at hand, thus ending the fantasy. You might instead accept his "invitation" to fantasize by expressing your own complaints after his. If others accept the invitation to dramatize, they would cocreate and coexperience a *fantasy chain*. These can be "fun," energy generating, and bonding experiences for grouping members who share a basic excitement from such a symbolic meeting of the minds. Members can feel closer as a result even if the manifest content of their complaint fantasy is that they are all being hurt by the requirements of their job.

The content of a fantasy chain is a *fantasy theme*. When grouping members engage in the construction of a fantasy theme, they portray people and events in the there-and-then. If a group feels that blame should be placed on the boss, she or he would be cast as a villain, while group members are portrayed in a positive light (i.e., as heroes or victims). *Fantasy types* may begin to be evident across a number of group meetings as stock scenarios with stock characters and situations are repeated again and again by the group. Fantasy types are a cluster of fantasy themes that help "shape" and "feed" the group's consciousness. Bormann (2003) says, "fantasy themes always put a spin on the facts, which are thus slanted, ordered, and interpreted" (p. 43). This symbolic convergence affects grouping members and helps effect group consciousness. Reflect upon your own experiences sharing fantasy with other group members during and after the completion of group work. Who receives praise for the group's accomplishments?

Who receives blame when the group struggles or fails? How does a group's climate or culture influence the way it dramatizes?

Thinking about and attempting to answer the questions provided in this section can help you to get a much better sense of what is really going on in a group. We provide more explanation for how to observe the two most fundamental bases for grouping, the Purgatory Puddle and The Way/Process, because that material is orientational for how you should observe a group well. To a large extent, you are now also prepared to help frame and conduct your observations of the final two Quadrad bases discussed below. We are much briefer in our description of the final two bases. That is not because they are unimportant, but rather because you should be getting the drift by now of the fundamental orientation you need to take and tools you can use.

❖ OBSERVING THE VISION/OUTCOME
AND THE SAVIOR COMPLEX

Because the most important observational processes for understanding and improving grouping activities and outcomes are found in tools that focus on Purgatory Puddle and The Way/Process, we spent the bulk of this chapter outlining a few of those options. In chapter 7, we provided enough detail about Vision/Outcome and Savior Complex exigencies, rhetorical strategies, and pitfalls to help guide your efforts to observe how well a group is co-constructing its Vision/Outcome and Savior Complex. Though these two are very important aspects of the group experience, the bulk of any effort to successfully co-construct them or to improve the group's ongoing co-constructions of them will necessarily manifest in Purgatory Puddle analysis and The/Way Process considerations.

Vision/Outcome represents the final products and purposes of the group. Evolving out of the task dimension of the Purgatory Puddle, Vision/Outcome exigencies are a bias toward action that serves as a magnet toward co-constructing and moving the group toward a Vision/Outcome. Vision/Outcome represents a readiness to respond to such exigencies with rhetorical efforts to attain the Promised Land, which must be attractive (promise) and substantive (land) enough to merit the group's efforts and to stand the test of time. The observational focal points are on: (a) whether the group's Vision/Outcome has sufficient salience to command group attention and effort; (b) whether the group's Vision/Outcome solves the problem or addresses the task or charge identified in the Purgatory Puddle; (c) whether the group outcome matches the vision the group has co-constructed of and for itself; (d) whether unfortunate disadvantages accompany the group's final fruits; (e) whether the group's vision was distorted by how they conceive of vision or because of exigencies that competed with the ideal group design; and (f) whether the group finishes its activities, assures that adequate feedback will be received regarding its fruits, and terminates itself properly. *Does the group test its outcomes to calculate how much of the problem they solve and how much of a disadvantage they accrue? Are procedures in place for gathering feedback on the performance of the group and its outcomes? Does the group distort its goals or highest purposes because of competing exigencies? Has the group worked to tie up any loose ends? What type of outcome (I, II, III, IV) does the group manage to finally accomplish?*

The Savior Complex involves how grouping members attempt to give and to receive direction while grouping. It represents the trust grouping members place in each other: in their agents of action. Beginning as the personnel dimension in the Purgatory Puddle, Savior Complex evolves throughout grouping processes as a complex amalgam of (a) the various conceptions grouping members have about the nature and importance of direction-giving and -receiving roles; (b) the processes of emergence or selection of direction givers; (c) the many choices made by direction givers including the type of direction giver they attempt to be (doer, follower, guide, manager, leader), their choice of style (autocratic, selling, consultative, democratic, laissez-faire), their choice of power base (referent, expert, legitimate, information, reward, coercive), and their orientation toward an appropriate balance of group functions (task, relational, individual); and (d) how groups prepare themselves for transition between direction givers. Savior Complex observations focus on how members negotiate the dance involved in deciding who will give and receive direction in their group.

These suggest a multitude of observational foci for your consideration of the Savior Complex. For example, *did the group find a way to co-construct acceptable direction-giving and -receiving roles? Do direction givers adapt to the various grouping exigencies perceived by group membership with appropriate choices in style, direction-giving type, use of power, and balance of grouping functions? What efforts are made to involve grouping members in learning to appreciate and understand the roles played by their colleagues? What opportunities are evident for grouping members to develop as potential future direction givers?*

❖ CHAPTER SUMMARY

The basic advice in this chapter is that you should strive to observe groups well. That can enhance your grouping skills, perhaps more than anything else. Use the questions you have to help determine what aspect of grouping is most important to you. Remember to narrow your focus and to try to triangulate your observations. Gather empirical observations over time. Do not rely entirely on anecdotes told by grouping members, though those can be interesting and useful. Record data regularly and objectively, and refer to those data as you draw and apply your conclusions. Respect the privacy of grouping members where possible and appropriate. Provide personal performance feedback privately when possible to help protect the egos of others and to help them make adjustments without getting too defensive. Improvise and stay alert! All group work is accomplished by grouping members who are actors in a grouping drama. As a skilled student of effective group processes, you understand how learning to observe groups well can enhance your own skills and your efforts to help others.

Notes

1. We modify the basic definition of a group that Hirokawa, Cathcart, Samovar, and Henman (2003) propose, which indicates four of the basic elements of our definition (purpose, boundaries, interdependence, communication), though we add *co-construction* and the three functions served by groups to their definition.

2. Such a metaphor is potent to the extent that recurring forms of dramatic action are represented. Nuanced interpretation should improve the metaphors "goodness-of fit" across situations. A representative metaphor is flexible: evocative both of key aspects and of varying interpretations of dramatic action. Flexibility provides greater usefulness to such terms. Their nuanced meanings enhance efforts to describe or to "anticipate" (Burke, 1945, p. xxiii) the dramatic action within the context represented (described and explained) by the metaphor.

3. Gastil includes voting as part of his definition of democratic groups, and, for very large groups, we agree. However, a "simple expression of preference" does not necessarily mean that "voting" should be used to end efforts to attain consensus; rather, it should mean that all must express their preference in discussions, and, that when a perception of achieved consensus is sensed by grouping members, it should be tested by "a simple expression of preference" to see if all really have come to a state of thinking in which they actually do all agree.

4. How well a group serves its relational and individual functions is determined by outcomes that are addressed elsewhere as aspects of grouping processes such as the co-construction of roles in chapter 5; the conformity, conflict, and consciousness concomitants of grouping (especially climate and cohesion) in chapter 6; the Savior Complex later in chapter 7; and observing communication networks, sociometrics of grouping dynamics, and the symbolic convergence in grouping culture in chapter 10 (also see the discussion of group culture in chapter 6).

5. An extended explanation of this warning may be helpful. Do not be misled by an appearance of continuity or sequence from one type of outcome in the Set of Potential Group Outcomes to the next. The outcomes in the set are based in important grouping dynamics, but they are not chronological or causal or linear in relationship to each other. The relationships among the

outcomes are limited. The only relationships are as follows. First, and most significant, every outcome dynamic has both good and bad potentialities. Second, an intentional and appropriate use of satisficing activity rather than its mindless and inappropriate use is depicted when moving from the Bad Satisficed Group to the Good Satisficed Group. Third, when moving from the Good Satisficed Group to the Optimized Group, a greater extreme in effort and quality is present. Fourth, lower quality is present when moving from the Bad Satisficed Group to the Failed Group. Beyond those relationships, the reference points in the set are only related by the topic: types of group outcomes. Groups do *not* necessarily proceed from Type I to Type II to Type III, then to Type IV outcomes in any consistent or predictable manner. Indeed, Type IV outcomes are possible from any grouping activity, regardless of other outcomes that might also manifest (e.g., a lifelong friendship could spring from a Bad Synergized Group). Type III outcomes are possible without Type II outcomes.

References

Allen, M., Mabry, E. A., & Halone, K. K. (2004). *Social loafing as a group commu-nication phenomenon: A meta-analysis and causal model of task and relational dynamics.* Paper presented at the annual meeting for the National Com-munication Association, Chicago, IL.

Bales, R. F. (1950). *Interaction process analysis: A method for the study of small groups.* Cambridge, MA: Addison-Wesley.

Bales, R. F. (1970). *Interaction process analysis: A method for the study of small groups.* Cambridge, MA: Addison-Wesley.

Bales, R. F., & Hare, A. P. (1965). Diagnostic use of the interaction profile. *Journal of Psychology, 67,* 239–258.

Bargal, D., & Bar, H. (1990). Role problems for trainers in an Arab-Jewish con-flict-management workshop. *Small Group Research, 21,* 5–27.

Barge, K. J., & Schlueter, D. W. (2004). Memorable messages and newcomer socialization. *Western Journal of Communication, 68,* 233–256.

Baxter, L. A., & Montgomery, B. M. (1996). *Relating: Dialogues and dialects.* New York: Gilford Press.

Benne, K. D., & Sheats, P. (1948). Functional roles of group members. *Journal of Social Issues, 4,* 41–49.

Bitzer, L. (1968). The rhetorical situation. *Philosophy and Rhetoric, 1,* 1–14.

Bormann, E. G. (1969). *Discussion and group methods: Theory and practice.* New York: Harper & Row.

Bormann, E. G. (1972). Fantasy and rhetorical vision: The rhetorical criticism of social reality. *Quarterly Journal of Speech, 58*(4), 396–407.

Bormann, E. G. (1975). *Discussion and group methods.* New York: Harper & Row.

Bormann, E. G. (1982). Fantasy and rhetorical vision: Ten years later. *Quarterly Journal of Speech, 68*(3), 288–305.

Bormann, E. G. (1996). *Small group communication: Theory and practice.* Edina, MN: Burgess.

Bormann, E. G. (2003). Symbolic convergence theory. In R. Y. Hirokawa, R. S. Cathcart, L. A. Samovar, & L. D. Henman (Eds.), *Small group communication theory and practice: An anthology* (8th ed.; pp. 39–47). Los Angeles: Roxbury.

Bormann, E. G., & Bormann, N. C. (1996). *Effective small group communication* (6th ed.). Edina, MN: Burgess.

Bormann, E. G., Pratt, J., & Putnam, L. (1978). Power, authority and sex: Male response to female leadership. *Communication Monographs, 45,* 119–155.

Brilhart, J. K., Galanes, G. J., & Adams, K. (2001). *Effective group discussion: Theory and practice* (10th ed.). Boston, MA: McGraw-Hill.

Brock, B. L., & Scott, R. L. (1972). *Methods of rhetorical criticism: A twentieth-century perspective.* Detroit, MI: Wayne State University Press.

Broome, B. J., & Fulbright, L. (1995). A multistage influence model of barriers to group problem solving: A participant-generated agenda for small group research. *Small Group Research, 26,* 25–55.

Burke, K. (1945). *A grammar of motives.* New York: Prentice Hall.

Burtis, J. O. (1989). Receiver as source: Stimulus evoked making of meaning. In C. Roberts & K. Watson (Eds.), *Intrapersonal communication processes: Original essays* (pp. 528–546). Scottsdale, AZ: Gorsuch Scarisbrick.

Burtis, J. O. (1995). Grouping and leading as citizen action. *The Journal of Leadership Studies, 2,* 51–64.

Burtis, J. O. (1996). Perceptions of leadership-conducive exigencies. In A. Woodward (Ed.), *Leadership in a changing world* (pp. 16–25). Burlington, VT: Association of Leadership Educators.

Burtis, J. O. (1997). Leadership-attaining strategies: A dramatistic taxonomy. In R. Orr (Ed.), *Leaders in leadership education* (pp. 205–214). Burlington, VT: Association of Leadership Educators.

Burtis, J. O. (2004a, November). *Organizational origins and vision: Four bases of exigencies and rhetorical resources for organizational leadership—the leadership-conducive system theory.* Paper presented to the Organizational Communication Division of the National Communication Association at its annual conference in Chicago, IL.

Burtis, J. O. (2004b, November). *Purgatory puddle germination and attractive leadership vision: Political exigencies, rhetorical resources, and leadership-conducive systems.* Paper presented to the Political Communication Division of the National Communication Association at its annual conference in Chicago, IL.

Burtis, J. O., & Turman, P. (2004, November). *The breakdown-conducive group theory and recurring bases for potential group pitfalls.* Paper presented to the Group Communication Division of the National Communication Association at its annual conference in Chicago, IL.

Burtis, J. O., & Turman, P. (2005, April). *A framework for potential group outcomes: Pitfalls and breakdown at the heart of group outcome.* Paper presented at the annual meeting for the Central States Communication Association, Kansas City, MO.

Buys, C. J. (1978). Humans would do better without groups. *Personality and Social Psychology Bulletin, 4,* 123–125.

Carron, A. V., & Spink, K. S. (1995). The group size-cohesion relationship in minimal groups. *Small Group Research, 26,* 86–105.

Cattel, R. B. (1951). New concepts for measuring leadership in terms of group syntality. *Human Relations, 4*, 161–184.

Cohen, A. M., & Smith, R. D. (1976). *The critical incident in growth groups: Theory and technique.* LaJolla, CA: University Associates, Inc.

Delbecq, A. L., & Van deVen, A. H. (1975). *Group techniques for program planning: A guide to nominal group and DELPHI processes.* Glenview, IL: Scott, Foresman.

DeStephen, R. S., & Hirokawa, R. Y. (1988). Small group consensus: Stability of group support of the decision, task process, and group relationships. *Small Group Behavior, 19*, 227–239.

Dewey, J. (1910). *How we think.* Lexington, MA: Heath.

DiSalvo, V. S., Nikkel, E., & Monroe, C. (1989). Theory and practice: A field investigation and identification of group members' perceptions of problems facing natural work groups. *Small Group Behavior, 20*, 551–567.

Elmes, M. B., & Gemmill, G. (1990). The psychodynamics of mindlessness and dissent in small groups. *Small Group Research, 21*, 28–44.

Evans, C. R., & Dion, K. L. (1991). Group cohesion and performance: A meta-analysis, *Small Group Research, 22*, 175–186.

Fiedler, F. E. (1967). *A theory of leadership effectiveness.* New York: McGraw-Hill.

French, J. R. P., & Raven, B. (1968). The bases of social power. In D. Cartwright & A. Zander (Eds.), *Group dynamics: Research and theory* (pp. 607–623). New York: Harper & Row.

Frey, L. R., Botan, C. H., & Kreps, G. L. (2000). *Investigating communication: An introduction to research methods* (2nd ed.). Needham Heights, MA: Allyn & Bacon.

Fuhriman, A., & Burlingame, G. M. (1994). Measuring small group process: A methodological application of chaos theory. *Small Group Research, 25*, 502–519.

Gastil, J. (1992). A definition of small group democracy. *Small Group Research, 23*, 278–301.

Gastil, J. (1993). Identifying obstacles to small group democracy. *Small Group Research, 24*, 5–27.

Gemmill, G., & Schaible, L. Z. (1991). The psychodynamics of female/male role differentiation within small groups. *Small Group Research, 22*, 220–239.

Gemmill, G., & Wyukoop, C. (1991). The psychodynamics of small group transformation. *Small Group Research, 22*, 4–23.

Gershenson, O. (2003). A family of strangers: Metaphors of connection and separation in the Gesher Theatre in Israel. *Western Journal of Communication, 67*, 315–334.

Giddens, A. (1979). *Central problems in social theory: Action, structure, and contradiction in social analysis.* Berkeley: University of California Press.

Goffman, E. (1967). *Interaction ritual: Essays on face-to-face behavior.* New York: Pantheon Books.

Gouran, D. S. (2003). Reflections on the type of question as a determinant of the form of interaction in decision-making and problem-solving discussions. *Communication Quarterly, 51,* 111–125.

Gouran, D. S., & Hirokawa, R. Y. (2003). Effective decision making and problem solving in groups: A functional perspective. In R. Y. Hirokawa, R. S. Cathcart, L. A. Samovar, & L. D. Henman (Eds.), *Small group communication theory and practice: An anthology* (8th ed.; pp. 27–38). Los Angeles: Roxbury.

Gruenfeld, D. H., & Hollingshead, A. B. (1993). Socio cognition in work groups: The evolution of group integrative complexity and its relation to task performance. *Small Group Research, 24,* 383–405.

Hall, E. T. (1959). *The silent language.* Garden City, NY: Doubleday.

Hall, E. T. (1983). *The dance of life.* Garden City, NY: Doubleday.

Hart, R. P., & Burks, D. (1984). Rhetorical sensitivity and social interaction. *Speech Monographs, 39,* 75–91.

Henman, L. D. (2003). Groups as systems: A functional perspective. In R. Y. Hirokawa, R. S. Cathcart, L. A. Samovar, & L. D. Henman (Eds.), *Small group communication theory and practice: An anthology* (8th ed.; pp. 3–7). Los Angeles: Roxbury.

Hersey, P., & Blanchard, K. H. (1988). *Management of organizational behavior: Utilizing human resources* (5th ed.). Englewood Cliffs, NJ: Prentice-Hall.

Hirokawa, R. Y. (1980). A comparative analysis of communication patterns within effective and ineffective decision-making groups. *Communication Monographs, 47,* 313–321.

Hirokawa, R. Y. (1990). The role of communication in group decision-making efficacy. *Small Group Research, 21,* 190–204.

Hirokawa, R. Y., Cathcart, R. S., Samovar, L. A., & Henman, L. D. (Eds.). (2003). *Small group communication theory and practice: An anthology* (8th ed.; pp. 1–2). Los Angeles: Roxbury.

Hirokawa, R. Y., Gouran, D. S., & Martz, A. E. (1988). Understanding the sources of faulty group decision making: A lesson learned from the Challenger disaster. *Small Group Behavior, 19,* 411–433.

Hirokawa, R. Y., Ice, R., & Cook, J. (1988). Preference for procedural order, discussion structure, and group decision performance. *Communication Quarterly, 36,* 217–226.

Hoffman, M. F. (2002). "Do all things with counsel": Benedictine women and organizational democracy. *Communication Studies, 53,* 203–218.

Janis, I. (1972). *Victims of groupthink.* Boston, MA: Houghton Mifflin.

Janis, I. L. (1982). *Groupthink.* Boston, MA: Houghton Mifflin.

Janis, I. L. (1989). *Crucial decisions: Leadership in policymaking and crisis management.* New York: Free Press.

Janis, I. L., & Mann, L. (1977). Anticipatory regret. In I. L. Janis & L. Mann (Eds.), *Decision making: A psychological analysis of conflict, choice, and commitment* (pp. 219–242). New York: Free Press.

Johnson, S. (2001). *Emergence: The connected lives of ants, brains, cities, and software*. New York: Scribner.

Kahn, R. L., & Quinn, R. P. (1970). Role stress: A framework for analysis. In A. McLean (Ed.), *Mental health and work organizations* (pp. 50–115). Chicago, IL: Rand McNally.

Keller, T. (1999). Images of the familiar: Individual differences and implicit leadership theories. *Leadership Quarterly, 10,* 589–607.

Kelman, H. C. (1961). Process of opinion change. *Public Opinion Quarterly, 25,* 57–78.

Keyton, J. (1999). Relational communication in groups. In L. R. Frey (Ed.), *Handbook of group communication theory and research* (pp. 192–218). Thousand Oaks, CA: Sage.

Keyton, J. (2003). Observing group interaction. In R. Y. Hirokawa, R. S. Cathcart, L. A. Samovar, & L. D. Henman (Eds.), *Small group communication theory and practice: An anthology,* (8th ed.; pp. 256–266). Los Angeles: Roxbury.

Knapp, M. (1984). *Interpersonal communication and human relationships*. Boston: Allyn & Bacon.

Knapp, M. L., Stohl, C., & Reardon, K. (1981). Memorable messages. *Journal of Communication, 32,* 27–42.

Krayer, K. J. (1988). Exploring group maturity in the classroom: Differences in behavioral, affective, and performance outcomes between mature and immature groups. *Small Group Behavior, 19,* 259–272.

Krips, H. (1992). Leadership and social competence in the declining years of communism. *Small Group Research, 23,* 130–145.

Lakoff, G., & Johnson, M. (1980). *Metaphors we live by*. Chicago, IL: University of Chicago Press.

Latane, B., Williams, K., & Harkins, S. (1979). Many hands make light the work: The causes and consequences of social loafing. *Journal of Personal and Social Psychology, 37,* 822–832.

Lord, R. G., & Maher, K. J. (1991). *Leadership and information processing: Linking perceptions and performance*. Cambridge, MA: Unwin Hyman.

Madsen, A. (1993). Burke's representative anecdote as a critical method. In J. W. Chesebro (Ed.), *Extensions of the Burkeian System* (pp. 208–229). Tuscaloosa: University of Alabama Press.

McGarty, C., Haslem, S. A., Hutchinson, K. J., & Turner, J. C. (1994). The effects of salient group memberships on persuasion. *Small Group Research, 25,* 267–293.

McMillan, J. J., & Harriger, K. J. (2002). College students and deliberation: A benchmark study. *Communication Education, 51,* 237–253.

Mead, G. H. (1964). Mind, self and society. In A. J. Reck (Ed.), *Selected writings: George Herbert Mead*. Indianapolis, IN: Bobbs-Merrill.

Meier, N. (1963). *Problem-solving discussion and conferences: Leadership methods and skills*. New York: McGraw-Hill.

Meindl, J. R., Ehrlich, S. B., & Dukerich, J. M. (1985). The romance of leadership. *Administrative Science Quarterly, 30,* 78–102.

Mitzberg, H. (1973). *The nature of managerial work.* New York: Harper & Row.

Moreno, J. L. (1953). *Who shall survive?* (Rev. ed.). Beacon, NY: Beacon House.

Moreno, J. L. (1960). *The sociometry reader.* Glencoe, NY: Free Press.

Mortensen, C. D. (1997). *Miscommunication.* Thousand Oaks, CA: Sage.

Mudrack, P. E., & Farrell, G. M. (1995). An examination of functional role behavior and its consequences for individuals in group settings. *Small Group Research, 26,* 542–571.

Newell, A. (1980). Reasoning, problem solving, and decision processes: The problem space as a fundamental category. In R. S. Nickerson (Ed), *Attention and performance, Vol. 8.* Hillsdale, NJ: Lawrence Erlbaum.

Offermann, L. R., Kennedy, J. K., & Wirtz, P. W. (1994). Implicit leadership theories: Content, structure and generalizability. *Leadership Quarterly, 5,* 43–58.

Olson, C. (1987). A case study analysis of credentialing in small groups. Unpublished doctoral dissertation, University of Minnesota.

Oxford Essential Dictionary. (1998). New York: Berkley Books.

Pace, R. C. (1990). Personalized and depersonalized conflict in small group discussions: An examination of differentiation. *Small Group Research, 21,* 79–96.

Patton, B. R., & Downs, T. M. (2003). *Decision-making group interaction: Achieving quality* (4th ed.). Boston, MA: Allyn & Bacon.

Pavitt, C., & Johnson, K. K. (2002). Scheidel and Crowell revisited: A descriptive study of group proposal sequencing. *Communication Monographs, 69,* 19–32.

Pearce, W. B., & Pearce, K. A. (2000). Combining passions and abilities: Toward dialogic virtuosity. *Southern Communication Journal, 65,* 161–175.

Poole, M. S. (1981). Decision development in small groups I: A comparison of two models. *Communication Monographs, 48,* 1–24.

Poole, M. S. (1983a). Decision development in small groups II: A multiple sequence model of group decision development. *Communication Monographs, 50,* 206–212.

Poole, M. S. (1983b). Decision development in small groups III: A multiple sequence model of group decision development. *Communication Monographs, 50,* 321–341.

Poole, M. S. (1990). Do we have any theories of group communication? *Communication Studies, 41,* 237–247.

Poole, M. S. (1998). The small group should be the fundamental unit of communication research. In J. Trent (Ed.), *Communication: Views from the helm for the 21st century* (pp. 94–97). Needham Heights, MA: Allyn & Bacon.

Poole, M. S. (2003). Group communication and the structuring process. A functional perspective. In R. Y. Hirokawa, R. S. Cathcart, L. A. Samovar, & L. D. Henman (Eds.), *Small group communication theory and practice: An anthology* (8th ed.; pp. 48–56). Los Angeles: Roxbury.

Poole, M. S., Seibold, D. R., & McPhee, R. D. (1985). Group decision-making as a structurational process. *Quarterly Journal of Speech, 71,* 74–102.

Poole, M. S., Seibold, D. R., & McPhee, R. D. (1986). A structurational approach to theory building in decision-making research. In R. Y. Hirokawa and M. S. Poole (Eds.), *Communication and group decision-making.* Beverly Hills, CA: Sage.

Putnam, L. L. (1979). Preference for procedural order in task-oriented small groups. *Communication Monographs, 46,* 193–218.

Putnam, L. L. (1982). Procedural messages and small group work climates: A lag sequential analysis. *Communication Yearbook, 5,* 331–350.

Putnam, L. L. (1994). Revitalizing small group communication: Lessons learned from a bona fide group perceptive. *Communication Studies, 45,* 97–102.

Putnam, L. L. (2003). Rethinking the nature of groups: A bona fide group perspective. In R. Y. Hirokawa, R. S. Cathcart, L. A. Samovar, & L. D. Henman (Eds.), *Small group communication theory and practice: An anthology* (8th ed.; pp. 8–16). Los Angeles: Roxbury.

Putnam, L. L., & Stohl, C. (1990). Bona fide groups: A reconceptualization of groups in context. *Communication Studies, 41,* 248–265.

Putnam, L. L., & Stohl, C. (1996). Bona fide groups: An alternative perspective for communicating and small group decision making. In R. Hirokawa and M. Poole (Eds.), *Communication and group decision making* (pp. 147–178). Thousand Oaks, CA: Sage.

Rosenfeld, L. B., & Fowler, G. D. (1976). Personality, sex and leadership style. *Communication Monographs, 43,* 320–324.

Salazar, A. J. (1995). Understanding the synergistic effects of communication in small groups: Making the most out of group member abilities. *Small Group Research, 26,* 169–199.

Sarason, S. B. (1972). *The creation of settings and the future societies.* London: Jossey-Bass.

Schultz, B., Ketrow, S. M., & Urban, D. M. (1995). Improving decision quality in the small group: The role of the reminder. *Small Group Research, 26,* 521–541.

Scott, D. K. (2003). The Eisenhower/Khrushchev rhetorical compact: Toward a model of cooperative public discourse. *Southern Communication Journal, 68,* 287–306.

Scudder, J. N., Herschel, R. T., & Crossland, M. D. (1994). Test of a model linking cognitive motivation, assessment of alternatives, decision quality and group process satisfaction. *Small Group Research, 25,* 57–82.

Shaw, M. E. (1981). *Group dynamics: The psychology of small group behavior* (3rd ed.). New York: McGraw-Hill.

Simon, H. A. (1955). A behavioral model of rational choice. *Quarterly Journal of Economics, 69,* 99–118.

Simons, H. W. (2001). *Persuasion in society.* Thousand Oaks, CA: Sage.

Snyder, M. (1974). Self-monitoring of expressive behavior. *Journal of Personality and Social Psychology, 30,* 526–537.

Steiner, I. D. (1972). *Group process and productivity.* New York: Academic Press.

Stohl, C. (1986). The role of memorable messages in the process of organizational socialization. *Communication Quarterly, 34,* 231–249.

Stohl, C., & Putnam, L. L. (1994). Group communication in context: Implications for the study of bona fide groups. In L. R. Frey (Ed.), *Group communication in context: Studies of naturalistic groups* (pp. 285–292). Hillsdale, NJ: Lawrence Erlbaum.

Sykes, R. E. (1990). Imagining what we might study if we really studied small groups from a speech perspective. *Communication Studies, 41,* 200–211.

Timmerman, C. K. (2002). The moderating effect of mindlessness/mindfulness upon media richness and social influence explanations of organizational use. *Communication Monographs, 69,* 111–131.

Ting-Toomey, S. (1988). Intercultural conflict styles: A face negotiation theory. In Y. Y. Kim & W. B. Gudykunst (Eds.), *Theories of intercultural communication* (pp. 213–238). Newbury Park, CA: Sage.

Ting-Toomey, S. (1991). Intimacy expression in three cultures: France, Japan, and the United States. *International Journal of Intercultural Relations, 15,* 29–46.

Volkema, R. J., & Niederman, F. (1995). Organizational meetings: Formats and information requirements. *Small Group Research, 26,* 3–24.

Vroom, R. H., & Yetton, P. W. (1972). *Leadership and decision-making.* Pittsburgh, PA: University of Pittsburgh Press.

Webster, D. M., & Kruglanski, A. W. (1994). Individual differences in need for cognition closure. *Journal of Personality and Social Psychology, 67,* 1049–1062.

Welch-Cline, R. J. (1994). Groupthink and the Watergate cover-up: The illusion of unanimity. In L. R. Frey (Ed.), *Group communication in context: Studies in natural groups* (pp. 199–223). Hillsdale, NJ: Lawrence Erlbaum.

Yerby, J. (1975). Attitude, task and sex composition as variables affecting female leadership in small group problem-solving groups. *Speech Monographs, 42,* 160–168.

Index

About the Authors

John O. Burtis (Ph.D., University of Minnesota) is a Professor in the Communication Studies Department at the University of Northern Iowa. He has taught courses in leadership and group communication at both the undergraduate and graduate levels and has been a consultant and trainer on related subjects in the private and public sectors. He has been the director of the Concordia Leadership Center and of the West Central Minnesota Leadership Program, the head of the Communication Studies department at the University of Northern Iowa, and the Director of Forensics at Kansas State University and at Concordia College.

Paul D. Turman (Ph.D., University of Nebraska, Lincoln) is an Assistant Professor in the Communication Studies Department at the University of Northern Iowa. He has taught courses in introductory group and advanced group communication at the undergraduate and graduate levels and has won numerous teaching awards at the regional, state, and university levels. His research interests include the examination of group communication variables within athletic teams and an assessment of the role of the coach as a facilitator for effective team interaction.